"With discontent uniting so man crisis demands real change, how polarization? How do we buil and the structures essential for us to take done a wonderful job in capturing so much. As a fellow '68er, I applaud his coherent challenge to keep organizing."

— **LARRY COHEN**, BOARD CHAIR, OUR REVOLUTION, PAST
PRESIDENT, COMMUNICATIONS WORKERS OF AMERICA

"Out of the ruins of neoliberalism and its vast human cost there emerged Donald Trump. He was denied a second term by disparate forces that, if properly united, offer real hope. In this superb analysis from the democratic (and romantic) left, sometimes withering, essentially optimistic, Anthony Barnett generously delivers a rebuke to the pessimism that is paralysing a scattered opposition. The centre and left must hold together. This passionately conceived book comes at a crucial moment, for the stakes could not be higher. If Trump and his grim surrogates around the world succeed then, among much else, climate change resistance is doomed, Barnett argues. He has given a lifetime to the cause of a saner, more democratic politics and his memory is long. Here, his mission is grand and big-hearted. He ranges widely to propose how we might act so the destructive, delusional folly of Trumpism shall not pass."

— **IAN MCEWAN**

"A wonderful book that tells a compelling story of a democratic awakening. Agency and possibility are back to reanimate the spirit of 1968. But also for the darker forces it unleashed, not least Trumpism, which seized on the nightmare America became for far too many. A worldly optimist, conscious of past defeats, Barnett sets out a possible route to a democratic future."

— **DAVID EDGERTON**, AUTHOR OF *THE RISE AND FALL OF THE
BRITISH NATION*

"Up against the wickedness of those who choose to abuse their wealth and power, Anthony Barnett sees a slender chance for hope in the USA, and challenges us to rethink how we do politics. I hope he's right."

— **CAROLINE LUCAS**, GREEN MP FOR BRIGHTON PAVILION

"Anthony Barnett writes beautifully and with sharp insight, and about the possibilities opened up by historical contingency and human creativity. Whether he is right about the rest of the contemporary juncture — and with such panoramic scope that is unlikely — he is blunt and stark on the threat posed by Trumpism, and clear-eyed about the struggle to prevent climate breakdown."

— **PROFESSOR NICK PEARCE**, DIRECTOR, IPR, BATH; HEAD OF THE PRIME MINISTER'S POLICY UNIT 2008 TO 2010

"*Taking Control!* is a moving exploration of political possibility and an essential guide for making sense of our historical moment, its potential and dangers. Sketching what he calls the "forces of humanisation," Anthony Barnett provides a terrific account of today's unequal global order, with the US at the center, as well as the potential for genuine change."

— **AZIZ RANA**, PROFESSOR OF CONSTITUTIONAL LAW, CORNELL UNIVERSITY AND AUTHOR OF *THE TWO FACES OF AMERICAN FREEDOM*

"*Taking Control!* is a marvellous book that reads like a thriller. It shows us how the fascist inclinations are innate to the neoliberal system and offers a solid way out of the global perils without hesitating to discuss the socialist option. It is clear from the tone that Barnett truly feels the pain of man-made troubles of our age and makes it his own problem to fight against them."

— **ECE TEMELKURAN**

TAKING CONTROL!

TAKING CONTROL!
Humanity and America After Trump and the Pandemic

Anthony Barnett

Published by Repeater Books

An imprint of Watkins Media Ltd

Unit 11 Shepperton House

89-93 Shepperton Road

London

N1 3DF

United Kingdom

www.repeaterbooks.com

A Repeater Books paperback original 2022

1

Distributed in the United States by Random House, Inc., New York.

ISBN: 9781914420269

Ebook ISBN: 9781914420276

Printed and bound in the UK by TJ Books

*For Rosemary Bechler
and the inspirations and arguments of a lifetime.*

Also by Anthony Barnett:

Aftermath: The Struggle of Cambodia & Vietnam (with John Pilger)
Iron Britannia: Why Parliament Waged its Falklands War (new edition, 2012)
Soviet Freedom
This Time: Our Constitutional Revolution
The Athenian Option: Radical Reform of the House of Lords (with Peter Carty)
Blimey, It Could Be Brexit!
The Lure of Greatness: England's Brexit and America's Trump

Edited books:

Debating the Constitution (with Caroline Ellis and Paul Hirst)
Power and the Throne
Town and Country (with Roger Scruton)

Contents

Introduction

You will never get anywhere by giving people truths on a plate; they won't thank you for it.
— Rosemary Bechler

Things are not as easily understood nor as expressible as people usually would like us to believe.
— Rainer Maria Rilke

Many of us, perhaps including you, have thought and said that COVID-19 is an alert, a cosmic signal that we need a course correction. In May 2020, as its economic impact hit America, Trump complained, "This is so unfair to me! Everything was going great. We were cruising to re-election!"[1] Indeed, he was.

Why he wasn't re-elected is at the heart of this book. It gives us grounds for optimism in an era of pessimism. Also, the response to the pandemic tells us we can create a different way of governing life on Earth. Not because there is a new "answer" to which we can turn or an old one waiting to be finally collected from left luggage. But because the potential of far-reaching change was being created all along, under governments of all political stripes, and has now taken us by surprise. This was due to forces of humanisation that resisted the marketisation of life and developed below the political surface of a world that celebrated the supremacy of the rich and powerful.

The monsters are frustrated not vanquished, which can

make them all the more dangerous. They currently seek to exploit the disruptions caused by COVID and its variants to double-down on their many existing advantages. The Biden administration would like to re-establish America's global primacy, which was a major cause of our problems in the first place. Nonetheless, something fundamentally positive is happening and his government is a critical part of it.

When change like this takes place, it has a strange quality due to the way our imaginations move faster and are more volatile than our everyday life. At first we think the differences will be dramatic. When they are not, we feel it's an anti-climax and conclude that nothing really changes. Ten years later and the world really is different. In 2011, a slogan at the Occupy Wall Street demonstration proclaimed, "This is the beginning of the beginning". Ten years later, and at last the beginning has begun: the beginning of a free, equal and inclusive world. The massive growth of official surveillance and the militarisation of police forces tell us that the authorities feel this as well and wish to prevent it.

There is another priority. Dramatic action is needed to prevent our current climate emergency from crossing the tipping point into irreversible overheating that will make human life impossible. We know it is happening. We know it can be prevented. What we have learnt from COVID, as Adam Tooze argues, is that "we can afford anything we can actually do".[2] We can shut down half the economy, we have paid people not to work. We could stop all coal burning now and assist those adversely impacted; we could cover Greenland in foil to reflect back the sun; we could halve the amount we drive overnight. We could, and this is what is needed, put in place a coordinated, national and international emergency. If we can do it, then we can afford it. It would be the equivalent of going on a war footing, only with and not against other countries.

But the fact that no accountant, or chancellor, or tabloid newspaper, or pundit, can tell us that we cannot afford to do what we are able to achieve, does not mean that we can do whatever we like. There are two lessons of COVID: that we have the collective agency to achieve objectives no one thought possible in 2019; and that there are objective realities, the first being that we are a vulnerable species who needs to tend the planet and take care of each other. We have the capability to protect ourselves and each other from being reckless — when we act in concert.

If we did do so, what would be the aim of such a "war effort"? What would we want to see on the other side, after we have mobilised to save our environment? By "we" I mean everybody, with all our tremendous differences and complexity, in a world where certainties are being dissolved.

To ask about purpose is to ask about politics and principles. So I'd like to open with some simple assertions.

The hyper-inequality of today's wealth and power is unacceptable. As is the way inequality is becoming ever more extreme both within and between countries. This should never have happened and it needs to be reversed — a view shared by a large majority of humankind.

It is unacceptable for at least three good reasons.

It is morally wrong. This is usually taken to be a pointless claim as it merely shows how powerless we all are. The response to COVID-19 and its variants, however, shows that assertions of simple humanity are not so powerless after all, and the objection is a fundamental one. It follows from the moral equality of all human beings.

It is now possible for everyone in the world to have the

basic securities of life, from hygiene to education, with time to make the best of our abilities. Instead, competing states linked to gigantic corporations and the fortunes of financiers, engender insecurity to impose a precarious, limited existence on most of us. Extreme inequality of power and wealth not only permits legal robbery, it steals from us our potential to enjoy being human.

Third, hyper-inequality is bad for everyone because it generates systemic crises from pollution to terrorism and warfare.

So if we can save the environment for human habitation, we need to ensure that the world that emerges from the other side of the climate catastrophe is not like the one we live in at the moment. Specifically, power must be rooted in real democracy and not monopolised by the few. My contribution to combatting the climate emergency is to seek to assess how we might start to achieve such a goal. I'd like the reader to share my sense of exploration of the issues.

The Chance of a Lifetime

Until November 2020, it seemed that nothing could be done, and that authoritarianism would shut down all hope. Instead, the initial victory of Joe Biden over Donald Trump opens up a slender portal through which it may be possible to create a sustainable and more equal world. This is a welcome, unexpected opportunity. The forces seeking to close it are formidable — in Beijing, Moscow, New Delhi, Jerusalem, Wall Street, London — it's not just the Republicans in Washington. To keep it open will take a generous and persuasive culture and good organisation.

My working premise is that the Republicans may win the mid-terms in November 2022 and take the initiative from

Biden, while the outcome in 2024 is uncertain and there is all to play for, because Biden's policies have already shown is that there is a majority for change. If liberals and progressives cooperate successfully the necessary transformation can begin.

Given that the leaders of the US Democratic Party were partners in the creation of hyper-inequality, how come Biden's election might open a path for its reversal? Biden's commitment to replace market fundamentalism took most of us by surprise because it could happen in no other way. No one could develop an explicit programmatic alternative within the existing parameters and run for president, let alone succeed. Bernie Sanders came close but would have been destroyed by the Murdoch-led media. For decades, in America and elsewhere, belief in democratic agency has been sucked out of politics and replaced by an ideology of "the market", in a manner so complete, and generating such widespread insecurity and helplessness, that it prevented the development of an effective counter-ideology. I will show how Trump is both an expression of this inhuman development and a response to its failures. But an open challenge to its political domination could not, initially at least, have come about "consciously". Any claim to be doing so would not have been believed.

Critiques and alternatives to the rule of "the market" flourished, however, along with multiple protests at the dangers and injustice of marketisation and calls for the protection of basic human and economic rights. Throughout the period since the 1980s, forces for humanisation grew. After 2010, they were expressed politically in the US by support for Bernie Sanders, and exploded in the manifestations of Black Lives Matter after George Floyd was murdered. There is a complex will to resist that propelled President Joe Biden into office —

a shift in mentality and desire, principally among younger Americans; a cultural change of temper and intelligence, especially around environmental issues, which is ahead of the political class, whose institutions are still locked in the past and are in hock to lobbyists and political funders.

I want to emphasise this by way of introduction because so much of what is happening is taking place beneath the surface of American politics. Commentators fall back on a familiar framework to describe what's going on. Biden's programme, for example, is likened to President Roosevelt's New Deal. There is no comparison. Unemployment in the US was below 5% in 1929 but had risen to nearly 25% in 1932 when Roosevelt was elected. It was an economic and social collapse. In his first hundred days, Congress passed whatever he proposed. Today the US faces a quite different form of crisis. Under Trump, parts of the economy were doing well. Black unemployment was in decline. A tyranny was on the verge of success. It means the US confronts a very different situation to that of 1932. Trump's legacy is still alive: his allies control the Supreme Court, a majority of the State legislatures, a rigged electoral system and the solid support of nearly 40% of the population; they have tons of money, and link up with authoritarians around the world.

Up against this, Biden's imperative is to prevent the US becoming neofascist under a return of Trumpism. The racist policies that have characterised the United States since its inception must be marginalised, and voters need to have a stake in good government — without which there cannot be the popular legitimacy required to confront the climate emergency and to begin the redistribution of wealth — the only lasting security against extreme reaction.

While Roosevelt delivered, he was a patrician. Should Biden

seek to reproduce the same paternalism, however progressive his policies, Trumpism will return. Voters will not accept being "told" what to do or think. They have shed their belief that those in charge know best, and have done so for good reasons. This matters greatly for progressive parties which lack a rhetoric of individual empowerment.

Since 1945, across the West, when established centre-left parties have gained office, they usually close down and "manage" any release of democratic vitality — to show the dominant system they are "responsible". The consequence has been that the positive reforms they have enacted have not been accompanied by enlarged participation. Instead, a sense of deadening disappointment is followed by demobilisation. The Biden administration will need to break from this pattern as well if it is to succeed.

Thanks to the threefold threat of Trump's nativist supporters, the need for a new politics of the economy, and the climate emergency, America's core freedoms and political liberty will only be preserved with popular, active support. This will be hard to achieve because what is now underway in the United States can be seen as a form of negative revolution. This is a crucial part of the story I try to tell. America cannot go back to the era of what is usually called neoliberalism. A contest is therefore underway over how to replace it. It is this which gives humanism — the opposition to the supremacy of profit — a chance.

The End of White Man's Rule

It is also a confrontation over the end of the white man's rule. This is literally the case in the USA — in the 2020 election Trump received the support of 60% of white male voters.

It is also true globally. The rise of China, alone, has made sure that white male pre-eminence is ending despite furious resistance. I welcome the termination of the white man's rule — the question is how this will come about.

I am conscious that because of my own limitations and the need for speed I have concentrated on developments in the USA, with supporting illustrations from my own country, the United Kingdom, where, in contrast to America, the state is undergoing a system breakdown not a renewal. It would have been much better if I had been able to incorporate the parallel but distinct experiences of Japan, Russia and especially the countries of the European Union. Above all, as Achille Mbembe rightly insists, the Global South witnesses the real workings of the world at large and this defining perspective is missing.[3] The knowledge that the world of the Global North must lose its privileged status runs through these pages, even though they are largely confined to developments within it.

A focus on the US may be justified. The fate of humanity will never be decided within one country, however strong and rich. Nonetheless, when global change is in the balance it can be tipped one way or the other by the direction taken by the currently wealthiest power. Had Trump won in 2020, he would have provided the keystone of an informal, international arc of authoritarian capitalist regimes prepared to control the world for a long generation, while life is fried by the climate emergency.

I want to emphasise the world context here as I don't address or try to analyse it in what follows except with respect to China. When he was in power, Trump's capacity to hog the limelight pushed his *de facto* planetary collaborators into the shadows. Now, relief at his defeat seems to have lifted concern about their collective existence. Yet the "Iron

Men", as Misha Glenny has dubbed them, oversee most of the world.[4] This remains the unlikely context of a moment of hope. They are not constrained by the basic framework of representative democracy: a free press, an independent judiciary, uncorrupt regulation and fair elections in which all can vote — or they are dismantling it, as Boris Johnson is doing in the UK, in so far as he can get away with it. They are many: Xi in China, Putin in Russia, Erdoğan in Turkey, Modi in India, Bolsonaro in Brazil, Orban in Hungary, Khamenei in Iran, Muḥammad bin Salmān and his father in Saudi Arabia, Lukashenko in Belarus, Duterte in the Philippines, el-Sisi in Egypt, Mnangagwa (the crocodile) in Zimbabwe, the list goes on. All claim a legitimacy based on manipulated support. All abuse state power to fix the economy. All mobilise hatred of foreigners, minorities and migrants to secure order. All lubricate their influence with illegal funding.

If Trump had won a second term, it would have been clunk-click for tyrants and tax havens around the planet. The unified globalist order under American leadership, also known as "multilateralism", would have been replaced by gangster pluralism. When he spoke, by video, to his fellow heads of state at the UN summit in September 2020, Trump told them, in the language of the mafia: "I have rejected the failed approaches of the past, and I am proudly putting America first, just as you should be putting your countries first. That's okay. That's what you should be doing."[5] An unpoliced world-city controlled by rival gangs of elites injecting themselves with the wealth of others would have taken over from "globalisation". In a hair-raising article, Alex Hochuli nails it as "Brazilianization":

The undoing of modernization through its principal process—the coming apart of formal employment and of the rise of precaritization—is the root of the whole phenomenon of 'Brazilianization': growing inequality, oligarchy, the privatization of wealth and social space, and a declining middle class [...] clientelism, and corruption.[6]

Each country might have his own type of authoritarian capitalism underpinned by surveillance.[7] Xi Jinping's one-party regime with its vicious systems of control is different from Trump's libertarian version. But that's okay too. As is boasting about the priapic qualities of your economy. What is mutually unacceptable to the "Iron Men" is any attempt to impose universal standards against which all can be judged, such as human rights, or freedom and liberty, or honest elections.

There has been a narrow, if temporary, escape. We have been saved from what was almost certainly an irreversible regime of reaction, not by the plague but by the way COVID-19 required good government. When mere competence was all that was demanded, Trump the "businessman" showed himself to be incapable. His failure to deal with the pandemic was central to his electoral defeat. With Biden in the White House, a breach has opened up in what would otherwise have been a global authoritarian enclosure. All of us who are democrats need to help secure the opening. To do so we must think afresh, act anew. We will need a coherent democratic politics, which enhances liberty and delivers economic and social justice that demand uncomfortable alliances. How do we go about achieving this — really achieving this — so that everyone has the opportunity to make the best of themselves while assisting others to do so? My hope is to convince you that this question must be asked, can be answered, needs to be answered, and has not been answered yet.

Any answer will need progressives to learn and change. To cooperate, for example, in the invention of new forms of representation that can win and retain majority support. It is a huge task: to turn our face towards humanity as well as the White House, the planet as well as party politics, culture and livelihood as well as production and platform corporations.

My Perspective

Underlying every book about our current affairs there is a presumption about the nature of humankind. Most authors, while critical of specific aspects of society, broadly accept that human life is naturally competitive and greedy, and capitalism is normal. A growing number tend to agree that we are also social and that there is an inherently collective aspect to being human. But the dominant presumption remains: that we are what we are, winners and losers.

Critics of the system-as-a-whole, such as environmentalists, anarchists, republicans (with a small "r"), Marxists and socialists — most of my friends in fact — usually feel that our existing societies represent a form of loss. Without shouting it out from the rooftops, they feel that we were more truly ourselves before the age of consumerism, that commercial values corrode our true, collective or shared nature, and that capitalist societies, driven and governed by corporate power which seeks to maximise its profits, are abnormal. This doesn't mean a rejection of market exchange, personal property, or the division of labour. Nor do such critics of the present-as-a-system desire to go back to times past. But they do want us to regain an "authentic" humanity. The more optimistic take a Hegelian view secularised by Marx that our inner collective nature will be released when capitalism meets its system breakdown.

I have a different perspective. I believe what it means to be human lies ahead of us in the full sense of being unknown. There is no essential human nature. We recognise what it means to be human when we meet its capacity, potential and joy. But there will always be different kinds of society and different ways of life so long as humanity exists. There is no intrinsic human nature to be unfolded, no collective singularity waiting to emerge from the contradictions of capitalism, nor an "Omega point" that our joint consciousness will arrive at. It is not that we don't yet know what our "true nature" is going to be — no such singularity exists or ever will.

The paradox of this uncertainty is that it makes us all the more, and in the best way, creatures of the past, which surges through our veins and synapses. We are not empty vessels waiting to be filled by the future. Far from it, we are above all historical animals formed by the unique attribute of language — my view is simply that at no point will we cease to be historically specific, as individuals/families, nations/tribes, and as a species, and therefore we will always be changing and in flux.

For fifty thousand years we apparently sang to each other with a full range of noises without language, making music a deep part of our being. For tens of thousands of years we talked without a written language and were civilised and skilful hunter-gatherers — some of us still are. Today, a majority of us live in cities; by this measure we became an urban not a rural species only recently, within my lifetime. The influences that preceded our becoming dwellers of the metropolis and its long suburban tentacles live on in us.

Yet our nature, while formed by these inheritances, is also changing. Today we'd regard it as shocking and *inhuman* to deprive a child of the capacity to read, girls and boys alike. But mass literacy is recent; in 1820 approximately 12% of the world population was literate compared to 85% today.[8] Gender equality is even more recent as an ideal — some societies still resist it. What we believe it means to be "truly human" is changing and quite fast. Soon, a majority of us around the Earth will regard it as "natural" that we text each other, as this becomes an essential part of our humanity. I hope that the fact that BlackRock controls £9 trillion in assets will soon come to be seen as inhuman, rather than, as today, "all too human".

Environmental biologists have recognised that the adaption of humankind is taking place at a far faster pace than regular biological evolution in terms of behaviour, culture and longevity.[9] I am interested in a related development, that of government and self-government: of power and democracy. Will there be a time when humans are able to say with shared confidence "These are the ways we take responsibility for ourselves and each other and give our voice to how we are governed"?

The most recent change came with the development of cyberspace, within which we now exist alongside the other domains of land, sea and air. It is clear that the internet empowers both the potential of a networked, supportive mutual-aid-based future and an antagonistic, denigrating, authoritarian and profiteering one.

The same unresolved character is manifest in the greatest issue of our time, the environmental crisis, which goes further than the climate emergency as it reaches the viability of the oceans and the sustainability of our food chains. What we know is that if we continue as we are living today, the Earth will call time on humankind as we know it.

This may then reduce us, although never completely, to a vile and vicious species — elitist, voyeuristic, demagogic and exploitative; in a state of war, or cold war, that we are unable to avoid waging on each other under conditions of human-generated "scarcity" and crises. Whether in the form of the hi-tech, bureaucratic authoritarianism of China, religious caste-based bigotry as in India, the brutal "free-market" oligarchy of the USA or a masked variety of the same in the European Union, it could be that this is our destiny.

It is also possible, and I hope likely, that a cooperative, intelligent, courageous, but also modest and open-minded, future can be achieved; a future based on the hard work of truthfulness rather than prejudice, so that we can delight in our differences and recognise our potential for wickedness; a future committed to a peaceful, shared, but not happy-clappy, existence, filled with aspiration, hard work and inventiveness but not systemically exploitative.

All we know is that the answer will not be simple and it will be mixed not white. We are transforming ourselves as a species with no inbuilt or inevitable destination. We are at a turning point and I am asking the reader to explore the reasons for this and the opportunities it creates. I've not tried to fence off the subject matter and I have tried to set out the issues in a conversational fashion, sometimes returning to themes such as the nature of the economy from different angles.

The tensions and dangers of the moment are creative ones. Perhaps the example of creative writing can free up the kind of political engagement I am searching for. In her wonderful account of the struggle to keep choice and intelligence alive in the aftermath of the Iranian revolution, *Reading Lolita in*

Tehran, Azar Nafisi recounts how she talked with her class about how empathy, even for "monstrous individuals", is found in fiction. A novel is democratic, she writes, "not that it advocates democracy but that by its nature it is so".[10] Philip Pullman put it even more strongly: "Writing is despotism, but reading is democracy […] The conversation a reader has with a book is none of the writer's business, unless the reader chooses to tell them about it […] They might read better than I can write. They might see things I was unaware of as I wrote them down. To limit a reader's permitted response to what the writer himself or herself knows about their own work is an infringement of freedom. Reading should be free."[11]

It is in this spirit that I offer these reflections, as a contribution to a free conversation. We are historical animals formed by a unique time and place without any inevitable destiny. We are creatures of the particular in networks of differences. I try to show how our possibilities are entangled in the granularity, unevenness and disparities of politics. This is not a denial of my responsibility — writers must choose their words and answer for their judgment and imagination. But the freer the reader feels to make and take what you will, the better.

My Background

An American friend who read a draft emailed to say that, especially as I argue the human is particular, readers have a right to know where I'm coming from. I am a 1968er. I marched against the Vietnam War in London, my home town, and this has connected me to American politics ever since. I'm an organiser not a theorist and worked on the practical side of the early *New Left Review* and then helped start a short-lived radical independent weekly, *7 DAYS*, in 1972. After it failed,

I researched the history of Vietnam and its conflict with Pol Pot's Cambodia as a fellow of the Transnational Institute, then under the leadership of Orlando Letelier (who had been Chile's Foreign Minister under Allende and was shortly to be assassinated by Pinochet). In 1980, a year after Pol Pot was overthrown by the Vietnamese and China invaded Vietnam to "punish" it (with the tacit assent of Washington), I visited and wrote about both Vietnam and Cambodia. This implanted a sliver of the "Global South" into my soul. Then, as my country embarked on a bizarre reconquest of the Falkland Islands in 1982, I turned to a short career in journalism. I wrote the "Islander" diary for the British left-wing weekly *New Statesman* and was rebuffed from becoming its editor by the Labour Party hierarchy.[12] It was a good setback and led to my leadership of Charter 88, a call for Britain to enjoy a democratic constitution. From 1988 to 1995 I turned it into a campaign, supported by tens of thousands, that influenced New Labour and the Liberal Democrats.

My motive was crystallised by Neal Ascherson, who had pointed out that we were less likely to achieve democratic socialism under the existing British regime than "induce a vulture to give milk".[13] The claim is salient for the argument in this book. Progressive policies today are always mangled by the overall state structure and party political systems of representative democracies, that have become irrational and captured by reaction. We need to change *how* we are governed, so that a democratic culture can breathe and learn to be effective. Campaigning for democracy confirmed my feminism and made me into a republican, not a liberal.[14] The difference being that liberals look at how society should best be run "from above", whereas republicans and feminists, while just as committed to freedom and liberty, ground them in the voice, agency and interests of regular people "from below". The Charter's initial priorities, a UK Bill of Rights, Scottish and Welsh parliaments and Freedom of Information, were achieved by the Labour government of 1997. But instead of seeking to renew the British state in a democratic fashion — Charter 88's main aim — the 'New Labour' Prime Minister Tony Blair and his collaborators Peter Mandelson and Alistair Campbell embraced what I described as corporate, manipulative populism.[15] It led Blair himself to become a zealot for market globalisation and military intervention in cahoots with Washington.

With Blairite philistinism in the ascendant, a group of us decided to use early cyberspace to resist. In 2001, after a year's planning, we launched a creative website for honesty and imagination: *openDemocracy*. Again and again across the two decades that followed, opposition to the increasingly unequal world of market fundamentalism arose, only to crash against the rocks and to recede leaving them intact: the World Social Forum as a counter to Davos; the Stop-the-War Coalition against the invasion of Iraq; repeated protests demanding action on the climate emergency; the Occupy movement against the 1%. #MeToo started to shift things and in 2020, Black Lives Matter was a turning point. But all in all, for more than twenty years of nonstop crises and top-down "shocks", even though we emerged with our heads held high, no political movement seemed close to delivering the necessary change of direction. I decided to write a book called *Adventures in Open Democracy* to reflect on the experience.

That is what I *was* writing. I find it hard not to comment on current events, a dangerous distraction if you are working on a book. But the scenes of the Trumpites' insurrectionary assault on the Capitol were too compelling to resist. Here were characters dressed like many of the anti-war ones I discussed, now abseiling the very portals of American hegemony in the name of reaction! In an article in *Byline Times* I called them Trump's Red Guards. The Red Guards were the "revolutionary" army of the Chinese cultural revolution in the 1960s aroused by Mao Tse-Tung's call to "Bombard the headquarters". The anti-elitism of their assault on "bourgeois culture" was a power ploy by Mao, the so-called "Great Helmsman", who used them to destroy his opponents. Then he shut them down and invited President Nixon to meet him and recognise the legitimacy of his communist China. Just as Mao called on the "revolutionary masses" to intimidate his well-educated opponents and destroy the institutions of authority in order to secure his leadership, so Trump deployed a similar, heady rhetoric of a besieged great leader, who called on his supporters to level the traditional elite so that he could remain supreme.[16] Only Trump lost and could now join my list of frustrated, twenty-first century protestors. It would make a fine, if ironic, concluding section.

It soon became clear that it wasn't like that. Not just that Trump had not lost, at least not yet, but also something more disruptive of my personal narrative was taking place. An alliance of progressives and liberals, of protest and opposition movements often linked to support for Bernie Sanders, had joined with trade unionists, and traditional Democrats reassessing after their 2016 defeat, to dispatch Trump from the White House. A post-2010 generation *might* be overcoming the division that had disabled both the radicalism of the left and the reformism of the centre. The activist, democrat left I am part of has been excluded from influence for decades.

Was this ending? Could this open the way to more genuinely participatory and just societies?

Asking this question demands an entirely different analysis, which I felt was the priority. It meant I had to abandon the retrospective account of my "adventures" so as to prospectively explore an historic opportunity. I am immensely grateful to my publisher, Tariq Goddard of Repeater Books, for the way he and his colleagues embraced the switch from an already announced title to this one, and to Judith Herrin for making sure the two of us held our nerve.

I had already begun the argument in an essay published in *openDemocracy*, then under the leadership of Mary Fitzgerald. It was edited by Adam Ramsay and called "Out of the Belly of Hell: Covid-19 and the Humanisation of Globalisation". Why, I asked, did governments shut down their economies to deal with the impact of COVID-19, when this was clearly against the instincts and training of world leaders, and had never happened during all previous pandemics? The real surprise is not that there was a financial crash — wise heads saw one coming, hedge funds shorted it — but that governments themselves brought it about by deliberate acts of policy. A previously inconceivable shutdown and rebooting of commerce was caused by politically ordered lockdowns. "No American economist I know would have predicted 'the non-market's' extraordinary multi-trillion-dollar interventions into 'markets' of all kinds — of goods and services, of finance, of construction, health care, housing and income", wrote one expert.[17] No scenarios had prepared anyone for what happened in 2020. Yet it showed that a latent capacity had developed that was not determined by market values. It seemed to me to be important to register this for the long term. As climate change closes in, I wanted people to hold onto the fact that

COVID-19 shows that our humanity can get the better of our inhumanity. I did not expect the showdown to become politically salient within the year.

Botley, September 2021

1. Three Questions

In November 2020, Donald Trump came very close to winning the US presidential election to secure a second term. Because the forces he personifies are now so popular, well-funded and deeply embedded, they may gain executive power over the USA in 2024, whether led by Trump himself or another Republican. The fact that he initiated an insurrectionary attempt to reverse the 2020 result makes this especially threatening. Not so much because it defied America's traditional constitutional culture and procedures that ensure a legitimate change of government, but because this is a prime reason for Trump's continued popularity. It means that should they regain the White House, Trump Republicans will feel justified in rewriting the rules to ensure they never lose it again. Nor is the possibility that Washington will bow to such tyranny a matter of concern only for those living in the United States.

The other side of tyranny is democracy. Not the zombie version we have suffered in the recent past, with undead candidates exchanging catchphrases sanitised by focus groups, but a living democracy that puts the market in its place and enables us all to make our joint claim on life. This is the upside of the danger that we face. The type of capitalist world we have known over the last half-century cannot reproduce itself. The contest over what will replace it has begun.

Like many, I watched the first results as they came in on Tuesday 3 November 2020 and witnessed the votes piling up for Joe Biden in the big states of New York and California and the narrow returns in the swing states that would decide the Electoral College. We live in England and have two daughters with whom, during COVID, we hung out on video. The eldest lives in the US and was taking a walk when the result was finally called on Saturday 7 November. We could hear the shouts of relief and ululations of delight as they echoed from the packed, suburban hills of north-east Los Angeles. The inhabitants of the city roared their approval and we shared in it.

The phoney transition followed, with Trump refusing to concede until the 6 January assault on the Capitol. As I watched the insurrection livestreamed, I became increasingly and wrongly confident that this would put an end to his political career.

I'd always thought that the attempt to impeach Bill Clinton was absurd. When he lied under oath about having sex with Monica Lewinski it was perjury, but it was also a politically harmless technicality that merely revealed his bottomless narcissism. It was not like Richard Nixon's 1972 use of a criminal gang known as "The White House Plumbers" to bug and burgle with the aim of destroying his Democrat opponents. An attempt to secure an election outcome and retain executive power by the use of force, taking advantage of the leverage of the presidency, is exactly what impeachment is designed to prevent and punish. The Republican representatives in Congress could see, as we all could, that this was what Trump attempted in plain air in January 2021. But most have ceased to be representatives, in the traditional sense of politicians who ultimately remain in charge of their own judgment. Reduced to being conduits of their supporters and funders, they were obliged to vote against initiating an impeachment process which their oath to uphold the constitution clearly obliged them to do. The Republican party's base and its tens of millions of voters had become inseparably loyal to Trump's supremacy. For them, it was his attempt at the intimidation of due process of a system in which they no longer believed that was a mere technicality. What really mattered was that the United States should be ruled by people like themselves.

Then Biden took office. I had expected, and dreaded, a second-rate return to the glamour of Obama, a continuity of appeasing the right so as to "get something done" while the necessary confrontations were held in suspense; a business-as-usual continuation of the last forty years, condemning the left to the familiar role of helpless doomsters and crepehangers. After all, Biden *was* the last forty years. I identified with the young Bernie Sanders supporter, Aaron White, who had been at primary school when a teacher came in to tell them about 9/11. The week before the election he wrote in *openDemocracy* that, "One in four young people in the United States seriously considered suicide in June. Around 52% of 18- to 29-year-olds are living with their parents — the highest percentage in more than a century. Those of us born between 1981–1996 own just 4.6% of wealth, even though we are 35% of the total workforce — the largest cohort in the labor force. In this collapsing empire, there's not much to look forward to."[1]

Instead, when Biden entered the White House he initiated a remedial programme that pointed in a good direction and began to implement it! I emphasise "pointed" and "direction". It's easy to conclude that he has not yet produced lasting results. But as Roberto Unger says, "In any programmatic argument, the direction of movement matters more than the rate."[2]

There are five essential processes needed to reverse Trumpism: average citizens must have more of America's extraordinary wealth; its super-rich must have less; everyone must be genuinely able to vote; its non-white citizens must be treated with real equality, from policing to housing; and the country needs to be carbon-neutral and assist the planet to become so as well. On all fronts the new president showed purpose and some initial delivery. I found this really surprising.

My Questions

At the end of January 2021, with Biden inaugurated, there were two developments I had not expected: the lasting strength and depth of Trumpism, and the range and seriousness of the Biden response. Together they pose three questions.

First, what lies behind Trumpism? The determination of support for Trump is impressive. It means the man isn't an aberration, he really does represent what a huge number of people and financial interests want. Worse, he links up with a worldwide development of authoritarians. Where does its strength come from, what keeps it going?

Second, what lies behind Biden's radicalism? If Trumpism is so strong, how come it was frustrated in 2020? This question seemed to me more important, less obvious and also harder to answer because Joe Biden presented himself as a consensual, "bipartisan" candidate, not as a clear ideological alternative. Yet he put together an administration apparently unified in its determination to implement a change of "paradigm", to quote Biden himself. A change to what? The new president and his team are centrists with decades of experience in dampening down calls for reform and squishing demands for paradigm shifts. If this is now their idea of a compromise, the demands they seek to contain must be volcanic. Where did these come from, why are they so strong and effective, when it seemed that progressives had been thoroughly crushed?

Third, a question I did not expect to ask but now delight in. Suddenly, progressives are in alliance with governing Democrats influencing domestic policy in the USA — as well as internationally with respect to the climate emergency. It's a contested alliance, on both sides. It is also novel and full of possibilities. How do we make the best of it?

2. The Shock of the 6th: Trumpism Frustrated but Defiant

Given the role of the spectacle in the American imaginary it is fitting that the final decades of the era when market values dominated politics have been bookended by two events watched live around the world. The opening salvo was the levelling of the Twin Towers of the World Trade Center. The final blast, the storming and occupation of the Houses of Congress. Both were forms of "propaganda of the deed". Both were initiated by cunning, fascistical narcissists — Osama bin Laden and Donald Trump — who apparently spent hours watching TV. Both were taboo-busting shocks played out on landmark structures of the USA, one being destroyed, the other desecrated.

The first saw Islamic fundamentalists on a suicide mission of protest against the US role in the Middle East, led by a man originally armed and trained by Washington. It was well organised while being undefined in its objective.

The second saw American fundamentalists march on Congress to "fight like hell" against the US establishment, led by a man who was the ultimate expression of the Washington swamp he claimed to oppose. It was poorly organised but had a clear aim.

Threads of violence and frustration link 9/11 to 6 January

2021, connections symbolised by Ashli Babbitt, a veteran of fourteen years' service in the US Air Force who did tours of duty in Afghanistan and Iraq, and earned twelve medals and ribbons including the Global War on Terrorism Service Medal, Iraq Campaign Medal, Air Force Expeditionary Service Ribbon with Gold Border and the Global War on Terrorism Expeditionary Medal.

She had backed Obama (Tweeting "I think Obama did great things […] I voted for him!…and I voted for trump [*sic*]. I could not vote for Hillary"). She followed Trump into his conspiratorial denial of the 2020 presidential vote. She paid to fly from California to Washington, tweeting "the storm is here and it is descending upon DC in less than 24 hours".[1] She celebrated listening to Trump at his White House rally, then marched on the Capitol and stormed into the building with her fellow believers. There, she pushed to the front of those clamouring to break into The Speaker's Lobby entrance to the House, and was lifted to the top of the makeshift security barricade that barred the mob from entering. It was guarded by a lieutenant in the Capitol police and before she could scramble over, he shot her dead.

In effect, she recycled bin Laden. Like him, she was trained by the USA, served in Afghanistan, turned against American power, declared that a storm would fall upon it, and was killed.

Babbitt's tragically short life reflects the link between 6 January 2021 and 9/11. The US responded to the levelling of the Twin Towers by occupying Afghanistan and then launching an insane, nationalist war on Iraq to demonstrate that its wounded hegemony was intact. As US forces crossed the Iraqi border and closed on Baghdad, Prime Minister Tony Blair wrote to President George W. Bush, "Our ambition is big: to construct a global agenda around which we can unite the world".[2] To legitimate their aggression the Anglo-Saxon powers proclaimed, falsely, that Iraq had weapons of mass destruction and they orchestrated a massive publicity campaign across all media to convince the public. Deceit and deception are normal in great power politics, but this was an obliteration of fundamental domestic norms. It opened the way to Trump's mendacity. It lent validity to his assertion that the media publicised fake news while the political system was rigged. For, as he pointed out on the campaign trail in 2016, he was part of it and he knew.

Unmeasurable Discontent

More important, the rigged system failed. The scale and intensity of support for Trump is rooted in the cumulative frustration of the huge American middle and lower middle classes which over decades had experienced income paralysis, intensified insecurity and military stalemate. The occupations of Afghanistan and Iraq were unmatched logistic and martial achievements accompanied by a colossal use of firepower that nonetheless turned into drawn-out strategic defeats. In 2008, the combination of dishonesty *and* failure opened the way for Obama, whose initial opposition to the invasion of Iraq gave him the standing to seize the Democratic Party nomination from Hillary Clinton, who had supported it.

Had the wars had been going well, Obama's Republican opponent, Senator McCain, would have beaten him. As it was, President Obama decided his role was not to cut America's losses immediately but to manage a withdrawal that preserved as much of Washington's influence as possible across the Middle East and worldwide. The result was eight years of global mortification overseen by a Black president who delivered only partial domestic change.

He was elected as the financial system crashed and was saved by the quantitative easing that he sanctioned. The middle of Obama's eight-year presidency was the turning point. The Tea Party was on the rise, the Occupy movement, which I will discuss later, had burst popular blindness to inequality. Yet in 2012 Obama still beat Mitt Romney to gain a second term. Among the ultra-rich Republicans of Greenwich, Connecticut this did not feel right. In a superb account in the *New Yorker*, Evan Osnos describes how one wealthy Republican, Lee Hanley, felt there was a "deep frustration with the status quo". He commissioned research to probe public feeling and go deeper than the usual polling. The investigation discovered that the "level of discontent in this country was beyond anything measurable".[3]

Ashli Babbitt is the maddened heroine of this unmeasurable discontent. It is reported that a fifth of those arrested for the Capitol Hill insurrection were, like her, veterans who had rallied to the flag of wars that were so misconceived as to be futile.[4] Many more were from the police and security apparatus who identify with the military and shared the frustration. After she ended her fourteen years of service Babbitt started a business and went bust, ripped off by a loan company. The *Washington Post* found a high proportion of the individuals who took part in Trump's mendacious assault have faced financial ruin: nearly 20% of those charged have been bankrupt, "A quarter of them had been sued for money […] 1 in 5 of them faced losing their home at one point".[5]

Many were down-the-line white supremacists giving insurrection a bad name. This was not the only way they bucked the stereotype of a rebellion against official power.

Those taking part in the early popular uprisings in eighteenth-century France were labelled the *sans-culottes* because they lacked the knee-breeches worn by aristocrats. The mob in Washington DC was no such mobilisation of the poor. They flew or drove in from across the USA, well equipped and clothed for the winter weather. They were, however, the new insecure, spun from a middle class whose businesses went bust, who witnessed the value of their modest wealth plunge, saw their debts rise and health costs skyrocket — and that's before we look into their sex lives and the ranting, paranoid tentacles of social media that has become their source of news.

In 2013, Lee Hanley "huddled" with Steve Bannon and the billionaire Robert Mercer in Connecticut, and considered the bubbling rage of millions of Babbitts that Hanley's research revealed. They wanted to use it to further increase their own advantage. Perhaps they were far-sighted enough to realise that if it crystallised around a left-wing challenger they might be done for. According to Osnos, they agreed that *they* needed "a populist challenger who could run as an outsider, exposing corruption and rapacity". It seems they knew Trump and thought him unsuitable. But he came through the primaries as the candidate that fitted requirements. This is the reality from which everything else follows. Trump is not the cause of America's discontent, he is its voice and expression, backed by billionaires who investigated the strength of the discontent and then exploited it.

A crucial moment came in the Republican primaries, when the favourite candidate was Jeb Bush, George W.'s brother and the ex-governor of Florida. In February 2016 during the early South Carolina primary debate, Trump confronted a hostile audience of Bush supporters who booed him continuously. "Obviously the war in Iraq was a big, fat mistake," he told them defiantly. "The war in Iraq, we spent $2 trillion, thousands of lives. We don't even have it. Iran has taken over Iraq with the second largest oil reserves in the world [...] We should never have been in Iraq. We have destabilized the Middle East [...] They lied. They said there were weapons of mass destruction. There were none. And they knew there were none."[6] He then stated that the trillions should have been spent on rebuilding America.

Democrats and progressives are wrong to ignore or dismiss the quality of Trump's boldness and judgment. Tens of millions of families across America have members who are veterans, or police and security officers. They are predominantly Republican. Trump was one of their own, and when he spoke like this some, if by no means all of them, lifted their heads, as did Ashli Babbitt. They felt he was right. He would put "America first".

Trump's opponents often ask how come Trump "had so much support among the public" especially when, with the exception of Murdoch's Fox News, the media and the establishment was so hostile to him.[7] The answer usually turns on the impact of the financial crisis. But class issues are mobilised and resolved within national frameworks. In a forensic interview by Zack Stanton, the veteran analyst of US voters, Stanley Greenberg, says how he was impressed at the way Trump brought in "all kinds of new voters" motivated to "save the country".[8] Top of their ticket was to save it from immigration and diversity. These were perceived as threats to the USA, a country of immigrants, because it seemed "weak" to let in more. Trump had a message that addressed the country's *national* reality and discontent. First and foremost, Trump spoke to the millions of patriots who, like him, believed in winning. He promised to be a tough, macho leader who would stop the waste, end the defeats, stand up to China economically and *withdraw* the US from being a loser in the playground of globalists. Two million had served, 6,500 had died and fifty thousand had been wounded, in fifteen years of victoryless conflicts. What pride could the Ashli Babbitts and their families and relatives take in the costs and anxieties they had been exposed to? Trump provided the self-belief they craved, his pledge was the answer they needed: "Make America Great Again" by ending wars overseen by the bipartisan elite that was responsible for the "big, fat mistake".

Then, of all people to run against this compelling call for restitution, the Democrats chose Hillary Clinton; the ultimate personification of failed intervention, who acted as if she was entitled to lead, yet could not even show the door to her lying, cheating husband.

The Historic Turnout of the 2020 Vote

Once elected, Trump delivered for his supporters. There were no new wasteful, endless wars. Taxes for the rich were cut, jobs boomed. Then COVID struck. Despite his grotesque mismanagement, denials and braggadocio, a tanking economy, hundreds of thousands of dying and his own illness, he fought back, campaigning to the end with demonic energy, and increased his overall vote by a staggering ten million votes. How could this possibly mean that he had not won?

Even more votes is the answer. Nonetheless, deploying all the influence of the presidency he sought to reverse the outcome. His attempt failed for four reasons.

First, the institutions and processes held: votes were counted and recounted accurately; officials did their job, even when they were Republicans they refused to be intimidated; courts threw out cases that had no merit in law, even when the judges had been appointed by Trump.

Second, many corporate and financial interests opposed Trump while Republican funders and supporters, not least Rupert Murdoch and his *Wall Street Journal,* who rely on a framework of law, did not feel threatened by Biden, and refused to support illegal breaches of due process. "Fuck him", was Murdoch's verdict when asked to approve Fox News calling Arizona for Trump on the night of the election.[9]

Third, a "huge coalition of activist groups" let officials know they would be held accountable if they caved in to Trump's pressures.[10] They were part of a dedicated, unprecedented effort to strengthened the dilapidated voting systems of the fifty different states and secure the integrity of the ballot as well as get out the vote.

Finally, there is President Biden's explanation in his inaugural address, that "we celebrate the triumph not of a candidate, but of a cause: the cause of democracy […] At this hour, my friends, democracy has prevailed."

Behind these answers is a determining factor which I want to say is feminism, as this would annoy Trump and his followers. In a way it was the work of feminism. Because the decisive answer is votes, tens of millions of votes, which in many cases came about thanks to the huge effort to register and get voters to the polls organised by women, especially Black women, led in Georgia by the exemplary Stacey Abrams, and also to a shift amongst women voters generally, who broke 57% for Biden and only 42% for Trump.

Nse Ufot of the New Georgia Project, describes, how they overcame the long legacy of voter suppression: "by direct voter contact — we knocked on over 2 million doors, we made almost 7 million phone calls, and sent 4 million text messages".[11] The campaign to reverse voter suppression in Georgia proved critical in winning the State for Biden in November and then, even more important, flipping its two Senate seats in January. This deprived Republicans of their majority in the upper chamber.

Before the 2020 election, the highest total won by any president was by Obama in 2008 when he gained 69.5 million votes. Eight years later, Clinton only got 66 million (all figures are rounded) and Trump 63 million. Last year, however, Trump won 74 million votes, nearly five million more than any previous presidential candidate had ever gained.

Except that Biden got 81 million.

Altogether, when third-party candidates are included, 23 million *more* votes were cast in the US in 2020 than in 2016 — a staggering increase.

In the low point of 1988, 91.5 million votes were cast in the US presidential election, making up barely half, a mere 50.3% of the voting age population. In 2020, the total votes cast were 159.5 million — 62% of the voting age population and 66% of those eligible to cast a ballot.

When I wrote *The Lure of Greatness: England's Brexit and America's Trump* in 2017, I argued that such was the extent of gerrymandering, corporate funding, and voter suppression, with millions who qualified being unregistered, and millions more effectively prevented from casting their ballot, that "America barely qualifies as a democracy". Four years later, it does qualify in terms of voter turnout, even if over eighteen million Americans of voting age are still denied registration.

A huge political and cultural shift took place as unprecedented numbers of voters on both sides decided their vote mattered. A multiracial network of civil society organisers reached out to those repulsed by Trumpism and called on them to say,

"Basta! Enough!" Their turnout came to fifteen million votes more than the previous highest total for a winning candidate. If they remain able to vote and continue to do so, this will forever alter the nature of what is still the world's major power.

Even though Biden won the popular vote by an astounding seven million, the 2020 US election outcome was terrifyingly close. To secure the influence of each of the fifty separate states, the US constitution mediates the popular vote through the electoral college system, in which the winner takes all of each state's votes. Currently this builds in an advantage for white conservatives, but never before to the degree of 2020. Trump lost Arizona by 10,457 votes, Georgia by 11,799 and Wisconsin by 20,682. He needed just 42,941 votes to win all three. Had he done so the Electoral College would have been tied. Vice President Pence was responsible for announcing the outcome and would urely have favoured Trump, despite his losing the overall ballot by 7,052,770. This is a measure of a broken democracy: a mere fifty thousand votes would have overturned a majority of seven million.

Furthermore, across America, Republicans made gains. They increased their support among Black men and Latinos, won the Governorship of Montana and control of the legislatures of New Hampshire and Alaska; they ousted fifteen Democrats from the House of Representatives and slashed their opponent's majority in the lower House of Congress to nine.

Bringing the War Home

For decades there had been little to choose between the main parties, as both served corporate interests and deployed marketing strategies to project winning "narratives". Low voter turnout and slim majorities confirmed the stagnant nature of the political domain. The closeness of 2020 in the United States terminated this stultification. Both sides burst the banks that had confined their support.

But then…

"We will not bend. We will not break. We will not yield. We will never give in. We will never give up. We will never back down. We will never, ever surrender!"

I saw a clip of President Trump saying this at his rally in Georgia on 6 December 2020, a month after the election. I didn't take any special notice as it seemed merely to continue the foul rhetoric he had spewed since he first ran. This was my mistake. It was a significant escalation. The US president had declared war upon his own country.

The Republican Governor of Georgia had just overseen the certification of the State's narrow majority for Joe Biden. The State's votes had been counted twice. Trump had clearly lost the count there and nationally.

The *whole point* of elections is that losers concede and don't arouse their supporters by telling them, "We will not break. We will not yield." Trump defied the primary attainment of America's political system.

At the height of the British Empire's confrontation with Nazism, William Beveridge was commissioned to write a report which became famous as it laid the basis for the UK's welfare system. In 1944, he wrote a book that deepened his argument, *Full Employment in a Free Society*. My father bought a copy which stayed on the family shelves. In its conclusion, Beveridge remarks, "the essence of democracy is effective means of changing the Government without shooting".

It's a striking definition. Beveridge was an upper-class liberal and this was the elite point of view. The democracy that his class developed in Britain, as across the Atlantic, was not about self-determination. Its essence was to ensure the peaceful transfer of power; academics call it "the minimalist theory of democracy".[12] It is a core achievement of representative systems, that preserves them from tyranny. Later, I examine the larger significance of this in the present context. It may appear banal to emphasise the point. Elections are *not* about "not yielding" or "never giving in". They are *not* about claiming, as Trump did, that you will "never, ever surrender". On the contrary, elections are purpose-made to decide who must yield. Nor is this a matter of "surrender". Instead they are designed to preserve, not eliminate the loser. The military terminology Trump used was itself an assault on the most basic — or minimal — procedure of democracy. Without it there is despotism.

When Trump made his December call of defiance in Georgia, he was not planning on leading a civil war. He was not *planning* on shooting to keep the presidency. For he never plans anyway. He wagers. His wager was that if he mobilised his supporters en masse this would be sufficient to intimidate the vice president, the Supreme Court, Republicans in Congress and State officials, and they would bin the result.

At the same time, to implement his wager he rallied his supporters to seize the Capitol. He knew they included supremacists, like those who marched by torchlight in a fascist parade at Charlottesville, whom he described as "fine people"; and also armed networks like the "Proud Boys", who in the first presidential debate he asked to "stand back and stand by". His supporters were not confined to such groups (nor was everyone who stormed the Capitol white). But he went out of his way to make them feel he was their man and they gave his campaign its cutting edge.

His wager culminated in the huge crowd of the "patriots",

as his daughter Ivanka called them, who responded to his call. They came to the White House on 6 January and then stormed Congress in his name.

Trump started no new wars and broke from the costly imperial globalism of his predecessors. But he declared a new belligerence. He savaged traditional allies, denounced the European Union as his "foe" and imported into America the violence it had exported abroad. He branded Muslims and Mexicans, pilloried the cultural "elite", hardened borders and permitted Russian intervention in domestic politics. He savaged anyone who crossed him and exacerbated militant antagonism within the country rather than without, in a relentless torrent of hostility, provocation and self-centred, great-man, swagger. In the heady days of the 1960s and the opposition to the US in Vietnam, militant leftists boasted that they would "Bring the war home!" Half a century later, Trump did just that as he reaped the harvest of the so-called 'War on Terror'. The Babbitts rallied to the call.

We are not used to thinking about politics in these terms. But the conflict has to be addressed in the quasi-military fashion Trump himself employed. On the field of force, hard-fought battles can leave both armies ready to prepare for another confrontation. Others may be close-run, but once one side is broken it turns into a rout that disperses the losers forever. This is the opportunity that we must hope the victors impose on Trumpism and therefore upon America.

A conservative side to partisan politics is essential to democracy. But Trumpism, however multilayered and capable of recruiting female, Black and Latino support, is racist and supremacist. The inner skeleton, spine and cortex of US power has long reproduced horrific treatment of those it defines as un-American, at home and abroad. Obama talked about what we can now call the Trumpian character of American behaviour, and would proclaim: "That's not who we are." Apparently he said this forty-six times when he was president.[13] The need to repeat it so often did not lead him to the conclusion that, no, such activities are American.

America's Dual Nature

Like Dr Jekyll and Mr Hyde, two American nations have coexisted in the same body since its inception. The reason the US got away with being oppressive, imperialist, racist, corrupt and determined by money and corporate oligarchy, was thanks to its genuinely law-abiding, open, energetic and tolerant institutions, which also defined its nature, extending a civilising munificence alongside its murderous claims upon the world.

When Trump won the presidency in 2016, the traditional elites, Republican and Democrat, in the media and across the departments of state, in the universities, policy centres and international corporations were appalled. They also presumed that thanks to his obvious limitations he would be tamed by office and Dr Jekyll would have his turn. Instead, Trump fired the generals and experienced staff whose role was to civilise him. He was blatantly corrupt, abandoned any pretence of support for human rights, recklessly trashed the principles of environmental safeguards and prepared to turn the US into a fortress of authoritarianism directed by his family; and he successfully defied the impeachment process he deserved. Instead of giving the cultivated Dr Jekyll his due, the monstrous Hyde sought to displace him entirely.

Trump represented a momentous cultural shift. But across the four years of his presidency, the political establishment (for want of a better term) hoped that he didn't. When he lost the election, they hoped that finally he and his supporters would play by the rules. Once again Trump escalated without restraint. He repudiated the legitimacy of the process and told his supporters to "fight like hell" and "take back our country"; "he assembled, inflamed, and incited his followers to descend upon the Capitol [in] an organized attack on the counting of the electoral college votes".[14]

It was terrifying that Trump was personally willing to use force to retain the presidency. It was alarming that the police and security services permitted his irregular army to surround and enter the Capitol, which they would not have done had the insurgents been Black. It was frightening to hear "the sound of pounding on the doors" from inside the gallery of the House of Representatives itself, as Rep. Jamie Raskin described it. A month later he was to open the impeachment indictment of Trump.

But the lasting shock came from outside Washington, D.C. and obliged most Republican representatives to question the election's outcome when they all knew it was valid. Mitch McConnell, the Republican leader in the Senate, could see that:

January 6th was a disgrace. American citizens attacked their own government. They used terrorism to try to stop a specific piece of domestic business they did not like. Fellow Americans beat and bloodied our own police. They stormed the Senate floor. They tried to hunt down the Speaker of the House. They built a gallows and chanted about murdering the Vice President. They did this because they'd been fed wild falsehoods by the most powerful man on Earth because he was angry he'd lost an election […] There is no question — none — that President Trump is practically and morally responsible for provoking the events of the day. No question about it.

Yet he led his fellow Republican Senators to vote against impeachment. His excuse, that the process should not be used against someone who was no longer in office. As Senate majority leader before Biden had been sworn in, however, McConnell himself had prevented the impeachment trial from taking place when Trump *was* still president! Every Republican Senator knew that Trump had committed a clearly impeachable assault on the electoral process itself. Yet few dared to raise their hand to say so.

They had talked with their staffs back home, and key local and regional supporters, who had talked with fellow voters, all had watched livestream the Capitol assault McConnell describes and then they backed Trump.

This was the shock of the 6th. Not the attack itself but the fact that a historic ruling party, its representatives, activists and supporters, when in full control of twenty-four of the US's fifty states and the legislatures of six more, whose presidential candidate gained 74 million votes, were willing to trash its most sacred procedure. The shock was that the American system had lost the consent of half its people.

A related process was underway in the Democratic half. It was exemplified by the success of Alexandria Ocasio-Cortez, known by all as AOC. After narrowly defeating a leading old-guard Democrat in the party primary for New York's Fourteenth Congressional District in 2018, she made her first impact when she tweeted from the induction sessions for fresh members of Congress. She asked why corporate lobbyists were involved but no one from the trade unions. Her poise and fearlessness made her the cutting edge of a new generation of radical left progressives. In 2020, the Democratic machine chose a young, attractive, experienced media personality, also with a double-barrelled name, Michelle Caruso-Cabrera, to run against her in the primary. The *New York Post* reported how "Some of Wall Street's biggest titans are pumping big bucks" into the challenger's campaign.[15] That failed. They switched to oust her in the election itself, and backed her Republican opponent, creating a $36-million fight, the second most expensive House contest.[16] The cornucopia of funding raised the Republican vote from nineteen thousand to 58,000, but AOC stormed through with 152,000 as she deployed an exemplary social media campaign.

The US corporate, political and media elite, who had previously used their wealth and power to designate those who opposed them as unacceptably "fringe" and unelectable, discovered that voters no longer complied. The public now see the panjandrums of Congress as corporate lobby fodder, and the rule of law a way of fixing the system. The machinery of state that had delivered world leadership with all its privileges and wealth to the country's elite was perceived as a hollow edifice not a genuine democracy. The broad consent essential to its stability had drained away among both Democrat and Republican supporters.

If America had been in fundamental decline, the subsidence of its polity would have continued (as has happened in Britain). Instead, in the 2020 election both sides fought it out to the full and split the Senate fifty-fifty. Their clash will terminate the coexistence of Jekyll and Hyde as the country's dual character is no longer sustainable. The twenty-first century world that the USA had been foremost in creating now demands America chooses between the two aspects of its character that have cohabited from the beginning — and are now irreconcilable. To see why we need to take a closer look at Trumpism.

3. Trumpism — Nativist and Minoritarian

To enable as many Trump supporters as possible to be weaned from Trumpism, the nature of their support has to be described in ways they can recognise. We need to respect the problems they wrestle with, without according the same respect to their answer. Not least because they powered effectiveness into voting and brought back US democracy from the phantom zone.

Many Democrat voters find this extraordinarily difficult. Trump fills them with such disgust that they consider any empathy with his supporters a concession to his politics. Such a reaction plays Trump's game, for he seeks the death of empathy.

This is a theme of Thomas Frank's recent book, *People without Power*. He notes that, "acknowledging that some Trump voters might be desperate and otherwise decent people became a thing unsayable" in liberal circles. He quotes Nicholas Kristof of the *New York Times,* on the "outpouring of rage" from his readers when he shared the grievances of Trump supporters. Perhaps now Trump is out of the White House, and the issue is how to ensure he stays out, intelligent understanding will be extended to the nature of Trumpism.

Exploring the reason for Trump's grip on his followers, Hal Foster suggests he is for them a "primal father":

there is a psychic dimension to his support that we must come to terms with. No doubt many of his voters—and remember that he received 63 percent of the white male vote in 2016—are sexist and racist, whether secretly or not; certainly, most are angry at elites, too. But they are also— they are primarily—*excited* by Trump, excited to support him: there is a positive passion here not just negative resentment. It may be difficult for progressives to see why, but one way is to suggest that he tapped into the 'the erotic tie' that binds the horde to the primal father.[1]

Although insightful, it is not the kind of understanding I'm calling for. Its approach may fit those who travel hundreds of miles to his rallies, or explain the related forms of love for Obama. But if you want to understand support for political leaders in democracies — however partial they may be as democracies — it is essential to see them as a matter of choice.

Voting is a Judgment Call

Why voters didn't select the *other* candidate is never irrelevant and often more important. Voters are making a judgment and appreciate the element of choice. This does not rule out identification, which does not have to be pathological. For example, you can dislike Trump personally yet like the way he hates the things you want to hate. Negative solidarity does not call for personal identification with Trump, to feel that he speaks for you in a field of alternatives. One reason Trump was partly disarmed in 2020 was that Biden had not been to Harvard and, although a man of cultivation, presented himself as from the working class and not a snob, which neutralised some of Trump's anti-elitism.

The judgment Trump supporters make deserves to be assessed at face value. Since 2016, I've been struck by the way many commentators who are well educated and relatively liberal find it necessary to "explain' why people voted for Trump or Brexit but don't see the need to "explain" why people voted for Clinton, or for the UK to remain in the Europe. The starting point for the democratic intellect is to respect everyone's public assertion of their views, not explain them away. Trump supporters declare that they want to "Make America Great Again". As a slogan it looks forward in only a vague fashion, but it is unambiguous about the past: it claims the country has failed. As a mantra, MAGA is a four-word *rejection* of the way the USA has been governed. The first question in considering why people voted for Trump is, are his supporters justified in their rejectionist judgment?

We have seen that in terms of the military calling of the USA, that means so much to them, the answer is "yes". It is also "yes", dramatically so, in terms of their economic experience. PBS Frontline published a set of striking charts in 2013, the year Trump prepared to run.[2] While the wealthy had got a lot richer, the income of the middle 60% of Americans who provide the core Trump vote, had fallen by 8% since 2000. Their net worth had plummeted; their average debts had risen massively; millions of good jobs had gone, replaced by the insecurity of part-time work in a land without public health care.

At the same time, people were being robbed by the rich on an astonishing scale. A recent report for the RAND corporation set out, in the words of its authors, to "quantify the scale of income gap created by rising inequality".[3] It documents the cumulative effect of four decades and estimates that in 1975 a US worker with a median income earned $42,000 a year. This rose to a mere \$50,000 a year in 2018.[4] If they were badly educated, it fell. By contrast the average income of someone in the top 1% was \$289,000 in 1975 and \$1,384,000 in 2018. Just as striking, the RAND analysts calculate that if growth had been as equitable over the four decades after 1975 as it had been in the two decades before 1975, the top 1% would be earning a hardly uncomfortable \$630,000 a year, while median income would have risen to \$92,000 a year and not remained at \$50,000.

In 2016, Hillary Clinton said, "We don't need to make America great again. America has never stopped being great."[5]

Imagine you are an average, male, late middle-aged, US voter. Had life continued as it was when you grew up, your income would be nearly *twice* as much as it is and instead of facing an old age of growing insecurity with your children in debt, they would be better off than you, just as you were better off than your parents. One candidate says, "I can make your life great again." The other tells you, "Your life has never stopped being great and there is no need for change." Who would you vote for?

The starting point for any understanding of Trump's popularity is to recognise that he called out American failure and it was right to do so. This is the material basis of his popularity. What is amazing is how badly Trump did and how much support Clinton got when she offered continuity. The reason Clinton did well and gained a popular majority is that Trump offered a false solution to the economic unravelling of the American middle class and its military humiliation. Most voters always saw that he was the wrong answer.

Racism, Religion and Money

The key to understanding his support, however, is to recognise that a call to terminate the way America was ruled was fundamentally justified. Only by acknowledging that he was the first to do this and that it needed to be done — that there had to be a political expression of the "unmeasurable discontent" over a crushing plunge in life expectations of middle America — can you avoid being hexed by the ogre himself. A canny and formidable operator, he role-played defiance of elite ascendency with a dangerous authoritarian nerve and originality. One of the ways Trump pulled this off is by provoking everyone to talk about him. In love with his own fame, he revels in the fixation of others with himself. He inundated the American mind with provocations calculated to exasperate opponents, delight supporters, and thus ensure reactions were always about him. It didn't matter if what he said was untrue, as he did not offer statements for mutual consideration of their veracity, even when he was alleging fake news. He spoke for the sole purpose of imposing TRUMP onto any perspective. If this maddened everyone so that they obsessed about him, that was a success! He wanted the world to regard him as the issue.

So the best way to assess the coalition that made up his millions is to turn one's gaze away from him and ask why they backed Trumpism. It demands a twin perspective. On the one hand they are right and brave to insist that the American system has become corrupt and ceased to deliver what was great about it for Americans. On the other, the prejudices and beliefs that enable them to think Trump is the answer are wrong and cowardly.

A considerable number are racist. A much larger number

are permissive of racism without feeling themselves to "be" racist (I wrote about them with Adam Ramsay before the November election[6]). As Stanley Greenberg observed, millions of new Republican supporters were voting to "save the country" — for themselves. Their "overwhelming motivation is a deep worry that Black people and immigrants will 'control the country', due to their own loss of security". At the same time, a "large portion of them want a welfare state that is dependable for working people".[7]

This may describe Trump's voters in general. Networks, interests and specific beliefs also got them to the polls. The Republican Party as such holds and retains influence across all fifty states, especially the thirty-one where they control the legislature and the twenty-four where they control the executive as well. Within and without the extensive party machine at least three sets of influence converge on Trump: evangelicals, the very rich and a previously alienated white power sentiment.

Evangelicals are a vital component of Trumpism. Their voice can be heard in the letter eleven members of Republican representative Adam Kizinger's larger family sent to him after he voted for Trump's impeachment.[8] "Oh my, what a disappointment you are to us and to God!" the letter began, as it went on to accuse him of working with Democrats and the "fake news media" who are part of the "devil's army". Hardly an allegation you can disprove. Evangelicals who believe they are chosen include those who have embraced the rapture and look forward to the end time. If you regard abortion, for example, as an intolerable sin that must determine your vote, not only do you want a president who supports you, but in addition it becomes God's work to drive those who disagree with you off the electoral register.

In her eye-opening book *Unholy*, Sarah Posner explains:

> Donald Trump constitutes the culmination of a movement that has for decades searched for a leader [...] He burst in at a critical moment, when top Christian right leaders were becoming painfully aware they were losing their demographic supremacy. In 2006, white evangelicals made up 23 percent of U.S. adults [...] A short decade later that number had dropped to 17 percent [...] But because white evangelicals are uniquely politicized and highly mobilized to vote, they can exercise an outsize influence on our elections and political culture if they unify around a candidate or cause. In the 2016 election, white evangelicals made up 26 percent of voters and fully one-third of Republican voters. Eighty-one percent of those people voted for Donald Trump [...] 73 percent of white evangelicals believed he was doing a good or even excellent job on race relations.[9]

From their point of view, he was indeed doing well on race relations! Posner recounts her 1986 meeting with one of the religious right's political architects, Paul Weyrich, who was a "mentor" to Trump's vice president, Mike Pence. Weyrich told her they would organise, "state by state, city by city, precinct by precinct, to realize conservative domination in politics". In 2001, he apparently oversaw a Christian nationalist manifesto which claimed, "We will not try to reform the existing institutions. We only intend to weaken them and eventually destroy them [...] We will use guerrilla tactics to undermine the legitimacy of the dominant regime."[10]

How could a benighted, religious cult possibly capture one of America's great political parties, and in the process governorships, state legislatures, Supreme Court justices and then the presidency? The evangelical Christian nationalists were certainly well-organised, but they met little resistance. They were like a lunatic invading force discovering that a once formidable enemy had already abandoned its positions. Including those in the traditional institutions of the Republican party itself, which had once upheld the values of conservative administration. Much of its self-belief, essential to traditional paternalism, crumpled as Reagan repeated ad nauseam that "Government is the problem" after his 1980 election. The militant alliance that forged Trumpism didn't need "guerrilla tactics" to secure their influence — the old conservatives that were their enemy had lost the will to resist.

A further web of sustained support for Trump are the very rich, anxious about a majority exercising the right to vote. Two of Trump's backers, who have been profiled recently, signal the staggering wealth of his key financial supporters.

Sheldon Adelson, the casino billionaire, died in January 2021. Apparently, he donated no less than $218 million to the Trump campaign and associated Republican causes, including an anti-Biden political action committee.[11] His *New York Times* obituary singles him out as a key influence in getting the US to move its Embassy to Jerusalem and ran a picture of him wearing a MAGA cap.[12] Adelson authored an op-ed for the *Washington Post* that claimed Trump, "has created a movement in this country that cannot be denied".[13] There are all kinds of movements, some are more deniable than others: in 2013, Adelson paid $47 million to the US government to avoid charges of money laundering, and so has not been found guilty of wrongdoing.[14] Perhaps he saw a fellow innocent in Trump.

As revealing is the role of Stephen Schwarzman. When, after the election, Trump claimed that he had won key battleground states that had been called for Biden, "senior business leaders alarmed by the president's claims that the election is being stolen" came together on a conference call hosted by a Yale management professor. About thirty chief executives of corporations like Walmart and Goldman Sachs heard Timothy Snyder, who has been outstanding in his scholarly warning of the tyrannical dangers of a Trump presidency. He told them a coup d'état was in the offing and business leaders could be crucial in preventing it. Their concerns were dismissed by Schwarzman, the billionaire founder of the aggressive Blackstone fund and an enthusiastic Trump backer, who had donated $30 million to the Republican campaigns. The combination of his influence and indifference was so shocking that three of the participants in what was a private conversation talked to the *Financial Times*, which front-paged the story.[15] On 1 March 2021, Reuters reported that Schwarzman "pocketed at least $610.5 million in 2020 from dividends and compensation".[16] I like the "at least" which allows for his other shareholdings.

Schwarzman and Adelson were not putting their money into encouraging the majority of American voters to express their judgment. They wanted Trump and what he stood for to continue in office. They were also aware of the support he aroused, which included a third element of Trump's alliance, the white power movement. In a compelling account, Kathleen Belew describes how after 1975 many veterans returning from the Vietnam War turned their military training, their horrible experience and their frustration with a defeat they regarded as a betrayal, into "a revolutionary turn within the white power movement". White supremacist vigilantism has "undergirded state power throughout US history". But even though it coincided with Reagan's anti-statism, his "moderation, as activists saw it, revealed conventional politics as unsalvageable".[17] White power supporters were the early shock troops of extreme alienation from politics. In their opposition even to Reagan, the white power movement gave this impetus a kind of libertarian authenticity. Their extreme hostility to government took a paramilitary form, culminating in Timothy McVeigh's bombing of the Oklahoma Federal office building in 1995, which killed 168 people and wounded more than five hundred. After that, they took to the hills, only to be brought back to the ballot box by Trump in 2020.

Trump is from the same generation as Vietnam veterans of the white power movement. The hard core is small in numbers, but their aversion to "Washington" was influential and has given the US a visceral anti-politics unequalled elsewhere. Later, at the end of the century, Peter Mair reflected on the way that the collaboration of all parties in pro-corporate politics opened up a gap between rulers and ruled that he termed "the void".[18] Voters were not apathetic so much as repelled by a system they understood as fixed against them. Anti-politics was a negative energy generated by the void. The US white power activists were its pioneers, opening up the frontiers of nothingness. The more their followers didn't vote, the more they felt justified as they watched the fiascos of Bill Clinton's impeachment and then George Bush's wars. Their influence spread especially among young men, whose personalised claim on citizenship was to have nothing to do with it except demand the right to bear arms. Fox News fed them consolation and confirmation. Trump was different and appealed to them. Many didn't trust him in 2016, suspecting he would be tamed by "the deep state". Uncounted by pollsters, they came out for him in unexpected numbers in 2020, after he proved that he was untamed. Proud and hostile, they had refused to lend the political process the legitimacy of their self-belief until Trump.

Critics of Trump have concentrated predominantly on the role of the right-wing media, especially the relentless corrosion of civic and civilised relationships associated with the tumbrils of Fox News and social media. Murdoch, degenerate but ruthlessly clear-sighted; Steve Bannon and the toxic messaging he orchestrated; Cambridge Analytica's penetration of all people's data profiles and abuse of algorithms to induce voters to abstain, analysed by Paul Hilder[19]; Putin's meddling; and uncounted dark money — all were surely essential to Trump's close victory in 2016. Outriders of Trumpism, the poisonous emissions of their relentless messaging will make democracy unbreathable should they succeed.

They are being investigated and exposed elsewhere. Our societies are not safe until this work is complete. Here, I want to pull back and ask what does the existence of this formidable set of the enemies of human kindness tell us? For they don't believe in anything except themselves and success. They would not have backed Trump if they had not suspected he could be a winner. They based this calculation not on their own capacities but on the energies and forces he was releasing. Racism, evangelicals, big money, white power sentiments and revulsion from the military and economic failure of the bipartisan order, were the main reasons for Trump's success, not the social media, cheating and lies that may have finally ensured his triumph. The dark forces, including the man himself, stirred and thickened but did not provide the ingredients that make up Trumpism — ingredients that remain ready to be stirred again.

Minoritarian Nativism

For all its clout, the most significant feature of Trump's popularity is its weakness: his core constituency is old, white and male. Thanks to his furious campaigning in 2020, he maxed out all the latent support within his demographics. It wasn't enough. A majority finds Trump himself repugnant. They always had, they always did, and they always will. From the middle of his presidency, when it was going well, he could see that he would not command an overall majority — and re-election would depend, as it did in 2016, on the Electoral College votes of swing states. Because his supporters were an overall minority, Trump had to mobilise them all to stand a chance. But mobilising them provoked a counter-reaction in the majority. Trump therefore began a preemptive campaign against the legitimacy of all such votes not cast on the day. From before COVID, Trump understood that for him and his supporters, power depended on preventing their opponents from voting.

There is a suitably ugly one-word term to describe this: minoritarian. Trump and his supporters actively seek to secure minority rule. It is difficult to overemphasise the significance of this limitation. The reason they turn to fascist tropes is that they can't win a majority. The "right" to vote remains ideologically important for them and so they declare they are the "real people" who have "legal votes". Perhaps the best term for this is nativism. Nativist minoritarianism appeals to large sections of the US population of all classes but especially to sections of the rich, the white suburbs, the religious, many — but not all — police and parts of the military, as well as racist zealots and social media addicts. A heteroclite set of the beastly, the fearful, the believing and the merely concerned, that Trump cajoled and conducted into his minoritarian alliance.

The dynamics of Trumpism are not those of a military dictatorship. On one hand, his alliance has a significant following: his rallies are huge; his followers, legion. On the other, it is not enough. This combination generated an embattled siege culture, to exclude and separate those who make up the majority: building walls, expelling immigrants, anathematising opponents, stirring fear and polarisation. In this way Trumpism generates political activism, while seeking to intimidate and paralyse the larger part of the population.

In the United States the ballot has been laced through with discrimination especially since 1890 when Blacks (and poor whites) were systematically disenfranchised and stripped from the electoral roles across the South. Today, the expansion of voting as witnessed in every state in November 2020, and in January 2021 in Georgia, means the incorporation of ethnic minorities of all kinds and hues. Trump's support is built on the desire to *prevent* this from becoming permanent.

A counterargument by Darryl Cooper was shared widely amongst Trump supporters. He wrote a 35-tweet thread on Twitter explaining why they think the 2020 election was stolen. Glen Greenwald asked Cooper to elaborate on his influential thread and published the essay on Substack. Its last paragraph reads:

> Trump supporters were led down some rabbit holes. But they are absolutely right that the institutions and power centers of this country have been monopolized by a Regime that believes they are beneath representation, and will observe no limits to prevent them getting it. I encourage people on the Left to recognize the once-in-a-lifetime opportunity in front

of them. You're not going to agree with the conservatives on everything. But if in 2004 I had told you that the majority of the GOP voter base would soon be seeing the folly of the Iraq War, becoming skeptical of state surveillance, and beginning to see the need for action to help the poor and working classes, you'd have told me such a thing would transform the country. Take the opportunity. These people are not demons, and they are ready to listen in a way they haven't in a long, long time.[20]

It's an important appeal especially as it expresses the class nature of many Trump supporters. But the price for listening to them can't be that one must accept the 2020 election was "stolen". True, many liberals in the power elite did what they could to defeat a man who attacked them. The key issue is not that. A good comparison is with those in Britain who narrowly lost the Brexit vote in 2016 and also regard it as "stolen". Russian influence, illegal payments, data sharing and lies almost certainly tipped the balance in Brexit's favour. Many therefore never accepted its validity and still feel just as Trump supporters do about Biden's win. But the vote was only narrow because London and Scotland voted heavily against Brexit. England without London backed it by an overwhelming 11% majority. This was genuine: in England there was an authentic democratic basis to the outcome — one most opponents of Brexit declined to recognise. A similar syndrome grips Trump supporters. They have condensed their attention onto the unfair operations of the other side. But they need to look around them. Trump was horrible to women and millions of Republican women refused to vote for him. Tens of millions more had enough of him and voted against him. Biden had a massive popular majority. So even if it were true that "the Regime" was responsible for the

42,941 votes that swung the three marginal states and "stole" it, there had to be millions of authentic votes of those who decided they had had enough of Trump to ensure it was so close. Cooper is right that many of Trump's supporters are not demons, have been treated unjustly, deserve respect and rightly distrust the rich. But the respect they deserve has to be matched with respect for the millions of Democrat voters who did not want Trump to be their president and are not patsies for the power elite and were without doubt in terms of the popular vote, the majority. Listening is a two-way process.

The real reason for the funding and media support for the allegations that victory was "stolen" from Trump is future oriented: its aim is to prevent majority success in the future. Whether or not they want Trump himself to head their party, his rich Republican backers across the USA know their power and wealth depends on reinforcing minority rule. For they face rising proportions of non-white ethnicities as well as whites, especially younger ones, opposed to supremacism. Future Republican victories in the state legislatures depend not only on dividing and demoralising their opponents but also on ensuring that they cannot vote at all.

Voter Suppression

After November 2020, the Republican machine decided to strike fast in a coordinated effort to suppress future votes. As early as 19 January 2021, Reuters reported that loyalty to Trump "was on display last week in the Texas state legislature as several Republicans introduced bills to restrict voting access, including limits on mail-in voting and early voting".[21] It was part of a "rush of new bills" from Republican state legislators, according to a detailed report in *The Hill*, justified by the need to "prevent fraud".[22] In Georgia it was already exceptionally hard to vote, as Mary Fitzgerald and Greg Palast have recounted.[23] In March 2021, the Republicans in the State Senate passed additional restrictions so blatant that the Republican Lt. Governor Geoff Duncan refused even to preside over the proceedings and boycotted them.[24]

In July 2021, the Brennan Centre reported "at least 61 bills with restrictive provisions are moving through 18 state legislatures. More specifically, 31 have passed at least one chamber, while another 30 have had some sort of committee action (e.g., a hearing, an amendment, or a committee vote). Overall, lawmakers have introduced at least 389 restrictive bills in 48 states in the 2021 legislative sessions", while "17 states enacted 28 new laws that restrict access to the vote".[25]

A wide variety of schemes are being deployed. In state after state similar key words are being used to justify them, such as the "sanctity" of the vote, the "integrity" of the process and a need "to restore confidence" — all signals of minoritarian nativism.[26] In *Mother Jones*, Ari Burman paints a gripping picture of how Republican state legislatures are redrawing Congressional districts to cement minority power, a danger echoed by Aziz Rana in *Jacobin*.[27]

Not all Republicans stumble into saying what they think in the same way as Republican John Kavanagh, who said, "everybody shouldn't be voting" and "Quantity is important, but we have to look at the quality of votes, as well".[28] Behind closed doors we can be sure they are more explicit as they calculate how best to strip Black families of their right to a say. A cold-eyed, shameless effort to reintroduce Jim Crow laws is underway by the wider political machine that took Trump as its leader.

I'll discuss the response to this in Chapter 6, on The Biden Surprise. What happened on the Republican side seems clear. In office, Trump had intensified his radicalism in one decisive fashion. The economic order until then had relied upon voter fatalism with enormous numbers staying at home. Indeed a key reason Trump won in 2016 was a social media campaign aimed at demoralising young Black voters about Clinton so they continued to abstain. Now his presidency provoked their unprecedented turnout. If this continues to benefit the Democrats as the proportion of Blacks, Latinos, Asians and large numbers of mixed-race citizens increases, the Republicans face extermination by pluralism. Especially because Trump's attacks on the ballot and the disruption of COVID led election officers to make special efforts to ensure as many as possible could vote securely and be counted accurately.

In response, Republicans in State legislatures use "the security of the ballot" as a smokescreen to discriminate against minorities in what is now a battle for the survival of nativist minoritarianism. To back voter suppression is to continue the 6 January assault on the Capitol by more serious means. There can't be a "bipartisan" resolution to such a conflict.

The showdown will also determine what replaces the larger economic order Trump brought to a calamitous close after his predecessors built and ruined a world system. The battle with Biden's "New Old Democrats" is a confrontation over the American political community that extends to the future of capitalism. We now turn to why this is so.

4. From Reagan to Trump: The Rise and Fall of Neoliberalism

When Trump gave his first press conference as president he said, "I am here to change the broken system".[1] When Biden made his first address to the nation from the Rose Garden as president, after signing the American Rescue Plan into law, he said:

> the theory was — we've all heard it, and especially the last 15 years. The theory was: Cut taxes, and those at the top and the benefits they get will trickle down to everyone. Well, you saw what trickle down does. We've known it for a long time. But this is the first time we've been able to, since the Johnson administration and maybe even before that, to begin to change the paradigm.[2]

On the one hand: the big time tax-cutter, white supremacist, climate-change-denying, America-Firster. On the other: the child-welfare, integrationist, environmentalist, democratic, America-leads-the-worlder. Opposites, yet both claimed they would implement a radical turn from the past: Trump denounces a broken system; Biden announces a paradigm shift from what has gone before. Each is in his seventies, has had a long and successful career and is an unlikely revolutionary. Yet when they occupy the White House, both turn their backs on the system that made them.

Backwards into Revolution

Neither is turning his back on capitalism. Far from it, both explicitly welcome the success of millionaires — only Biden says they should pay their taxes and strengthen democracy. The issue in play is how to take American capitalism (and therefore much of world capitalism) forward politically. The underlying difference is over how the US economy should be governed, for what aims and ends. The electoral defeat of Trump in 2020 hardly guarantees that the authoritarian nationalism he advocates will not sweep back, under him or someone else because this is the answer that much of white America believes it needs. The threat of such a comeback obliges Biden to propose a bold programme of popular reform — of the kind his Democratic predecessors anathematised and many of his Congressional colleagues oppose. Beneath the shout-out to all Americans that each is making lies a deepening conflict.

Both Trump and Biden have had to abandon the claim that the market knows best, while politically they take opposite directions of travel. We can't expect them to spell out what they are doing; the money-laundering showman and the professional politician are not theoreticians of the future. An uncertain contest is unfolding, one that can be upturned by the shocks of international affairs and the uncharted dynamics of cyberspace, surveillance, AI, climate change and variants of COVID. What we can be sure of is that Trump and Biden represent conflicting responses to the explosive failure of the way American capitalism has been governed since the 1970s.

Each in his own way has been obliged to repudiate the political form of the economic system that shaped most of their lives — with contrasting claims about how to mend it — in order to express the desires of their energised supporters.

A historic divergence of this kind is full of danger. There is a myth that revolutionary transformations take place when the oppressed and discontented rise up against an established order which they find intolerable. This is not what happens. System change occurs when all parties and classes, including those within the established power structures, realise that the dominant form of government is broken, but differ over how to replace it. Such a collapse is rarely instantaneous, as various efforts are made to resist change. Eventually, as these become more extreme, it becomes clear that society is faced with a choice between fundamentally different futures.

To repeat, this does not come about only because the status quo is challenged but when two conditions are fulfilled. First, that there is a consensus, reluctantly embraced by many, enthusiastically by some, but nonetheless accepted across the board, that the old order has lost its mandate and cannot continue. "Consensus" is perhaps inappropriate as it implies a reasoned agreement. For most working people, there is rage and despair as insecurity and loss of hope kick in. Second, that there is a deep disagreement within the dominant order as to how the status quo should be replaced, rather than broad agreement as to what to do next. When these two factors combine, the way a society is governed will change significantly *in one way or another*.

As the nature of the choice of direction is clarified, the breakdown of the old certainties intensifies under the pressure of the necessity of their replacement. On both sides there will be young and old, the poor, middle classes, intellectuals, organisers and the wealthy mobilised around those elements they hold dear, in opposing cross-class alliances. All will proclaim they are the true expression of the country as a whole. Whoever wins will in fact redefine it — except that "redefine" does not communicate the inevitably unintended consequences, as it suggests preconceived intention.

The dynamics of negativity drive an unpredictable process. There will be much positive and inspiring rhetoric about the way forward — often genuinely intended. But sincerity is not the motivating factor within the competing alliances. Many prefer their side primarily because they find the alternative abhorrent and unbearable. This is one reason why change is often poisonous. Everyone proceeds backwards, repelled by the other rather than desiring the transformation required by the direction they are taking. Each becomes radicalised to ensure the necessary defeat of the other, while their conflict has been set in motion by the irreversible system failure.

Walter Benjamin wrote of the Angel of History whose wings are pinned back by the gale, "The storm irresistibly propels him into the future to which his back is turned, while the pile of debris before him grows skyward. This storm is what we call progress." He penned it in 1940, at the bleakest moment when Nazism was all-conquering and the Soviet Union had signed a pact with Hitler's Germany. Marxists like Benjamin felt betrayed and had to flee or face capture and concentration camp, or in his case take a fatal dose of morphine. By then, there was only one storm: Fascism. His use of "progress" is bitterly ironic. In a period of transformation like our own, the outcome is still in play and there are reasons to hope. "In every era", Benjamin continues, "The Messiah comes not only as the redeemer, he comes as the subduer of Antichrist."

The people of America find themselves divided over who is

the Messiah and who the Antichrist. So too does everyone in countries like mine, which are under US hegemony. To take full measure of the clash we have to look first at the system failure that generated it.

The Advent of Neoliberalism

To do so we need to take a further step back in time. For a societal-wide system to have failed means it must previously have succeeded. What was it that *worked* that is now broken? We know when it broke, in October 2008, when the global financial system caved in. The central bank governors and finance ministers of the G7 met together in the US Treasury. They were told that people in Germany were saying they had seen the fall of communism and now they were witnessing the fall of capitalism. After listening to an appeal from President Bush, they agreed on coordinated action and initiated the rescue of capitalism with unparalleled, coordinated government-backed central bank largesse. Mark Carney, who was a leading participant and became Governor of the Bank of England observes, "The crisis and its aftermath marked the end of the market fundamentalism in finance that began with the Reagan-Thatcher revolution and which grew to the point where the answer to any market failure was to build more markets and/or to deregulate."[3]

They saved the day for capitalism. To do so they had to terminate adherence to the market fundamentalist principles that had guided their collective oversight of it for three decades. This double movement — of successful rescue and radical cessation — set the stage for what has happened since. Capitalism was saved by abandoning the way it had been run. This took place pragmatically, without any explanation to the millions of people who were not "in finance" but who continued to be subordinated to the cruel priorities of a now decapitated market fundamentalism. Eventually they would have their revenge.

Crises, crashes, bubbles and busts are as much part of the nature of capitalism as profitable booms. 2008 was different. Like 1929, the crash threatened to move out of the stock exchanges and money markets into the entire, real economy. In the UK, for example, the ATMs were hours away from being switched off, unable to dispense cash, while the movement of food to the cities would have frozen. The rescue operation mounted by the central bankers and finance ministers prevented an immediate catastrophe and long-term economic depression with mass unemployment. They were able to salvage capitalism because of the enormous, material achievements which had taken place under it over the past half century. Yet their actions struck a blow at the way this had been overseen.

After 1945, the United States emerged from the war with enormous confidence in the capacity and effectiveness of its government. Aside from the 13% who were Black, it delivered high employment, rising wages, unemployment support, access to health and basic welfare and housing. Up to the 1970s and the Nixon presidency, politics governed economics. After the crisis years of the Seventies a different approach took over that Carney refers to as market fundamentalism and is also called neoliberalism. It began to dominate policy internationally through institutions like the IMF in the 1970s and then, in the 1980s, under Ronald Reagan and Margaret Thatcher, the economies and societies of the USA and the UK.

I'm going to be talking about neoliberalism throughout

the book, returning to it from different angles. The view I'm taking is that neoliberalism should be seen as a politics that disarmed the potential of democracy to influence government by inducing popular fatalism. Voters internalised the belief that there was no way they could influence the "realities" of the market, that nothing could be done politically to improve their lives, that they could *only* better themselves by individual effort and competition, that there was indeed "no alternative". This was the bedrock of neoliberalism and its bleakest achievement.

The presidency of Bill Clinton was critical for the supremacy of neoliberalism because he led the Democrats and represented the party that stood for government being on the side of working people rather than the rich. Instead, in his first inaugural in 1993, he proclaimed, "It is time to break the bad habit of expecting something for nothing from our government". In his State of the Union address three years later, he announced, "Government is not the problem, and government is not the solution. We, the American people, we are the solution." This incorporated Reagan's cry of "government is the problem". In case it could be misinterpreted, a week later Clinton told his fellow Americans, "the era of big government is over," and went on to re-election.[4]

Bob Borosage has written, "Most liberals still don't realize how bad Bill Clinton was. Virtually every major decision he made: austerity, financial deregulation, repeal of welfare, mass incarceration, corporate-defined policies on trade and globalization, unleashing Harvard boys on Russia, failing to pass labor law reform (lost by one vote and he didn't produce the vote of the Democratic Senator from Arkansas) — were not just wrong, but disastrous."[5] The policies were only half of it. Because he led the party of the left, Clinton's embrace of the ideology that big government "is over" closed down the space for politics as such. As James Meadway observes, "The peak neoliberal governments – those that perfected the form – were not Thatcher and Reagan's, but those of Blair and Clinton. And the peak neoliberal moment in history was not the defeat of the British miners' strike, but the entry of China into the World Trade Organization in 2001... It wasn't the most ideological governments who were the most neoliberal: it was those who came afterwards, who proclaimed themselves to be 'beyond ideology' or 'beyond Left and Right'".[6]

Neoliberalism propagated powerlessness. Under the welfare capitalism that preceded it, the kind of government you voted for shaped the economy you would live in. Voters felt they were agents with some choice over the direction of travel. Mass parties had strong loyalties and some inner life of debate that shaped policy. From the 1980s onwards, under neoliberalism, the realm of public choice narrowed to the point of disappearance. Supported by the media, the role of government was seen as being to serve and protect market competition domestically and internationally. It was a decades-long process. At its zenith in 2007, one of its overseers, Alan Greenspan, was asked how he would vote in the 2008 US presidential election, and replied, "[we] are fortunate that, thanks to globalisation, policy decisions in the US have been largely replaced by global market forces. National security aside, it hardly makes any difference who will be the next president. The world is governed by market forces."[7]

The young Greenspan, a follower of Ayn Rand, had worked for Richard Nixon's campaign for the presidency in 1968. Reagan made him the head of the federal reserve in 1987, and he was reappointed by Presidents Bush, Clinton and Bush junior through to 2006. He was one of the foremost architects of the neoliberal order. What he helped achieve and revelled in was a political system in which "we are fortunate that" voting "hardly makes any difference". He said it with complacency because voters were not rebelling against this but were resigned to it and could see no way but to accept it: it was a system of closed democracy.

A year later, the system Greenspan had played a central role in constructing was a smoking ruin. In October 2008, at a Congressional hearing on the causes of the financial crash, he was asked whether, "your view of the world, your ideology, was not right, it was not working". Greenspan replied, "That's precisely the reason I was shocked, because I have been going for 40 years or more with very considerable evidence that it was working exceptionally well."[8]

Comment at the time focused on his admitting error. I think we should stress his observation that for forty years things had been going "exceptionally well". Over the forty years from 1979 to 2019, real wages for men in the United States *fell* by 3% for median earners and by 7.7% for those in the bottom tenth.[9] Greenspan is describing a class system at work, one that worked "exceptionally well" only for those at the top.

Neoliberalism presents itself as an economic theory about how the market works best. It has been developed and written about by economists (including its critics). Naturally perhaps, most think of it as a branch of economics. Whereas really it is a theory of politics, of individual freedom and the role of the state, disguised as economics. At its core it regards the state as a threat to individual freedom. As democracy is expressed through the state, society and citizens must be depoliticised — its foremost spokesman, Milton Friedman, even denounced one-person one-vote (an incident I will come back to).[10]

Today, the flaws in the economics of "neoliberalism" are increasingly familiar and its trajectory and debates are being mapped by those expert in them. But perhaps because economists are the authors of these critiques, there is an assumption that while the wrong argument won, nonetheless neoliberalism gained the upper hand because economists persuaded policymakers of its vitality. Naturally, thinkers who favour neoliberalism believe this too. It is the other way around. As an economic theory for advancing the general good, a neoliberal approach is ridiculous (as in the suggestion that wealth will trickle down) and blatantly greedy. The problem to which it provided the solution was political. After the Sixties, governing classes needed to roll back what they experienced as the threat of democracy. Neoliberalism provided an answer: the depoliticisation of politics. This was not an unintended consequence; it was the objective. Except that it was not conceived as a fiendish scheme but embraced in a trial-and-error fashion. The appeal of the "democracy of money" diverted public rejection of elitist class systems into the market place, leaving privilege intact. I will return to this.

The best way to understand the supremacy of neoliberalism, therefore, is as a politics that remained in command but at one remove: its role was to disempower voters (not just unionised workers) and disperse collective agency into market choice, so that individualism became "common sense".[11] As Wendy Brown has argued, neoliberalism sought to replace political men and women with economic men and women; not because capitalism needed to up the rate of profit but because it wished to neutralise the challenge of self-conscious democracy.[12]

Greenspan's sense of triumph in the creation of a world order had been shared. Two months earlier, in 2007, Gordon Brown, as he prepared to become prime minister, made his tenth and final annual speech as the UK's Chancellor to the assembled representatives of Britain's financial centre. He told them how he was proud that he had supported deregulation and encouraged risk-taking across "an era that history will record as the beginning of a new golden age for the City of London […] And I believe it will be said of this age, the first decades of the 21st century, that out of the greatest restructuring of the global economy, perhaps even greater than the industrial revolution, a new world order was created."[13]

Hindsight makes it easy to laugh at the hubris — the new world order was just about to tumble. But we have to distinguish what genuinely succeeded from what was about to fail so catastrophically. The initial expansion of credit that floated the Atlantic economies had turned into a bloated development of financial instruments. But the deregulated expansion of speculation that Brown saluted and was shortly to implode was parasitic upon unprecedented real-world achievements of organised investment, scientific development, engineering accomplishment and the hard work of increasingly educated and trained women and men. This enormous material success gave the political leaders and central bankers the confidence that the world's economy had to be saved from "the crisis of market fundamentalism in finance".

From its early beginnings in the 1970s through to 2008 the neoliberal era saw an enormous expansion of the world economy. International financial organisations like the World Bank and the IMF imposed the "Washington Consensus" on developing countries. Adam Ramsay has argued that, historically, the role of neoliberalism was to replace colonialism as a way of extracting wealth from the Global South.[14] It was certainly accompanied by militarisation with annual world arms expenditure outside the Middle East rising from $800 million in 1968 to today's $2 trillion a year, along with the growth of state and non-state violence.[15] This expenditure alone shows it to be a system of power and domination rather than the rule of "the free market".

Six Aspects of Neoliberalism's Success

Neoliberalism successfully imposed its anti-political framework on the Anglo-Saxon North Atlantic thanks to at least six broad processes: the achievements of the great acceleration; the collapse of Communism; the professionalisation and marketisation of politics; the role of the media-entertainment complex, within whose parameters war and hostility to immigrants became part of the spectacle; the corruption of politics; and the way that despite its role neoliberalism escaped being named.

The Great Acceleration
From the beginning, market fundamentalism succeeded politically because it accompanied what is known as "the great acceleration". The exponential expansion of production and productivity after 1950 turned into vertical growth. Most big-picture surveys stress its environmental recklessness, but there are other factors as well: the success of corporate organisation in the application of research, development, manufacturing and trading; the building of hundreds of millions of heated homes and apartments with running water; the achievement of many small and medium companies in working within local, regional and global markets, supplying a range of foodstuffs and commodities that many people — and not just in the developed world — now take for granted.

In 1950, the world's population was 2.5 billion. In 2020, it was 7.8 billion. In the mid-twentieth century an estimated half of the world's population had no formal education, most women were illiterate, most people lived on the land and most of today's countries were colonies. Today, while 10% of us still have no basic education, this is regarded as shocking.[16] Nearly two-thirds of us have mobile phones, most of us live in cities or towns. An enormous improvement in the human condition has taken place. Neoliberalism exacerbated the uneven features of this process and sabotaged ways in which it could have been made far more humane; nonetheless, it gained legitimacy from it. Ironically, it gained enormously from the economic rise of China, even though China itself resisted market fundamentalism and chose a superior form of developmental capitalism. Over the forty years from 1980 to 2020, China grew from an economy of $200 billion to one of $14 trillion: neoliberalism surfboarded a great wave of capitalist growth for which it was not responsible.

The Collapse of Soviet Communism
The American claim to be the country and system of "the future" seemed to be confirmed by the Soviet system collapsing in 1989. It took the wind out of liberal and social democratic parties and the Democrats in the US caved in to neoliberalism's hegemony. By doing so they closed down electoral opposition to it and vindicated Margaret Thatcher's battle cry, "there is no alternative". A diarchy of left and right now shared the fundamental need to ensure public austerity, international trade and marketisation. Under its sway, end-of-the-century democracy achieved something never deployed before in popular politics with such effect: fatalism. The notion that there is no alternative would echo from 1979

down the decades to Tony Blair in 2005, when he told the Labour Party conference, "I hear people say we have to stop and debate globalisation. You might as well debate whether autumn should follow summer." By globalisation he meant the domination of the world by finance. Political parties no longer even pretended to be vehicles for agency, planning and solidarity, and the blood ran out of electoral choice. Colin Crouch dubbed it *Post-Democracy*. There were critics, warnings and lamentations but a democratic route out of neoliberalism was closed off by the absence of influential organisations advocating such a course; those who did so were outside the pale.

The Marketisation of Politics

Capitalism always seeks to enlarge the market place. Deregulation, privatisations and the expansion of finance, were all underway well before Reagan and Thatcher initiated the politics of prioritising the free market in 1980.[17] Marketisation as a set of economic priorities pre-existed the two leaders, just as it continues to this day. What they introduced — which I am calling neoliberalism — was a politics that disarmed the public's natural opposition to market priorities. While insisting that government was the problem, they used the state to deploy business methods and corporate presentation to persuade the public that the market ruled. Elections were prepared for with intensive research using advanced methods of advertising, public relations companies, secret opinion polling and focus groups, in order to shape the presentation of policies. Manifestos and messages became products. Political language was sterilised as parties sought to become brands.

The "punters" (to use English slang) know they are being played. Even the best marketing can never guarantee success.

It is only when everyone plays the same game that there is no escape from it. The problem was not with any particular campaign, therefore, but the way choice itself was reshaped so as to lack meaning. Up against the apparent modernism of the cult of ownership, historic parties of the left found that their old-fashioned, policy-heavy approach lost elections. New leaders embraced the marketisation of politics with the cold enthusiasm of outsiders. Bill Clinton and his "New Democrats" adopted "triangulation" to retain the presidency in 1996. His political advisor, Dick Morris, is credited with the approach which he described as taking policy positions that "not only blended the best of each party's views but also transcended them to constitute a third force in the debate". A polished way of describing filthy opportunism. Tony Blair embraced Clintonism and turned triangulation into "The Third Way", generating a rash of conferences and a small library of mystification. In 2008, Obama's cry of "Yes We Can" appealed to a desire to break out of the miasma. By 2010, he felt he had to use his State of the Union address to deny that he was triangulating — he needed to because he was; only now he and his advisors were sensitive enough to recognise that, post-crash, voters no longer appreciated being gamed.

In Britain, Blair, along with his key political advisor Peter Mandelson, developed a "manipulative corporate populism".[18] This turned Her Majesty's subjects into consumers not citizens. Within various government departments, genuinely redistributive policies such as "sure start" for children and the child trust fund were initiated. But without an overall justification, the public did not take possession of them emotionally and they were easily abolished after Labour lost the 2010 election.

It seems a paradox. When Reagan and Thatcher first commercialised politics it was experienced by many as empowering. Communities were destroyed, but people also felt freed from the confinement of class and locality — they were offered meaning, even if it was just as competitive individuals. When the centre-left parties adopted and then implemented the same approach and globalised it, a sense of emptiness and loss of meaning followed. The shallowness of party politics as it became a wrapper for capitalism was not a fault — it was successful packaging. The market has to have a container of laws and the consent of the population, the point of neoliberal politics was to ensure this was paper-thin — democratic enough to bestow legitimacy on an economic system that was intrinsically anti-egalitarian and anti-democratic. The process enabled an intensification of inequality that could never gain political approval — no one thinks it is *right* that while an average American CEO earned twenty times more than their employees in the 1960s this should rise to 350 times more in 2017.[19]

In 2010, in a case known as Citizens United, the Supreme Court ruled the law that prevented corporations from funding political action committees was unconstitutional, as it constrained "free speech" — as if corporations are individuals. In a chilling analysis, Wendy Brown shows how the Court's majority decision reinterprets elections as a political marketplace, and turns the democratic right of free speech into an "unhindered capital right", "remaking political life with market values".[20]

The Political Media-Entertainment Complex
The de-democratisation of politics was reinforced by the role of the corporate media, in what became a joint enterprise between proprietors and politicians. Neoliberalism is the period of colour TV. It opens and closes with two US presidents,

Reagan and Trump, who learnt their media communication in television studios. Voters became consumers before they were citizens and, as consumers, were excited by popular competitive culture and new products mediated by the small, bright screen which became flatter and larger and brought the technological revolution into our homes across the four decades. Media culture shifted the relationship of political authority; reporting gave way to opinionizing. In 1988, the US Federal Communications Commission lifted the Fairness Doctrine that required broadcasters to ensure their coverage was balanced. Talk radio with shock jocks like Rush Limbaugh took off, triggering the polarisation we are now familiar with. In 1996, Murdoch created tabloid television with Fox. It became a force for libertarian market values with a loathing of government and helped give neoliberalism its popular, prejudiced base, projected in strident tones reinforced by bullet points, news flashes, and stock exchange-style tickertape, emitting a culture that anathematised collective organisation.

The media was an integral part of the political success of neoliberalism from the beginning. One small episode symbolises the relationship. On 4 January 1981, Rupert Murdoch met with Margaret Thatcher, at his request, and they had lunch at Chequers, the British prime minister's country house, along with her husband and Bernard Ingham, Thatcher's aide and press secretary. Ingham's memo of the "salient points" is typed on plain paper, not official notepaper, and is headed COMMERCIAL — IN CONFIDENCE.[21] All the participants denied they had met, until the memo was published in 2012.[22] Thatcher had been premier for less than two years and was not popular, Reagan had won the election in November and was forming his administration. Murdoch offered to facilitate introductions. "Much of the discussion was concerned with Mr. Murdoch's (favourable) impressions of the embryonic and developing Reagan administration". He singled out "Stockman (Budget) about whom he was particularly enthusiastic". This was David Stockman, known as the "father" of Reaganomics, who was the engineer of tax cuts and launched austerity. The "main purpose of Mr. Murdoch's visit was to brief the Prime Minister on his bid for Times newspapers". He set out how he believed he could make the *Sunday Times* profitable, would put pressure on the *Observer* (then Thatcher's main critic) and promised to keep the *Times* going, although this would need reduced manning levels and new technology, two things Thatcher responded to with approval.

Thatcher told the Cabinet that there was no need to refer Murdoch's bid to the Office of Fair Trading even though he owned the *Sun*. He became the most powerful media proprietor in Britain. With the cornucopia of the *Sun*'s profits, he left for America and its media opportunities. Within the framework of neoliberalism, certainly in the UK, the media owners "went into coalition with government".[23] This was especially important when it came to war. A year after Murdoch and Thatcher looked forward to the coming Reagan revolution, the Falklands/Malvinas islands were invaded by Argentina. The *Sun* led the pack in topless celebration of Thatcher's task force, sent to rescue British pride. More than an alliance was forged. The early lesson was that polarisation against enemies, immigrants and outsiders, the more dramatically belligerent the better, brought readers and revenue, and created loyalty outside the marketplace that could be used to "defend the free market". Twenty years later, every single one of Murdoch's worldwide empire of 175 papers supported the Iraq War.[24] By then, in the UK, the government was Labour and a tabloid journalist, hired as Blair's media controller, had become one of the most influential people in the land.[25]

The larger point is that the media generated a depoliticising culture of tabloid energy as consumerism was sexed up and anti-elitism celebrated. By turning politics into a game show, democracy was disempowered.

Corruption

Corruption, dark money, tax havens, money laundering, have lubricated the expansion of the global economy and are arguably the greatest threat to democracy in world terms as they enrich authoritarian regimes whose leaders then cling to power. I'm just going to signal a financial sideshow of this hugely important process that helped ensure the success of neoliberalism by delegitimising politics in the UK and US.

Media corporations were at the forefront of the rise of top salaries that accompanied the intensification of inequality. It meant that when ministers were interviewed about important issues like defence or education, or the national budget, they found themselves interrogated by people earning three or four times their salary. While this reflected the shifting balance of power, it was only natural for the politicians to feel that they were being underpaid.

In the United Kingdom, to save the Thatcher government from the embarrassment of raising their salaries when it was attacking public sector pay, Members of Parliament were given a permissive policy towards their expenses and encouraged to take second jobs. This weakened their capacity to hold the executive to account. When, finally, freedom of information legislation came into force, a lone investigator, Heather Brooke, forced the compilation of their expenses. These were then leaked in unredacted form to the *Telegraph*. An enormous scandal humiliated the House of Commons as the money-grubbing behaviour of most members of parliament was exposed (to give just one example, David Cameron — already a wealthy man, married to a millionaire and shortly to be prime minister — charged taxpayers for planting wisteria in his country home). Politicians were suborned and then pilloried for being suborned, thus demonstrating the uselessness of politicians, which in turn makes voters feel helpless as corporate interests set the parameters of the possible.

In America, serious money comes into play. The Clintons, for example, made $125 million from speeches between 2001 when they left the White House and 2015.[26] After she lost the presidency, Hillary was asked why she took $675,000 for three confidential talks to Goldman Sachs as she prepared to run in 2016. She replied, "men got paid for the speeches they made. I got paid for the speeches I made."[27] It is true, the fuss made about her payments had a twist of misogyny. The men did get paid and this was the norm — it had been so for decades. When British Prime Minister John Major lost office in 1997, he was quietly recruited, apparently by ex-President George Bush senior, onto the European Board of the Carlisle Group, a huge private equity fund that specialised in the arms industry, as well as various international banks. Major became a millionaire. No one has ever questioned him about it.

The process of corruption is systemic and much of it is legal. The epicentre of shady corruption and global money-laundering, turning dark and illicit funds into openly tradeable assets, is the City of London. A political system that accepts, indeed expects, such behaviour has been corrupted. Everyone knows it is wrong. Again and again, we are told about reports that express concern with how the public has "lost trust" in politics, as if voters are to blame for making a good call. It led many in the US to choose Trump as being the real thing.

Say the Word

The domination of neoliberalism rested on it gaining political acceptance despite its unpopularity. One way this was achieved was by scorning the use of the term. There is nothing wrong with being "ideological"; we all are — we all have beliefs that govern our lives. What is evasive and deeply subversive about neoliberalism is the way it denies its own nature. Which is convenient if you want to avoid being called out. Those who sought to use the word were, to use the latest description of censorship, "cancelled". This worked for decades. Finally, after half a century of imposing its harsh realities on developing countries, the IMF published a report in May 2016 in which three of its economists surveyed the influence of the Fund's "neoliberal" agenda across fifty-three countries and named it as such. The report said the IMF's "neoliberal" policies had seen millions brought out of poverty and privatised inefficient state industries. But the accompanying austerity, competition and deregulation "had not achieved very much" while it had increased inequality to the point that this hurt sustainable growth and lead to "the pervasiveness of booms and busts". The *Financial Times* ran a furious editorial, its anger aroused not by learning of the cruelty of IMF-imposed policies on poorer countries but at the use of a word: "neoliberalism". This, the Editorial thundered, was an "all-purpose insult", that had "lost all meaning" and led to "navel gazing [and] childish rhetoric". It turned out to be a cry of rage at the rising of the sun as it cleared the fog. Within a few months the paper was publishing articles that referred to neoliberalism without embarrassment. The episode is telling as it demonstrates the ferocity of the long years that protected neoliberalism from being named.[28]

Think of the term "neoliberalism" as a doorway. It tells us that there is somewhere else that is not neoliberal, somewhere where it is possible to be governed democratically and not by the market. When Thatcher said there is "no alternative"; when Clinton said "It's the economy, stupid"; when Blair said globalisation could not "be debated", they were all saying there is no such doorway. Hence the importance of the word and the effort to make it unspeakable.

The Dangerous Failure of Neoliberalism

Across forty years of unprecedented economic expansion, neoliberalism ruled the roost. It was an awesome achievement organised by a hegemonic USA, supported by the UK, as the City of London became a strategic epicentre of America's financial overlordship. The era of market fundamentalism witnessed unprecedented global expansion; tore down international barriers; replaced competing colonialisms with a single, international system of wealth extraction from poorer countries; generated inequality as well as an emancipation from poverty; and incorporated political leaders from across the spectrum, marginalising those who resisted it. In the process it retained the pacified assent of the US public despite flatlined incomes. Global corporations ensured that the priorities of neoliberalism dominated the media sphere and were reinforced with tabloid intimidation, as use of the term was repressed. Its spirit of untouchability and its claim to express human nature reinforced widespread fatalism. For the final twenty years of its supremacy, between 1989 and 2008, it did indeed seem that there was no alternative.

Yet today neoliberal politics is a shattered Ozymandias, its "wrinkled lip, and sneer of cold command" broken on the sands of our own experience; its "values" of giving priority to a rentier economy, served by a rentier state, for the benefit of unregulated rent holders, held in contempt by the younger generation.

There is a danger in premature celebration of this downfall. The massively unequal financial and corporate order it permitted and protected still stands. The transformation of capitalism carried out in its name has not been rolled back. In some ways it has been strengthened now that the state and government instead of being denigrated are shamelessly deployed to prop up finance and corporate revenues after COVID-19, while inequality has been intensified. But the political formula that disarmed opposition and got capitalism to this point is no longer operable. Neoliberalism was a politics that gave capital the use of the state while persuading voters they were powerless. They no longer accept that they are.

Four Strikes

Four developments brought down neoliberal politics: the financial crash, the success of the Peoples Republic of China, the climate emergency and the COVID pandemic. Without the first two, Donald Trump would not have become president; without the second two, he would still be president.

Before looking at what undid neoliberalism, three things need emphasis. First, its claim that human nature is essentially competitive and greedy is wrong — most of us prefer producing for use and sharing; we like aspiration, not profit maximisation and its insecurities. Neoliberalism's unpopularity is rooted in a wise recognition of its inhuman character.

Second, voters' revulsion from its inhuman ideology demanded a continuous effort to ensure its domination. Peasants revolted only rarely. Thanks to religion, lack of education, poverty, hunger and the brutal power of their lords, they were obliged to live out their fate. But neoliberalism needed globalised, urban, educated women and men as consumers. It needed to motivate them to acquire, take on debt and rent or buy property. It therefore stimulated peoples' agency in the marketplace. This intensified the need to keep a lid on them politically.

Third, the combination of encouraging insatiable desires and suppressing self-determination, generates mental illness and addiction. Even to accept you are helpless demands considerable energy in managing shame and reining in wishes so as to prevent disappointment. Eventually, the frustration exploded in baleful, inhuman and reactionary forms.

Thus the legacy of neoliberalism lives on: both in the power systems of national capitalisms and global finance and the inequality they generate and also in our personal lives and beliefs. We may have left its rule; we have not yet left its world.

Neoliberalism Undone by the Crash

The decisive rupture of neoliberalism as a political ideology occurred with the financial crash. Some, like Ann Pettifor and Nouriel Roubini had predicted the disaster. Roubini specifically tagged the US house price bubble as a likely trigger. No one foretold the nature and scale of the response. Western governments and central banks bailed out the threatened institutions and printed money on a breathtaking scale to rescue the system. At a stroke the two core claims of neoliberalism were shown to be worth less than tissue paper: instead of "the market knows best" and "government is the problem" we had the market fails and government is the solution.

Market fundamentalism as a theory has never recovered. But those who saved the system had been formed in its mental universe. They presumed that the public's fatalism and depoliticisation, on which they had built their careers, would continue. Instead of reversing neoliberal social policies, the US and UK ruling elites intensified the imposition of market "realities" on the electorate.

In the UK, a Conservative-Liberal alliance took over from Labour in 2010. The rescue of a bloated banking sector had led to the world's largest deficit increase as a proportion of GDP. Instead of blaming this on New Labour's reliance upon the City of London for tax revenues, the coalition led by David Cameron, George Osborne and Nick Clegg (respectively prime minister, chancellor and the Lib-Dem leader) accused Labour, falsely, of overspending. They then assaulted public spending, accelerated the marketisation of the NHS and savaged local government funding. The already impoverished regions were hit hardest. Later they would map with uncanny correlation as the areas that voted most strongly for Brexit.

It is worth pausing on this sideshow for a moment as it sheds light on the main story. Gordon Brown, the Labour premier in 2008, had been a cheerleader for neoliberalism. But he was formed as a young man in left-wing debates and had strategised Labour's embrace of globalisation after 1989. When the financial crash occurred, Brown played a leading role in the international rescue operation because he had a measure of the need for public spending to rectify the damage.

By contrast, Cameron, duplicitous and worthless; Osborne, cunning and avaricious; Clegg, vain and shallow, were young, smooth men who had been entranced by Blair. They loved politics as the plaything of the financial markets. For them, high public office was a career move to gain the experience and connections that would open up the massive rewards of being on the boards of global funds and corporations (as, indeed, has happened). Voter discontent with the aftermath of the financial crash lifted them into office. Then, incapable of their own strategic thinking, they proceeded to govern as if the priorities of neoliberalism were still intact.

People are already beginning to look back and ask, when did the United Kingdom cease to be a serious player and become petulant, narcissistic and self-harming. The answer is with Cameron, Osborne and Clegg. Not just because this is what the three men are, but because it led them to intensify the anti-democracy of market fundamentalism upon the United Kingdom, just as people woke up to the fact they had been sold a false prospectus. The coalition carelessly abandoned that aspect of political life in Britain which had ensured its historic continuity and validated a modern state without a modern constitution: namely, a deep sense of reciprocal consent. Through wars and general strikes and slumps and booms, the British public has had to put up with a lot of bad government. But there was still a belief that those who rule us care about us and, to use an old-fashioned word, as this is a pre-modern sentiment, that they were gentlemen with some integrity, or at least desired to be. This was true of Thatcher and Major and even Blair as well as Brown. But Cameron, Osborne and Clegg were laughing at us. They had completely absorbed the neoliberal idea that markets ruled the world, that voting was a form of entertainment, that party politics was a branch of corporate power, and they knew best. Thanks to the stupefying way they imposed neoliberalism on the country after neoliberalism had had its day, the historic Britain that fell into their hands is now beyond recovery.

The most grievous imposition of a neoliberal politics after the crash, however, occurred in the USA. There, the banks and lenders were bailed out with astronomical largesse. But, "9.3 million American families lost their homes to foreclosure, surrendered their homes to a lender, or were forced to resort to a distress sale".[29] Most of the nine million were connected to other families via parents, children, siblings, friends and colleagues. As the banks were rescued the families of middle-America were failed, and the politics of neoliberalism lost its credibility across swathes of American opinion. According to one account, a former Federal Reserve vice-chairman proposed rescuing many of the vulnerable home owners, as happened under Roosevelt. He said that he "was laughed out of court".[30] In an excruciating review of a study of the housing crisis, Larry Summers who presided over Obama's National Economic Council in 2009–10, claims he organised monthly meetings to try and find ways to assist homeowners and failed.[31] His special pleading about the costs, and Obama's second-guessing of what could get through Congress, betray the reality: the banks — and bankers — *had* to be saved; the homeowners did not. For decades, US voters had accepted flatlined incomes because there was no alternative. Now public money flooded into the pockets of billionaires who had screwed up, while the bailiffs tossed a neighbour's belongings into the street or a relative lost their home and the savings they had invested in it.

David Stockman, the instigator of neoliberalism when he

was Reagan's Director of the Office of Management and Budget from 1981–5, was scathing about the way Goldman Sachs was rescued after the crash in 2008. In 2011, he told an interviewer, "Once the broad public sees that the cronies of capitalism are bailed out by their friends in Washington and the Fed, why should they believe that the system we have is fair or is working in their interests?"[32] It's a point that many critics on the left made, before the crash as well. Coming from the right, it was a harbinger of Trump. The system never was fair, but it had been accepted as such by many in the US public. They thought it was rough but not rigged. They had been sold neoliberalism by Ronald Reagan as an emancipation of the American dream of self-reliance from government regulation. Now government was pouring money into the pockets of the rich. Although the word neoliberalism had never and probably will never pass their lips, they had accepted depoliticisation and thus fulfilled its political purpose. Now, on the right they were to mobilise around the Tea Party, on the left around Occupy Wall Street, and in 2016 they upended political fatalism at the ballot box.

Neoliberalism Undone by China

The growth of China since Deng Xiaoping became its leader in 1982 is the single most significant improvement in one country's living standards in human history, accompanied by the most massive one-generation migration from the land to the city, and the longest sustained period of economic growth. In her important account, *How China Escaped Shock Therapy*, Isabella Weber shows that while the ruling communists opened up the country to marketisation, after an intense debate they refused to implement the neoliberal agenda. I'm going to come back to the importance of this for the Biden presidency in the next chapter. Unlike Russia, the Chinese did not relinquish political control as they embraced capitalism. They planned and directed it and sought to manage the release of energy and investment it instigated. It proved an extraordinary success. Much of the world's expansion in trade, from which the financial sector in London and New York benefited, stemmed from China's colossal growth.

If you compare China's achievement to what happened across much of the developing world where, according to its own report on its "neoliberal agenda", the IMF "had not achieved very much" apart from "the pervasiveness of booms and busts", you get a measure of how much better the world would be if the epoch of the great acceleration had not been dominated by Wall Street and overseen by Ayn Rand addicts like Greenspan.

Through the Nineties, however, and as China joined the World Trade Organisation in 2001, the conceit in the West was that an economic process was underway that would inevitably lead to China's integration into, and therefore subordination to, a dollar-denominated neoliberal order. Instead, while US policymakers permitted the dismantling of manufacturing across their country, arguing that cheaper goods benefited consumers, China consolidated its amazing expansion and began to invest strategically in advanced technology. After Beijing survived the financial crash, American rulers began to realise that a communist state was a capitalist competitor — gaining on the US in overall economic influence and pulling ahead of it in key technologies, *and* hollowing out the "American way of life", thanks to US permissiveness.

China disrupted neoliberal nostrums across the board. It showed that an active state ensured more effective and sustained growth of a market economy. Its success meant

America needed countermeasures. The challenge did not have as great an impact on popular sentiment as the disillusionment that followed the crash of 2008. But across Washington the whole political class began to realise they needed government to be active in the economy after all. If the crash ended market fundamentalism "in finance", China ended it in trade and manufacturing.

Neoliberalism Undone by the Climate Emergency

Since the 1970s, the fossil fuel corporations have been aware that pollution endangered life on Earth. A clear public understanding of this would lead to efforts to restrain their business. This would cut the profits generated by the extraction, processing and sale of energy. They lobbied massively, consistently and successfully against the regulation of carbon emissions. An unmeasured and perhaps unaccountable part of the long reign of neoliberal recklessness is due to the automobile, mining and oil industries' subversion of political parties and government officials. By undermining the need for good government, market fundamentalism assaulted the wellbeing of the planet for the advantage of capital. They endangered human existence for short term gain. The mainstream media, above all Rupert Murdoch's, supported this and played a big role in perpetuating the catastrophe.

While the scientific evidence has become irrefutable and extreme weather events more frequent, it was the tireless efforts of campaigners that slowly convinced the public and policymakers. In the second decade of the twenty-first century the consequences of unrestrained exploitation of Earth's resources and mass-chemicalisation of the environment ceased to be a matter of prediction. Floods, fires, palpable climate change, cyclones, cancers, smog, droughts and humanitarian disasters are now frequent. The case for action has ceased to be about preventing what might happen and became a call to limit what is already taking place. The imperative need to respond to the climate emergency caused by the way capitalism has expanded cannot be left to the market. Capitalism may well be renovated and given a new lease of life thanks to subsides, state aid and the planning of a sustainable, carbon-zero economy. But not by neoliberal politics.

Neoliberalism Undone by COVID-19

I am going to look at the impact of the SARS-CoV-2 virus on the rise of Biden in the next chapter. Here I just note that the pandemic forced the universal abandonment of the neoliberal principle of government abstention from the economy. This concluded the process that had begun in 2008.

Trump: Neoliberalism in One Country

Now we can return to the arrival and power of Trump. He is a product of two aspects of the economy generated by neoliberalism: corruption and the spectacle. As a property speculator and developer, he manipulated businesses that gained from money laundering and the conspicuous consumption generated by extreme increase in super-wealth. As an entertainer, he gained a fortune from 50% of the profits made by The Apprentice, a reality TV show launched in 2004, which was a "huge hit" and in which he starred; its culture celebrated desire, money making and insecurity and helped him leverage his reputation into a brand. After it saw his tax returns, the *New York Times* calculated "that between

2004 and 2018, Mr. Trump made a combined $427.4 million from selling his image".[33]

By 2015, the shine had worn off The Apprentice and Trump explored elevating his image into the ultimate hall of fame by running for the presidency. As an outsider he rode the tiger of "unmeasurable discontent". Rather than induce a further state of comatose indifference in the average voter, as the Republicans' favourite son Jeb Bush was doing, Trump aroused them. He made voting matter and torpedoed neoliberal fatalism, as his rallies became media events in the form of a revivalist crusade, with those who had seen and videoed him spreading the word as clips transmitted the drama of his appeal.

His second audacious move was to call out neoliberalism globally. His frankness was integral to his appeal. Having sunk Jeb Bush with the blunt truth about the Iraq War, as we've seen, Trump went on to give devastated communities across America a clear picture of what the internationalisation of their capitalism had done to them. Campaigning in Pittsburgh, Pennsylvania, a key state in his eventual victory, he said, "Our politicians have aggressively pursued a policy of globalization — moving our jobs and our wealth and our factories to Mexico and overseas. Globalization has made the financial elite who donate to politicians very, *very* wealthy. I used to be one of them [...] But it has left millions of our workers with nothing but poverty and heartache." When Trump accepted the nomination, he told the gathering of Republicans at the convention, "special interests [...] have rigged our political and economic system for their exclusive benefit [...] My message is that things have to change and they have to change right now [...] Nobody knows the system better than me, which is why I alone can fix it." And he added, "Americanism not globalism will be our credo".[34]

Trump's political attraction was his shameless account of how things were. It turned minoritarian nativism into an apparently legitimate claim on the world as his supporters experienced it as truthfulness. When people voted for him, part of the attraction was that he personified opposition to the hypocrisy of the neoliberal elite pretending there was no alternative. For many Trump is still a refreshing and, in this sense, an honest figure.

An interesting "might have been" is what would have happened had Bernie Sanders managed to win the nomination. He made similar speeches to Trump's in Pennsylvania, as he too called out corporate globalism and demanded a break from the past. And he would have pointed the finger at Trump as a plutocrat.

But Sanders and the left spoke the truth about globalisation not just to end fatalism but also to replace it with a revival of democratic politics. Trump's rhetoric was self-centred and reinforced the long-established flow of market fundamentalism: its anti-politics. It's a paradox. He ended fatalism. He made elections matter by generating a real choice. He stirred people up and smashed the political methods of neoliberalism but not its underlying culture of celebrating individual market success, while his aim was to preserve its gains for the rich and corporate interests. Naomi Klein puts it well when she sees him as the "culmination" but also the "logical end point" of the epoch's culture: "That greed is good. That the market rules. That money is what matters in life. That white men are better than the rest. That the natural world is there for us to pillage. That the vulnerable deserved their fate and the one percent deserved their golden towers. That anything public or commonly held is sinister and not worth protecting. That we are surrounded by danger and should only look after our own. That there is no alternative to any of this."[35] Except for that last sentence. He may have wanted there to be no alternative but because Trump was a such provocation, you knew there had to be one.

As Branko Milanović observes in what for him is an optimistic as well as an insightful column, "Trump tore off the curtain which divides citizens, the spectators of the political game, from the rulers and displayed the wheeling-dealing, exchange of favors, the use of public power for private gain in an open, in-your-face manner, available for all who attended the show to see." He continues, "While in the past administrations such illegal and semi-legal actions, as receiving money from foreign potentates, moving from one to another lucrative position, cheating on taxes were done with discretion and some decorum, with the curtain lowered so that spectators could not see and participate in the malfeasance, this was now done in the open. These are unpardonable sins. Sins enjoyed in secret are acceptable or overlooked; sins flaunted are not."[36]

However, while Trump's kleptocratic, authoritarian and misogynistic behaviour may have been unpardonable to many, others loved it. More important, many funded it and not just because as a rebarbative candidate he divided voter support, using the age-old rhetoric of racialising the dangers of the "other". In the Noughties, I also underestimated the power of Trump's flaunting of his malfeasance. While in New York for *openDemocracy*, I looked out on mid-town Manhattan from a small room high in the UN Plaza hotel. There were the shining skyscrapers of the great city, built on borrowed money, funded by anonymous financiers. And sticking out from amongst them there was a monolith with someone's name — TRUMP TOWER. I thought it was ridiculous — uncouth, childish and unprofessional. The function of New York City's neoliberal cityscape was to present its structures as geological facts — the achievement of a system that could not be personified or questioned. You can marvel at their engineering, but the ranks of towers spelt out that even the sky has to submit. Amongst all this, he was an obvious crank consumed by phallic insecurity and defiance, or so I thought.

Donald Trump surprised us. He grasped the leadership of a United States groggy from the financial crash, bleeding its hegemony in the Middle East, astonished by the rise of China, polluting its glorious landscape, and failing to pay its working citizens more in real terms for forty years. He brought home market supremacy with a vengeance, yet reversed the resignation that had once ensured its acceptance. He closed the welcoming gates of the "City of a Hill" that claimed to be a beacon to the world. He assailed NAFTA and TPP, denounced globalism and levied tariffs on China, the EU and Canada. He cut taxes for the hyper-rich and corporations (like his own), let regulation wither, packed the judiciary with reactionary white Christians and lavished billions on all branches of the military.

Large sections of US capital opposed him, the law-abiding, liberal, open to talent, international as well as domestic companies both traditional and hi-tech. But the decades of market fundamentalism had bred another capitalism, of gambling, drugs, pornography, arms sales and real estate; 9% of America's billionaires, together worth a combined $210 billion — either directly or through their spouse — pitched in to assist the costs of Trump's 2020 campaign.[37] Trump was their candidate thanks to his uncanny ability to make the blatantly wicked extraordinarily popular. For me the still shocking symbol of this was the way he ran down the IRS, the Inland Revenue Service, so that even legally due taxes were not levied from the wealthy while many who did pay them voted for him and, in effect, for being robbed.

It worked. He generated an economic recovery sufficient to win a second term and consolidate his grip domestically and internationally. After decades of flatlined incomes, job losses, rising health costs and mounting debts this may not have been hard. But he did it. According to the *Wall Street Journal*, "During the first three years of the Trump presidency, median household incomes grew, inequality diminished, and the poverty rate among Black people dropped below 20% for the first time in post-World War II records. The Black unemployment rate went under 6% for the first time in records going back to 1972 […] Low unemployment produced cascading benefits. Wage growth accelerated, and opportunities for low-skilled workers grew."[38]

Thanks to this, as in 2016, he would have retained the swing states needed to win in the electoral college. An Iron-Men international awaited his re-election. It would not have been a world of Nazism, because Trump opposed expansionism. But an authoritarian, racist globe was in the offing, policed by the stormtroopers of social media, backed by the deep pockets of billionaires and perfectly capable of upturning the historic procedures, checks and balances of the US Constitution, with massive domestic support in America itself. The Nazis were young, fresh and came to power a little over a decade after the party was formed, led by a 44-year-old Hitler. Trumpism is the gnarled consequence of decades of market fundamentalism, that had planted its tentacles deep into the fabric and mentality of America, led by a 70-year-old master of its arts. How is it possible, therefore, that Trumpism has been frustrated — at least for now?

5.   Out of the Belly of Hell

In November 2019, a year before the presidential election, Trump was set to win a second term. There was no evidence that his support would rise above 50%, but 46–47% was the Plimsoll line on which he could float back to office. And nothing he did seemed capable of driving his support down below the low forties, which would have made his defeat inevitable. Wages and employment were rising, and Trump's was a strong narrative about success and making America great.

He had already launched his campaign against the validity of the ballot because he wanted to legitimate his ongoing, minoritarian rule. As the master of the pre-emptive strike and the tactic of accusing your opponent of the misdemeanours you are about to commit, he asserted the election could be stolen. At one rally he toyed with the idea of an unconstitutional third term. At the back of his mind may have been the calculation that fuels the stubbornness of every authoritarian — only by retaining presidential immunity would Trump be able to protect himself from the possible jail sentence so many of his associates had already experienced.

He had good reason to think long term. The Democratic opposition seemed to pose little threat. Its most able candidate was an intelligent, left-wing woman, Elizabeth Warren, already the object of his scorn and designed to inflame his base. The most effective, with the strongest counter-narrative, was Bernie Sanders. His gentle, social-democratic programme and willingness to address "the system" ensured that Murdoch and Fox news (now untrustworthy and tiring of Trump's antics) would annihilate him. "Sleepy" Joe Biden seemed like a deadbeat from the past.

Meanwhile, Trumpism was backed by organised religious congregations, rich supporters, the racially prejudiced, judicial reactionaries, Republican officials across all fifty states, often in governing positions, foundations, think-tanks and public relations professionals pumping out a polarising torrent of fear and distortion as well as the worldwide kleptocracy (Russia's Vladimir Putin had enough details on his dodgy funding to blow him out the water[1]). Trump had every reason to look forward to reinauguration, and just as important, the Republican movement under his leadership was poised to consolidate its power, something the relatively better "down the ballot" results for the House and the Senate confirmed in November 2020.

Trumpism was set to establish itself as the long-term, post-crash authoritarian replacement of globalist neoliberalism in the United States. It did just this in the United Kingdom. The Boris Johnson government won a large parliamentary majority in December 2019 with only 43% of the popular vote. Behind Johnson was the similar alliance to the one that backed Trump: Rupert Murdoch's media, the UK's tax haven based hedge funds, Putin's helping hand, a frustrated longing for better times. Coverage of the UK often flip-flops from excessive admiration for its "effortless" royal superiority to unjustified contempt for its miserable fall from grace. It should be seen as a considerable middle-country with an experienced military, an independent judiciary and an advanced financial sector that has exploited its location and language to become a world centre for money management. What it suffers from, like the USA, is a nineteenth-century winner-takes-all political system designed to create an exceptionally powerful executive — an arrangement that makes both countries susceptible to institutional capture, the UK especially so as the checks and balances were cultural and moral and not codified in a basic law or constitution. Westminster is now in the grip of a quasi-dictatorship rewriting the rules and imposing voter suppression, whose leader lies to parliament.[2] What has happened in the United Kingdom was about to happen in the United States.

Then a terrible misfortune occurred that saved America from the triumph of Trumpism.

Pandemics

A virus that would soon be known as SARS-CoV-2 entered someone still unknown in central China's Wuhan, the capital of Hubei province, in late November or December 2019. While he or she had no obvious symptoms, it spread on their breath and a deadly pandemic was unleashed. The microorganism's origin may have been from a zoonotic transmission of a mutation that had jumped from a bat to another species and then a human, or directly from a bat. It may have been the product of an experiment in the Wuhan Institute of Virology which then escaped the laboratory. An analysis of the probabilities by Nicholas Wade in *Bulletin of the Atomic Scientists* suggests the latter. Others say evidence points to Wuhan's wet markets. Eighteen academics, most of them distinguished biological scientists, say both theories are "viable". A careful analysis by Zeynep Tufekci adds the suggestion that it was caught from a bat by a lab worker.[3] What really happened needs to be properly researched without any anti-Chinese prejudice.[4]

However it emerged, the new coronavirus was a side effect of globalisation: either a consequence of the exponential expansion of the human population with its demands for food and resources forcefully impinging on other species; or the rapid international development of knowledge, including experiments with the minute building blocks of life. Yet it was also natural in that it was an external event not generated by human will. Deadly pandemics are a regular feature in history. In the past not much could be done about them except suffer the consequences and restrict movement to slow down the rate of contagion. Fatalism of both government and people was the norm. Logically, therefore, a pandemic that proved the limitations of state power should have been a perfect backdrop for regimes like Trump's and Johnson's.

A hundred years ago, when perhaps fifty to 100 million died in the 1918–20 flu epidemic, governments were not blamed. In 1943, the British government did not feel responsible for the Bengal famine that took two million of its subjects' lives, continuing an official indifference to genocide that goes back to the Irish famine. In 1957–8, a flu pandemic killed around one million people worldwide. In the UK estimates of deaths vary from 14,000 to 30,000. Before it arrived from Asia, a *British Medical Journal* report noted, "The public seems under the impression that nothing can be done to prevent the calamity",[5] and indeed in the UK the Macmillan government managed not to be bothered.[6] In 1968, the Hong Kong or H3N2 flu virus killed over 700,000 people worldwide, around 100,000 in the US.[7] But there were no mass shutdowns of national economies.[8] It seems to have made little impact and is now largely forgotten.

In Britain, resignation was official policy. In October 2016, a three-day simulation codenamed *Exercise Cygnus* assessed the UK's preparedness for a flu pandemic. It foresaw between 200–400,000 excess deaths over a few months, with the health services overwhelmed. The results were regarded as too shocking to be published and remained secret, a sign perhaps of an underlying shift in attitude. But the policy of acceptance remained unchanged.[9] Although it identified shortage of ventilators as a critical issue, new orders for them were later cut back as a "necessary" cost-cutting measure. *Cygnus* showed that government passivity was built into the presumptions of future disaster management.

Both the Trump and the Johnson administrations did their best to continue in this hands-off tradition when they got the news of COVID-19. Neither had serious domestic political opposition at the start of 2020. Both leaders were masters of the media and ruthless in their dealings. Yet by mid-March, each of them gave the go-ahead for massive economic lockdowns and agreed to subsidise the costs for business — policies they loathed.

I want to identify what imposed this turnaround. Before doing so I'll examine the gruesome ways Trump and Johnson sought to evade acting as they did, as this shows how strong the forces were that frustrated them.

The Virus Arrives

On 7 January 2020, Chinese researchers isolated the SARS-CoV-2 virus and published its genetic sequence. On 23 January, just ahead of the Chinese New Year that sees the largest annual mass movement of people on the planet; Wuhan, a city of eleven million, was locked down. On 24 January,

Cheng Wang and colleagues published "A Novel Coronavirus Outbreak of Global Health Concern" in the *Lancet*, the independent, London-based, peer-reviewed medical journal. It compared COVID-19's already known "case-fatality" ratio in China to that of the 1918 influenza pandemic with its tens of millions of victims. The authors' conclusion: "Every effort should be given to understand and control the disease, and the time to act is now."[10]

Four days later, on 28 January, President Trump was told by his National Security Advisor, "This is going to be the roughest thing you face." The advisor's deputy, the Chinese speaking Matt Pottinger, agreed and reported that his Chinese contacts had even compared it to the 1918 influenza. Evidently, he had yet to be shown the *Lancet*. He advised an immediate ban on all incoming travellers from China. On the same day, Dr Tedros, the Director General of the World Health Organisation, visited China and met President Xi Jinping. When he got back to his colleagues on 30 January, the WHO declared an official PHEIC: a Public Health Emergency of International Concern.[11]

On 2 February, Trump claimed, "We pretty much shut it down coming in from China."[12] The weasel words "pretty much" meant he knew it was incomplete. Five days later, he talked with Xi Jinping himself on the phone. "We had a great talk for a long time. But we have a good relationship. I think we like each other a lot," Trump told Bob Woodward that same evening. "The Chinese were very focused on the virus," Trump told him. "you know, it's a very tricky situation […] It goes through air. That's always tougher than the touch. You don't have to touch things. Right? But the air, you just breathe the air and that's how it's passed. And so that's a very tricky one […] It's also more deadly than even your strenuous flus."[13] It was a private conversation with Woodward, one of a series for the book he was writing.

Xi alerted the US president to the danger in no uncertain terms at the start of February 2020, confirming what Trump's own national security team had told him. Looking back, we can see that this was an extraordinary moment for authoritarian collaboration. The two leaders could have issued a joint alert for the world: wear masks, stay distant, quarantine if ill, freeze international travel, no exceptions. Millions of lives would have been saved. Trump would have been re-elected, because voters everywhere supported incumbents who sought to unify their country in the battle against the virus. Xi would have gained recognition as a world leader alongside the US president in an authoritarian diarchy.

To appeal to all Americans with such a policy demanded a culture of government. Trump's brand was the opposite: boastfulness, competition and blame. You have to credit Trump with integrity — he was true to himself and his base. There was no coordination with China. He decided to let America ride it out. Three days after talking with Xi he announced, "I think the virus is going to be — it's going to be fine." On the same day he said, "looks like by April, you know in theory when it gets a little warmer, it miraculously goes away". On 24 February, "The Coronavirus is very much under control in the USA"; on 26 February, "the 15 [cases in the US] within a couple of days is going to be down to close to zero […] This is a flu. This is like a flu." He knew it wasn't. In public he said the opposite of what he himself had told people in private.[14] In March, he said to Woodward, "I wanted to always play it down." Asked why, in the run up to the election, he told reporters, "We have to show calm […] We want to show confidence. We have to show strength."[15]

It was weakness: he had to show his base he was not for turning, let alone due to a minute foreign virus. Also, there was no longer an all-American "narrative" for Trump to appeal to from the right. Obama had tried from the centre left. Trump's supporters now regarded such genuine appeals to "all Americans" as the threat of a "takeover" by outsiders. Minoritarianism *is* minoritarian. An enemy had to be blamed. It was "a Chinese virus"; to wear a mask was un-American.

Boris Johnson's response was a more cultivated but equally irresponsible expression of free-market repugnance at the idea of government intervention. On 3 February, ten days after the *Lancet* article warned of a worldwide pandemic, Johnson spoke to the world's ambassadors in London. The aim was to celebrate Britain's liberation from the clutches of the European Union now that Brexit was "done". The venue was the suitably baroque painted hall at the old Royal Naval College at Greenwich, restored to its early eighteenth-century colours, covered in aptly undressed bottoms and breasts for the prime minister's wandering eye. Nelson's body had lain nearby after the Battle of Trafalgar.

Johnson attacked suggestions that international borders should be closed to contain the coronavirus as "bizarre autarkic rhetoric" that went "beyond what is medically rational to the point of doing real and unnecessary economic damage". The juxtaposition is revealing: the economy came first. The UK had not left the supposed imprisonment of the EU's regulations to clamp down on business. On the contrary, heroic Britain would rescue the world itself from any such a fate, Johnson claimed, if necessary as a lone global Superman. Please bear with me, it is deeply embarrassing to be governed by such a figure. But the UK's prime minister literally told the assembled ambassadors to think of Britain as "Clark Kent" about to take off its spectacles and enter a phone booth to emerge, "with its cloak flowing as the supercharged champion of the right of the populations of the Earth to buy and sell freely among each other".[16]

The grotesqueness of such bloviating should not distract us from its purpose. Johnson is a master of fluttering brightly coloured verbosity like a matador's cape to distract attention. We should focus on his sword. His intent: to put moneymaking first. Like Trump, he exemplifies the last stage of neoliberalism: he terminated the fatalism essential to its acceptance to double-down on its proclamation of market supremacy. Humiliated by the 2008 crash, financial capitalism could no longer secure its hegemony by banishing democracy to the limbo of depoliticising entropy. Instead, like Trump, Johnson wanted to save the dominion of finance by hyper-energising voters behind a populist version of "super-charged" market freedom.

This was Johnson's aim when he finally addressed the wider public about the advent of COVID-19. He joined a popular breakfast television show on 5 March, more than a month after the WHO had issued its worldwide public health emergency. His cold-blooded purpose startled his two hosts, "Perhaps you could take it on the chin, take it all in one go and allow coronavirus to move through the population without really taking as many draconian measures" he told them. He described this as "a theory" about how best to respond. He did it with enthusiasm, oozed reassurance, delighted in shaking hands, and insisted that for most people COVID is only "a mild to moderate illness".

The words that most chilled me at the time were "move through the population". He talked about us like a colonialist chatting about the natives catching smallpox. A week later, on 12 March, as other countries in Europe were going into lockdown, Johnson ended testing for the public and limited it to only those ill in hospital. His "let it move through the population", the so-called herd immunity approach, was a decision to put the economy before life.

It could not be sustained. This is the important point. As with Trump, many of the positions Johnson adopted were shocking but true to form and intrinsic to his success. This time, however, as with Trump, what both men wanted was not allowable. Four days later, on 16 March, Johnson called on non-essential workers to stay home. On 23 March, it was an "order" that became law on 28 March 2020, more than two months after the *Lancet* had reported that "the time to act is now".

Dominic Cummings, who worked for Johnson, has provided an account of the UK's decision to lockdown. Johnson resented it even after he himself was ill enough with COVID to be hospitalised and oxygenated. When the failures of his first, delayed shutdown became evident after the summer of 2020, he faced the same problem again with demand for a second. He made his attitude clear: "No more fucking lockdowns — let the bodies pile high in their thousands!"[17]

The equivalent, lethal voice of Trumpism, in public at least, was left to others. Fox commentator, Glenn Beck, "I'd rather die than kill the country," or the just elected lieutenant governor of Texas, Dan Patrick, on grandparents like himself dying for the economy: "If that's the exchange, I'm all in."[18]

Here is the Question

So here is the question that needs to be answered. Historically, letting the bodies pile was the way it was. Pandemics were not the state's fault. Its responsibility was mitigation — not to damage the economy further through its own actions. Since the 1980s an anti-government, hands-off approach had been consolidated into the hegemonic ideology. Independent institutions that sought to determine outcomes in terms of non-market values such as veracity, historical and scientific truth, academic excellence or even the pleasure of the commons, were undermined, financialised or driven to the margins. The role of the state was to put its influence behind the market and "free" the economy from any impediment to its penetration. This was the core principle of the two Anglo-Saxon powers and many others. A new pandemic, therefore, should be a moment of confirmation not crisis; a moment when the "realities" of the market legitimised the pain of illness and mortality. Grandparents would die for the economy. We would all take it "on the chin". To govern was to "interfere" with our fundamental freedom. This was Trump's wager when, even after what he heard from Xi Jinping and his National Security advisors about the massive, deadly impact of COVID-19, he announced, "I think the virus is going to be — it's going to be fine."

But it wasn't fine. The deaths and spread of the disease came as expected. What surprised the Anglo-Saxon leaders was how unacceptable their approach proved to be. Somehow, a force that was not an ideology, and it still doesn't yet have a name, defeated two hard-nosed exponents of market fundamentalism, president and prime minister who discovered there was "no alternative" to *shutting down* much of the economy. They joined governments round the world. Between January and May 2020, the *Economist* reckoned, "over a third of the world's population has at one time or another been shut away at home". March 2020 was the height of the catastrophe. In one week, ten million Americans lost paid employment. Between February and April, unemployment in the US rose from 3.5 to 14.7%.[19] Peter Baldwin mapped what he calls "government interventions on a scale unparalleled outside wartime", and quotes the *Economist*, "It is hard to think of any policy ever having been imposed so widely with such little preparation or debate."[20] Prepared or not, in the USA and the UK it is impossible to think of any such policy imposed on the president and prime minister despite their reluctance. They were obliged to agree that their governments and central banks pour rescue stimulus into their economies on an unprecedented scale.

Part of the reason they had to act as they did is that public opinion in the West demanded they follow the example of China. The leadership in Beijing certainly believes in economic growth but also claims to be in command. China has an ageing population. COVID is disproportionally fatal for the old; even in a country with ancestor worship it was a chance to thin them out. In 1958, over thirty million died thanks to the so-called Great Leap Forward, yet Mao never answered for it and the losses were glossed over. The treatment of the Uyghurs shows such ruthlessness has not been stilled in today's Beijing. But Xi and his Politburo decided the Chinese should not take the coronavirus "on the chin" although Beijing's system of party control and surveillance could have imposed this. Instead, when it became clear that the spread of infection and its mortal consequences could neither be covered up nor easily contained, the Politburo realised the days of the Great Leap Forward were over. What could once be unleashed on the dispersed, immobile rural settlements of a fatalistic peasantry, or today imposed on a religious minority, was not going to be tolerated by the smart populations of connected metropolises dedicated to improving their lives.

There is now something akin to public opinion in the most populous country on Earth. To retain its support, the Communist Party launched a China-wide lockdown. Growth targets, the key to the regime's success, were abandoned. China's economy has expanded by an average of close to 10% a year since 1979 — an astonishing record.[21] In the first quarter of 2020, it shrunk by over 6% as the brakes were slammed on. So complete were the closures even pollution temporarily diminished. The Politburo understood that its legitimacy depended on it demonstrating that nothing mattered more to it than the lives of its people.

China has a political system that believes in government and a population that agrees with taking collective action when necessary. South Korea showed this does not need dictatorship. A parliamentary democracy of over fifty million people, South Korea recorded its first case of the Coronavirus on 20 January — the same day as the US. By the end of April, it had limited mortality to five COVID-19-linked deaths per million of its population and its capital Seoul — bigger than New York City and with twice its density — was not under curfew. It had even managed to hold a general election. By comparison, the US had had 207 deaths per million and its great cities were silenced. (The UK had officially recorded 419 deaths per million.) Just as important, while the economy of South Korea started to recover, both the US and UK were staggering under lockdowns.

One measure of the surprise is that two of the countries worst hit by COVID-19 are America and Britain. At the turn of the century, they were confident that they "represented the future". That South Korea was capable of making better television sets or generating weirdly popular girl bands and dance routines could be put down to its unique location between China and Japan. The virus has revealed that if you measure a society's success by its ability *to look after its people in freedom*, then South Korea's embrace of modernity is superior to the Anglo-Saxons'.

Had you asked any expert of any persuasion in 2019 whether governments around the world would impose the steepest recession in history and then flood their countries with credit to keep businesses afloat in response to a contagious but survivable disease that was mainly fatal for the old, ill and obese, they would have said it was inconceivable. In the UK, the small number who knew about Exercise Cygnus would have confirmed that policy was to accept the "reality" of a pandemic.

Instead, the human reality of COVID-19 swept aside the principles of market fundamentalism. To slow down the loss of life and secure health services, political leaders everywhere were obliged to shut down their economies; neoliberalism be damned.[22] They did not discard capitalism. On the contrary, they acted to ensure its survival. But this demanded an ideological upturn. In the financial crash of 2008, government, not the market, was deployed to save finance. After 2016, the USA deployed government, not the market, to save trade and manufacturing from China's influence. Now, government had to save the people themselves from the danger of going to work or restaurants or entertainment, by funding businesses and paying them to furlough their employees. Deliberate policy measures, however reluctantly taken, badly run and limited in scope, precipitated the sharpest recession in history as even Trump and Johnson were obliged to put peoples' lives and health before profits.

An Anthropological Moment

For this to have happened, four historic shifts were necessary: governments had to be seen by the public as having responsibility for the economy; people had to expect their governments to ensure the availability of health services, including modern hospital support for citizens who need treatment to survive; people needed a relatively clear idea of what was happening which governments could not suppress; and people had to believe that everyone had a right to life.

Together these detonated the political framework that governed the world.

The first head of state to spell out the moment's "anthropological" significance was France's President Emmanuel Macron. In April 2020, he told the *Financial Times,* the impact of COVID-19 "makes us refocus on the human aspect. It becomes clear that the economy no longer has primacy. When it comes to our humanity, women and men, but also the ecosystems in which they live, and therefore the emissions of CO_2, global warming, biodiversity, there is something more important than the economic order." To emphasise the shock of this, he did not draw back from describing what was happening. "We are going to nationalise the wages and the profit and loss accounts of almost all our businesses. That's what we're doing. All our economies, including the most liberal are doing that. It's against all the dogmas, but that's the way it is."

Macron's observation that "all" economies are breaking with the dogma recognises that it was a globally correlated shock from which there was no escape. The market can force a country to follow its structures when it can threaten capital flight (as happened to France under President Mitterrand in 1983). When a shock is global, capital has nowhere to go and cannot dictate. By "dogmas" Macron means neoliberalism. When he says "the economy no longer has primacy", he means abandoning what he, and all other leaders of our era, believed up until the start of 2020. He said, "I think it's a profound anthropological shock [...] We have stopped half the planet to save lives, there are no precedents for that in our history [...] it will change the nature of globalisation, with which we have lived for the past 40 years [...] it [globalisation] was undermining democracy."[23]

For an Englishman whose comic book prime minister had just compared himself to Superman, the contrast is painful.

Macron is disliked in France as an upstart who struck lucky when France had a poor choice of candidates and became a "president of the rich". But traditional politicians who spend half a lifetime manoeuvring must calibrate what they say to ensure approval of their constituencies. Macron's lack of any hinterland of obligations is an advantage in fast-changing circumstances. It makes frankness easier. Few other right-wing politicians would dare admit openly they have just discarded their dogmas.

Before the vaccines were in everybody's arms in the rich countries, let alone around the world, concerted efforts began to re-establish the old dogma. The impact of the pandemic has intensified not levelled existing inequalities. There are already proposals to "depoliticise budgetary decision-making" across the European Union as the COVID emergency programmes, which Macron first demanded in that *Financial Times* interview, begin to wind down.[24]

Such efforts to re-establish a depoliticised order are unlikely to succeed. The need now is for political government, and COVID demonstrated its feasibility. It was the evidence that he did not know how to govern that shifted opinion about the US president. His incapacity exposed, Trump felt support slipping away in May 2020 and complained: "This is so unfair to me! Everything was going great. We were cruising to re-election!"[25]

Combined Determination

Trump stormed back and nearly won while the Republican party as a whole did better than him in 2020. Whenever there is a close outcome it is common to blame or praise a single factor or event as the winning or losing cause. In fact, when an outcome is in the balance, it means that no single cause dominates. Instead, it is always the case that *combined determination* is at work.[26] The fifty-fifty division of the US Senate symbolises how two mighty sets of forces came to a head in the US in November 2020. The more you fear one as most powerful, the more the other must be almost as formidable, in order for things to be on a knife edge, as they are.

We've looked at the well-endowed and deep-seated strengths galvanised by Trump's audacious response to America's post-crash predicaments, and his answer to the identity crisis they generated — *Make America Great Again*. What counterforces were galvanised to push back with equal energy to displace him from the White House?

The question has a twist because, after Bernie Saunders was disqualified, the opposition to Trump lacked both a clear, post-crash message equivalent to "MAGA" and a candidate with the charisma to match the ogre. What kind of America did Biden want, what were his answers to the multiple crises? His campaign strategy was to gather the support of everyone whose response was "Not Trump!" This seemed both intrinsically weak and high risk and needed Trump to self-destruct. In the first presidential debate he nearly did, then recovered from COVID and campaigned with fury to raise his 74 million votes.

In fact, Biden had a definite strategy for office: to be what Jake Sullivan, now his National Security advisor, described as a "New Old Democrat". In a long 2018 article in *Democracy,* Sullivan set out the need to revive government activism and twinned this with a well-presented call for an international strategy that pulled back from the military activism of the Reagan to Obama era.[27] The underlying ideological coherence of the Biden team gave its campaign discipline and helped to ensure it was error free. Absences do not generate media coverage and are therefore little discussed. But Trump was deprived of even the smallest of blunders that he and his social media trolls are so good at using to destroy their opponents — an important reason for Biden's success.

Two elements of Sullivan's *Democracy* article stand out. The first is his claim that:

Democrats do not have to […] pay too much heed, when political commentators arch their eyebrows about the party moving left. The center of gravity itself is moving, and this is a good thing. The government's role in checking the excesses of the free market and supporting workers and families *should* and *will* be redefined in the years ahead. The question is how […] There's something profound happening in American politics right now. A tide is moving […] Democrats have a rare opportunity to set bold goals and meet them.

The second, that his policy suggestions are preliminary and wonkish, whereas "one of the key takeaways from the 2016 election is that a few, simple, canonical policy ideas—'build the wall'; 'break up the banks'—are much more powerful than a long list of elaborately explained proposals and programs".

No canonical ideas were offered. The Biden campaign had no story that appealed to voters' guts. Even before he was elected it was impossible to recall any significant policy slogan or defining message of the Biden campaign. I have never known a centrist candidate to be elected with such low expectations.

It worked because Sullivan's 2018 analysis was correct. America was shifting leftward. Only now the growing desire for government action was reinforced by the need for a coherent response to COVID. It was this rising progressive tide that lifted team Biden to its slender success. When Bernie Sanders was brought in to help build the platform, it wasn't just an old-fashioned tactic of alliance building plus neutralisation, as most of us assumed. It was a strategy to ride with the movement of American society. Presumably polling told them that if they issued hats saying, "Turn Left With Joe", it would have frightened essential support and the media would have assaulted it. They did not attempt to define themselves with a few simple, powerful ideas, even if they could have. Instead, they relied upon a shift of judgment by a majority of voters fed up with the cult of the market, its inequity and insecurity. The Biden campaign was a masterful exercise not of leadership but of followership.

Seven Aspects of the Humanisation of Humanity

In order to understand the combination of forces that frustrated Trump in 2020, therefore, we have to turn to the deeper shift of opinion that Biden rode. Macron described it as "anthropological". The word is well chosen. It means an alteration for the whole human species. Below the monstrous surface of neoliberal dehumanisation, a massive undertow was being generated, itself made up of various undercurrents that came together in response to the pandemic. There are at least seven of them. They didn't create a programme. They are not yet an ideology. They expressed the general interest of humanity in a way that had not happened before. All of them, like neoliberalism itself, has been continuously energised by the great acceleration. All seven are ways in which our relationship with each other and our environment are being transformed. None on their own would have altered the balance of power. Taken together, they are why Trump is not currently in the White House. Life resisted the necrophilism of neoliberalism. I'm not attempting to be encyclopaedic — there may be other forces too — my description of each is suggestive not comprehensive. All I seek to show is that instead of observing each in its disconnected silo, as our commercial culture does, we consider the way they mingle within each of us in different proportions and together empower a potential, living resistance to market values that does not belong to the past.

1. The Creation of Cyberspace

When, during the Cold War with the USSR, the Pentagon developed its strategic doctrine, it sought "full spectrum dominance" in all four domains of land, sea and air and space. It has now added a fifth domain: cyberspace. This is the best way to think about our ubiquitous electronic relationships which are more than a means of communication or entertainment. We now live in a fifth domain, connected to it by the internet, the web, our smartphones, where we have an additional identity. Our capacities to experience ourselves and each other are being transformed. This has thrown up new concentrations of power while old media have fought to reframe their influence. The nature of public space has expanded at the same time as it is enclosed, creating new freedoms and forms of relationship even as these are commercialised (*Minecraft* is an example). It changes relationships outside of cyberspace as, thanks to video especially, we know what it is like for others in a way that is far more expansive. Atrocities like the murder of George Floyd become world events thanks to cyberspace. The experience of family is expanded. In China, which has the most efficiently controlled cyberspace, the Politburo knew they could not prevent knowledge of what had originated in Wuhan from spreading.

I start with the advent and growth of cyberspace as it highlights the dual nature of these forces of humanisation. Facebook, for example, is ruthlessly commercial and intrusive as it seeks to lock its users into its marketplace even as it relies on them to gift their pages and networks, and freely share their love, support and appreciation of each other.

2. Feminism

The "long 1968" which I discuss later was the formative political moment of the era of acceleration. Its most lasting political influence was the second wave of feminism that began in reaction to the macho culture of commercial and sexual freedom. It initiated a movement for full equality that has still to achieve liberation from patriarchy but has transformed the relationships of men and women in the course of a worldwide claim by women for their rightful place as political, economic and moral equals. Before the 1970s, the workplace in industrial countries, whether blue or white collar, was hierarchical and predominantly male, and men came home and took it out on their wives, reproducing a culture of obedience, with women often seeking solace in religion. In poorer, agricultural societies gender authoritarianism was also widespread. The change has been profound and is lasting — a model for progressives everywhere that I will discuss in the conclusion. The passive acceptance of victimhood that marked previous pandemics was accepted in part because family structures were built around stoicism and subordination. Today, across the world, the demand for access to lifesaving treatment is a refusal of such resignation, and feminism has been a crucial part, perhaps the crucial part, of the claim to basic entitlement by men and women in families of all classes that distinguishes modern urban civilisation.

3. Human Rights

The success of feminism is associated with the diffusion of belief in human rights. They became a battleground of the neoliberal era: claimed by democrats while being used to confine democracy. Usually, discussion of human rights starts with the Enlightenment or with the 1948 United Nations Declaration of Human Rights. The latter provides "rights" with an anti-fascist foundation that is not revolutionary and bypasses awkward questions about complicity in imperialism's non-stop atrocities. It is best to begin, as Paul Gilroy does his discussion of rights, with a salute to the short-lived four-page monthly *Human Rights*, published in New York by the abolitionist Elizur Wright from 1833–38. The starting point, historically and for our contemporary world, is to ground human rights in the repudiation, in the name of humanity, of racialised slavery and its many after-forms.[28] Human rights express resistance to oppression, exploitation and the dehumanisation of the market, which is why claims of rights almost always accompany popular uprisings. This "activist citizenship of rights" is an expression of our humanity.[29]

Righteousness, however, thrives in the shadow of rights and also seeks to confine them to legal tramlines. Official power sought to expropriate "rights" in the signing of the Helsinki Accords of 1975 that technically brought the war in Europe to a close and recognised East Germany. The Accords included a commitment to human rights. On both sides this was cynical. The Americans sought to reburnish their liberal credentials, now that they had ceased bombing South East Asia, while the Russians regarded Western hypocrisy as so blatant it could not represent a threat. Thirteen years later, when Presidents Reagan and Gorbachev met in Moscow they sparred about human rights in just the way their predecessors would have expected, "Reagan raising both general and particular humanitarian issues in the Soviet Union, and Gorbachev referring to the unemployment statistics of American Blacks and Hispanics and the per capita income difference between Whites and Blacks in the US".[30] After this ritual they returned to their negotiations. By then, however, the skids were under communism. The crushing of the Prague Spring in 1968 had seeded a dissident commitment to basic liberties. In 1977, within two years of the Helsinki gathering, Czechoslovak intellectuals launched Charter 77 to demand that their country enjoy the human rights which the Accords had pledged. In this unexpected way they prised open the apparatus of bad faith that passed for "People's Democracy" in Eastern Europe. And while the core demands were for legal rights such as freedom of speech and travel, Charter 77's conclusion was a moral claim for all citizens "to work and live as free human beings". A sign of the intrinsic subversiveness of human rights.

Western media that had never dreamt of energetic support of human rights at home (for example, in Northern Ireland) delighted in doing so behind the Iron Curtain. Political cynicism turned to human rights for cover, and unwittingly gave the notion of fundamental rights a degree of traction its adherents have never since relinquished. But, as Samuel Moyn has analysed, references to human rights rose in the 1980s as mentions of socialism nosedived. A notion of rights "accompanied" neoliberalism, depoliticised claims of property and safeguarded privilege.[31] While they promise the same protections to all, whatever their inheritance, sex or race, they ring-fence claims from democracy, strengthen paternalistic authority and seem powerless against the rise of inequality. When they are seen as inherently individualistic, they share with neoliberalism a scepticism of the need for collective choices. Notoriously, in the 1990s, human rights were weaponised to justify Western military interventions — a process that reached a crescendo after 9/11 and the "war on terror".[32]

However, the demand for our rights is also a claim by the powerless, one that fuels demands for equal treatment and raises expectations that are, ironically, all the harder to oppose because they are "unpolitical". So while the neoliberal era elevated human rights as an international principle to reinforce depoliticisation, it created an alternative non-market or human fundamentalism as it brought a call for human equality in from the cold. People like the idea that their humanity entitles them to universal norms and this opens up a space to show that the equal rights of each demands the equal rights of all.

An example of how the ideals of rights survived under neoliberalism as a form of resistance to it, is clear in the influence of the political philosopher John Rawls. In the early 1970s, he published *A Theory of Justice* which set out how justice — a system of fair social cooperation among equals — could be justified in terms of an imagined "contract". It sold over 400,000 copies, generated thousands of academic papers and was widely translated. It idealised the presumptions of the liberal section of the elite after a quarter-century of success. But as Katrina Forrester, the historian of his influence, points out, his "vision of society as characterized by a consensual core was always an idealization, but it lost its grip on reality as the reality itself transformed". Later she expanded the point, writing that "It is also a ghost story, in which Rawls's theory lived on as a spectral presence long after the conditions it described—and under which it emerged—were gone."[33] Rawls insisted that liberty and equality are companions and not, as the neoliberal theorist Milton Friedman claimed, incompatible. Unlike him, Rawls stood for public reason not private profit. If only as an uncanny presence he helped inspire spaces like the *Boston Review* for radicals to debate and succour belief in equality as a human right; a belief that claims for the market were unable to extinguish.

4. Anti-Racism

The struggle for race equality has yet to change behaviour to the extent that feminism has achieved. In many countries racism remains ingrained and even official when it takes a religious form as in Israel and Iran. Despite nominal legal equality there are structures of racism in all societies, which lock us into an authoritarian framework. It was this that the breadth of the George Floyd Black Lives Matter protest called out, generating energy that strengthened opposition to voter suppression in the USA. The change over the last fifty years has been considerable. Everyone on Earth has surely now thought about whether those with different skins and facial features are "like us". The "other" has been humanised by the question. One of the greatest weapons of reaction and exploitation — that people of a different ethnicity are disposable — is being disarmed.

5. *Environmentalism*
In 1970, the first Earth Day saw a widespread expression of environmental consciousness. The greatest tragedy of the fifty years since then may be the defeat of the movement to stabilise the ecosphere for human habitation, despite all its foresight and practical intelligence. It is especially important as the most political of the forms of resistance to market priorities. Also, it has ensured that everyone has the capacity to think on a planetary scale. It's said that when eighty million in China viewed David Attenborough's Blue Planet II, it slowed the internet. Knowledge that the Earth is vulnerable makes us feel powerless. When COVID struck, one reason for the spontaneous willingness to lockdown was that here, finally, was a way of taking personal action against something worldwide.

6. *Science and Medicine*
Today, there is hardly a family on Earth which has not experienced the benefits of medical intervention, whether to secure the life of infants, extend that of the elderly, repair an

accident in the healthy or secure recovery from a dangerous disease. It's a double transformation backed up by advances in knowledge and medical technology; the mRNA vaccine is the latest example. Reactionary "anti-vaxxers" may get the headlines but there is an under-recognised rise across the public of all classes of respect for medical professionalism as an adjunct to our lives. Images of Popes, Rabbis and Muslim clerics, the holiest representative of their respective religions, wearing face masks signal the supremacy of scientific knowledge. It isn't the law that made them feel obliged to do so; it is their experience of successful treatment. During the flu epidemic of 1918, there were no intensive care units, which were first developed in the 1950s. The ability to oxygenate patients — which saved the life of the British prime minister — is relatively new. The capability of intubating for long periods while a patient is fully sedated is even more recent. It saved the life of the popular English children's poet laureate, Michael Rosen, who was hours from dying of COVID and was kept unconscious and on life support for forty-seven days until he recovered (By contrast the epidemic of 1918 killed Egon Schiele, Austria's Picasso, at the age of twenty-eight; and two years later Max Weber, the great sociologist, aged fifty-six). Medicine has become a form of collective agency. At the same time without the capacity to save lives in this manner the problem of overwhelming hospital services would not exist. Lockdowns were necessary to slow the rate of infection so that the recently developed forms of treatment would be available for those in need.

7. Consumerism and the Body

Ecological consciousness and medical developments were accompanied by another change familiar to all of us and theorised by feminism, but little considered in global politics: the rise of body-consciousness. Drawing on perennial practices of humanity, the emporiums of the nineteenth century turned our bodies into a playground for commerce: women's bodies first, starting with soaps, scents and makeup; followed by men's in the twentieth century, especially via sports. The commodification of intimate life and personal appearances stimulated demand for attractive appearance and then healthy physiques. The word "jogger" entered the English language in the early 1960s and only became widespread in the latter part of the decade as "personal fitness" took off. Across the last half-century, as the human species became urban, individual wellbeing, from diet, including intelligent vegetarianism, and more recently consciousness of mental health, became a central part of modern life, reinforced in all sorts of ways, from domestic pets to gardening. Outside of the United States, where racism prevented the emergence of a shared national community, it was natural for developed societies to create universal health services.

Consumerism empowers and energises our relationship to our bodies as it seeks to expand demand, enflaming our sense of agency as it privatises our needs in a marketplace it can control. Fitbit monitors are an example, with similar technology now integrated into smartwatches. Our health, sexuality, hygiene and diet are also lived relationships with others in a social and ecological environment. As issues they are mostly excluded from what passes for democracy. This makes politics less relevant and reinforces depoliticisation. But outside of the routines of party political consciousness emasculated by neoliberalism, there is a growing sense that we, as members of families, have a right to our health and emotional life that cannot be measured by market values and that this claim should be grounded in our societies and how they are governed.

A striking expression of this shift has been popular support for the right to gay marriage. This is more than a permissive acceptance that homosexual relationships should not be banned, for it redefines the character of the most sacred social relationship of all, one that is specifically designed to create a set of obligations outside of the marketplace once the knot is tied as "two bodies become one flesh". The right to be different has become a potentially unifying sentiment along with the right to breathe.

These seven arenas of change are part of hypercapitalism even as they are also springboards for opposition to it. The World Wide Web was created by Berners-Lee as a virtual commons — Zuckerberg's Facebook seeks to enclose it. Feminism has Sheryl Sandberg, "leaning in" to corporate privilege, as well as Dawn Foster's "leaning out" to collective change. Human Rights can be double-edged, empowering yet depoliticising. Anti-racism can lead to exploitative Black capitalism. Greenwash and guilt-trip recycling leaves the main culprit, corporate pollution, unaffected. Medical advances are commercialised. Bathrooms overflow with quack creams and useless pills. Identity is privatised into a singularity when it is social and plural.

But connect the seven together and you can see that the collective agency of humankind across most nations has been transformed since the 1960s. While societies have been systematically deprived of democratic voice by neoliberalism, peoples have made themselves, not profit, the centre of value. When COVID forced a choice between the economy and human life — a choice made possible by the changes of the last half-century — the economy came second.

Socialism: The Dog That Did Not Bark

In 2000, to mark the start of the new millennium, the leading Marxist journal, *New Left Review,* relaunched itself. To mark the occasion, its founding editor, Perry Anderson, surveyed the battlefield of the previous decades and declared complete defeat for his own side: "For the first time since the Reformation, there are no longer any significant oppositions — that is, systematic rival outlooks — within the thought-world of the West [...] neo-liberalism as a set of principles rules undivided across the globe: the most successful ideology in world history."[34] Twenty years later, as a governing world outlook neoliberalism lies in ruins. So much so that the *New Yorker* publishes long and elegant essays describing people discussing the fall of America's "neoliberal order".[35]

It is a strange downfall. The thought-world of the West is now full of proposals for alternative forms of capitalism.[36] There are as yet no systemic rival outlooks — apart from "Xi Jinping thought". Meanwhile, the dark processes that reinforced the domination of neoliberalism continue to perpetrate their harm. Corruption is rife and networked, fertilised in British tax havens. Militarism and wars are fed by arms sales that also turn police into paramilitary forces. Authoritarianism is reinforced by surveillance and Pegasus-powered spying. Financialisation is cashing in on the pandemic. Terrorism is far from over, and America's global killing machine remains in operation.[37] Migration and tourism, while hugely improving our societies, feed xenophobia and ecological harm. Religious claptrap can exploit widening insecurity, rather than alleviate it as community-rooted religions can do. To begin to list the bleak side of things makes the prospect of any positive outcome seem remote.

The seven arenas I've listed, and there may be more, generated a humanitarian pushback that ended the neoliberal form of capitalism. Perhaps the best overall term for this achievement is *resistance*. But resistance has a weakness. It does not generate the collective learning needed for replacement. A prisoner who takes up drawing as a way of surviving a life sentence; a teenager taking drugs to recover from bad schooling, are resisting. They also express helplessness. In authoritarian bureaucracies there is another well-known form of defiance: the spoken or written word, in an article, book, video, movie or song, followed by censorship, arrest, and in Russia assassination. What we lack is a politics of humanisation that is both a way of learning and transformation.

What is missing is the dog that did not bark: socialism. Despite its claim to be the main historic opposition to capitalism, the broad socialist tradition gave birth to none of the seven counter-currents whose cumulative impact shattered the politics of neoliberalism. Socialists eventually supported them. But, historically, most working-class parties resisted feminism. The green movement was excoriated as anti-production. Human rights were seen as "bourgeois" even by social democrats. The fight for racial justice took place within and against the left. Socialists have not known how to respond to the positive energies of consumerism. And the development of science and technology and cyberspace took place "un-politically" because there was no popular rethinking of the relationship of capitalism and science. When, in the end, the sweeping but diffuse combination of counter-currents called time on "the most successful ideology in world history", it was humanity, including many who see themselves as liberals or on the right, who blew the whistle, not "the left".

Yet without left-wingers, where would these forces be? For the heartbeat of the left since the Levellers in seventeenth-century England, or since *The Communist Manifesto* proclaiming that "the free development of each is the condition for the free development of all", is the emancipation of humankind. And after their defeat many socialists aided the seven processes of humanisation even if they did not do so *as* socialists.

The eviction of Trump from the presidency, however, took conscious, strategic organisation. Thousands of experienced women and men from all the seven arenas of humanisation collaborated in a massive and sustained effort to evict him, assisted by a crucial addition: representatives of the trade unions. This novel coalition fills what is now happening in America with the promise of a modern alliance for egalitarian democracy.

In a report for *Time Magazine*, Molly Ball describes how Mike Podhorzer, an adviser to the AFL-CIO trade union federation, began to build a progressive network in 2019, before COVID, when he understood Trump's game plan. By 2020, according to Ball, Podhorzer's weekly Zoom meetings "became the galactic center for a constellation of operatives across the left who shared overlapping goals but didn't usually work in concert […] The invitation-only gatherings soon attracted hundreds, creating a rare shared base of knowledge for the fractious progressive movement." Those logging in for the two-hour sessions included organisers from "the labor movement; the institutional left, like Planned Parenthood and

Greenpeace; resistance groups like Indivisible and MoveOn; progressive data-geeks and strategists, representatives of donors and foundations, state-level grassroots organizers, racial-justice activists and others".[38] An observer who joined some of the Zoom calls told me that while Ball's narrative overdid the centralisation, the people from the organisations mentioned, "alongside thousands more, all played critical roles in defeating America's wannabe dictator". He was most impressed by "how bottom-up the whole process was". In response to the "flood of dark propaganda from the right wing", progressive US civil society "developed increasingly effective network organising capabilities". Groups on the left forged links with Silicon Valley technology experts and concerned business people. By 2020, "there were thousands of organisations and leaders involved in anti-Trump networks, operating mostly without any coordination with the Biden campaign — and they knew how to play well together."

Another "network of networks" that organises against Trumpism, is Our Revolution which supports and "empowers" progressive candidates. Justice Democrats is smaller and organises for Democratic candidates who pledge not to take corporate funding. Their aim to use the primary system to get left-wing Democrats into Congress. Alexandria Ocasio-Cortez was their first success in 2018. In a *New Yorker* article about them, Andrew Marantz writes: "Justice Democrats is one of a handful of like-minded organizations—others include a climate-action group called the Sunrise Movement, a polling outfit called Data for Progress, a think tank called New Consensus, an immigrants'-rights group called United We Dream, and an organizer-training institute called Momentum—that make up an ascendant left cohort. Their signature proposal is the Green

New Deal".[39] He goes on to describe how they have pulled the whole Democratic party in Congress to the left.

Perhaps most important of all, there was the registration and turnout of Black voters organised across America. LaTosha Brown and Cliff Albright of Black Votes Matter helped win the decisive cities that broke for Biden thanks to Black turnout.[40] Stacey Abrams, whose organisation Fair Fight played such a critical role in Georgia, tweeted on 6 November:

> So many deserve credit for 10yrs to new Georgia: @gwlauren @fairfightaction @nseufot @NewGAProject @ AAAJ_Atlanta @GALEOorg @BlackVotersMtr Helen Butler @GeorgiaDemocrat @RebeccaDeHart DuBose Porter @ DPGChair. Always John Lewis. Charge any omissions to my head. My heart is full.

The Neoliberal Whale

In 1939, George Orwell was writing a long essay on contemporary writers as war broke out in Europe. He called it "Inside the Whale". Its focus is the possible future reputation of Henry Miller, the American author of a famous pornographic novel *Tropic of Cancer,* published in Paris in 1935. Orwell found the book exceptionally memorable. He felt the experiences it relayed are "recognisable". That the novel's voice spoke without humbug or fear. It was the book of a man who is happy and says "I accept". Orwell found Miller repugnant and fascinating. A literary magazine the American helped edit described itself as "Non-political, non-educational, non-progressive, non-co-operative, non-ethical, non-literary, non-consistent, non-contemporary". Orwell felt "Miller's own work could be described in nearly the same terms. It is a voice from the crowd [...] from the ordinary, non-political, non-moral, passive man. Later, Orwell describes it as "the view-point of a man who believes the world-process to be outside his control and who in any case hardly wishes to control it". Today we can see this describes a neoliberal citizen: a person who consumes but makes no claim on society. With his bleak grasp of how attracted people are to laziness, passivity, viciousness and even evil, Orwell foresees the triumph of this view-point. Although Miller is a "completely negative, unconstructive, amoral writer, a mere Jonah, a passive acceptor of evil", his book will become the future of successful writing. Especially if the only alternatives were banal, "fanciful" literary posturing or the emptiness of political fiction proposing a "true vision".

The reference to Jonah gives Orwell's essay its title. He says that Miller positively wants to be away from it all "inside the whale":

> being inside a whale is a very comfortable, cosy, homelike thought. The historical Jonah, if he can be so called, was glad enough to escape, but in imagination, in day-dream, countless people have envied him. It is, of course, quite obvious why. The whale's belly is simply a womb big enough for an adult. There you are, in the dark, cushioned space that exactly fits you, with yards of blubber between yourself and reality, able to keep up an attitude of the completest indifference, no matter *what* happens [...] there is no question that Miller himself is inside the whale [...] he feels no impulse to alter or control the process that he is undergoing. He has performed the essential Jonah act of allowing himself to be swallowed, remaining passive, *accepting.*[41]

I find this description strange. Orwell emphasised *accepting.*

Far from being cosy and homelike, what could be more abhorrent and feel less safe than being confined inside a beast capable of diving at any moment to the lower depths or digesting you forever? This is certainly how the Bible describes the experience for "the historical Jonah" if such there was. For it says he cried out for help to his Lord "from the belly of hell".

This is where we have been for decades, swallowed by the whale of neoliberalism. We have been too passive, but we have not been *accepting.* Many of us have cried out fruitlessly. Then, just as it seemed it was about to digest us for good, the whale got COVID-19 and spat us out. Here we are, astonished, on the shoreline, still covered in neoliberal slime but whole and in one piece, unsure if we can believe in our escape.

Where and how we are to live now is still unknown, except for one important thing: we are not going back.

The plain speaking Biden is the first elected leader to stagger out of the whale and try and wipe away the slime, saved by the seven forces that shape the changing nature of humanity and developed, despite everything, in the belly of hell. How his administration hopes to replace Trumpism for good is the next part of the story.

6.   The Biden Surprise

It's important to remember that this has been a 60-year battle to make
voting more accessible, more available to Americans across the country, and
our effort, the president's effort to continue that fight doesn't stop tomorrow
at all. This will be a fight of his presidency.
— Jen Psaki, White House Press Secretary, 21 June 2021

The most striking aspect of Biden's administration on taking
office was its inner coherence. It did not have a strong external
projection of its purpose, a significant weakness exposed by the
Afghanistan withdrawal. But from the start it had a consistent
approach to economic growth, taxation, climate change,
migration, race, democracy, military deployment and foreign
policy. In July 2001, soon after Biden announced his anti-trust
programme, Rana Foroohar of the *Financial Times* interviewed
Heather Boushey, a member of Biden's Council of Economic
Advisors. As well as being a co-editor of a collection of essays
on Piketty's *Capital*, Boushey is the author of *Unbound*, a
critique of inequality and a call for public voices of all kinds
to engage with economic policy. Foroohar asked her, "You talk
about four crises that need to be tackled — healthcare, the
economy, climate and racial justice and equality. Is there a
unified field theory to dealing with all those things within the
administration? Is there a theory for the 'work, not wealth' era
that is emerging?"[1]

Boushey's answer details how their aim is to deliver "a
stronger middle class", and how the economy is "basically this

three-legged stool: it's land, it's labour and it's capital", and too much assistance had gone to capital "for the past 40 or so years" and not enough to labour. This is a class approach although unclear on the question of land; e.g. housing. And while not a "unified field theory" it signals the Biden administration's desire to grow the economy in a way that is racially inclusive and favours workers and their families.

The administration announced a Rescue Plan, a Jobs Plan and a Families Plan. The first was passed in March 2021, with elements of the family policy included. The second two were amalgamated into a "Reconciliation" package scheduled for the autumn 2021 (when this book will be at the printers) and a bipartisan infrastructure act that has Republican support. The Families Plan is modest by European standards. The US remains the only developed country without government-mandated paid leave for new parents, and support for families is wretched despite its importance for advanced economies.[2] But post-COVID there is a novel upturn in what people, especially the young, want and expect from work. A revolution in expectations could have huge impacts on the effectiveness of economic programmes. Getting past the road block of Congress is only the first stage of a major set of reforms.

Legislation to support voting rights is similarly being subject to compromise and may not pass at all – this battle too may inflame unpredictable expectations. Received wisdom says that unless Biden gets the legislation he wants, the Democrats will lose their slim majorities in the House and the Senate in the 2022 mid-term elections and the administration will be lamed, as happened with Obama. Such a prediction could be wrong in both ways. Even if the economic programmes are signed into law they still have to deliver and larger global events could prevent this; while an ill-managed crisis might ruin Democrat support even with voting rights secured. On the other hand, as Mitch McConnell, the Republican minority leader told the Senate, Biden's plans are "an effort to move our country to the left forever".[3] Should McConnell prevail, he will prevent them being passed. But, if the country is moving leftwards as Jake Sullivan claims, the Democrats could win the mid-terms by running as the opposition.

What is impressive at this early stage is the change of direction and the break from the politics and principles of neoliberalism. It is not premature to ask: Do they mean it? Is Biden sincere?

The first thing to say is that any such turn represents a massive win for Bernie Sanders and vindicates his persistent dedication. Biden's policies do not go nearly far enough for Sanders. Yet his approach, regarded as quixotic in 2016,will now be crucial for any successful Democratic strategy, after being steeled by the fire of primaries and national campaigns.

That other Democrats helped perpetrate neoliberalism does not make them today's hypocrites. It's a mistake to underestimate intelligent people's capacity to reflect and do things differently.[4] A guiding principle of the early Biden administration is that they must not repeat the Obama trajectory most of them took part in. So when Boushey and her colleagues say policy must change "from the past 40 or so years", left unstated — because they are, after all, Democrats — is an acknowledgment of the terrible measure of Obama's failure: he led to Trump.

Obama himself quickly sought to climb on board the Biden Express. He told Ezra Klein of the *New York Times* that Biden's team is "essentially finishing the job" which he began, and then went on to say, "Sometimes I have my friends in the Democratic Party who criticize us, who misapprehend this idea that we had sort of a — what's it called? Neoliberal perspective. That we had some ideological aversion to pushing the envelope on policy. That's not the case. We had just political constraints we had to deal with".[5] An instant expostulation from David Sirota on *Daily Poster* set out how Obama whitewashes his record. Far from being "angry" about the banks in 2008, as he claims in the interview, Obama backed Wall Street to the hilt.[6] What I found striking is the artful way the ex-president uses the royal "we" and a version of the double-negative to position himself as an opponent of neoliberalism all along. It's a salute to Biden's claim to be implementing a change of "paradigm" that his predecessor now offers his approval — in the form of asserting continuity when there is a significant change of direction. For Obama most certainly did perpetuate a "What's it called? Neoliberal perspective".

Does Biden himself grasp what his team is committed to? An interesting picture of him emerges in George Packer's *The Unwinding*, a beautifully written account of the hollowing out of America, written in the interregnum between the financial crash and the advent of Trump, and published in 2013. One of Packer's characters, who are selected to represent the American experience, is Jeff Connaughton, who was inspired as a student by hearing Biden in 1979 and went to work for the young Senator and helped with fundraising. He witnessed Wall Street undermining Washington and lost his passion for politics in the process. Connaughton ends up writing *The Payoff: Why Wall Street Always Wins.* Biden is simply observed as part of the background. He emerges as dedicated and professional, not always pleasant to work for, obsessed with becoming president but not with money (unlike the Clintons) and not a bigot. Biden became Obama's "employee of the month" in his predecessor's humiliating phrase;[7] selected to be on his ticket as vice president because he knew the ropes of Congress, was diligent and clean. Biden only flickers across the pages but leaves a clear image of someone obsessively ambitious yet not devious. Ted Kaufman, who figures in the book and was, like Biden, a former Senator from Delaware, told the *New York Times*, "It's usually best to listen to what he says. Because that's usually what he thinks."[8] When Biden says he wants a "paradigm change", whatever it means, it isn't just cynical positioning, even if he fails.

One reason why the shift from neoliberal priorities is credible is generational. Biden has compared his proposed legislation to President Lyndon Johnson's Great Society programme of the mid-Sixties, as if it was a prequel to his own infrastructure aims and voter registration effort. In doing so, he is not just looking back to a far-off time in history when politics mattered, government did things and results were to be expected. It was when he entered politics! The current shift in US policy is being led by politicians, like him, who are so old they were formed by that earlier period: Nancy Pelosi, who leads the House, born 1940; Chuck Schumer, Senate leader, a youngster born 1950; Bernie Sanders, Chair of the Senate Budget Committee, born 1941; Biden himself, born 1942. Grandparents all, they have seen neoliberalism come and now go, and have witnessed how "politics-led-by-the-market" does not deliver. Why should they want to repeat what failed them in middle-age?

Instead, they are enabling a handover to a post-Iraq generation. In his account of the Biden surprise, Ezra Klein highlighted the underlying shift: "A younger generation revived the American left, and Bernie Sanders's two campaigns proved the potency of its politics [...] Washington is run by 20- and 30-somethings who run the numbers, draft the bills, brief the principals […] [they] came of age during financial crises, skyrocketing personal debt, racial reckonings and the climate emergency". The last is a crucial factor. The urgency of the need to save the environment, when the risks were established in the 1970s, is indisputably a consequence of neoliberal failure. There is an imperative need for a politics that governs the planetary totality for all our sakes. Brian Deese heads the National Economic Council and "is notable for being a climate wonk who's now in charge of the nerve center of White House economic policymaking". Born in 1978, he is thirty-six years younger than his president. He told Klein, "It has to be that Americans see and experience that the investments in building out a more resilient power grid actually improve their lives and create job opportunities for them, or their neighbors".[9]

A tension races like referred pain across the Biden administration and its media allies — can they preserve the control of the Washington political elite? The need to abandon neoliberalism and counter the influence of Trump's energetic base means they need active progressive support — does this have to be spoilt by the involvement of *actual* progressives and activists? I will come back to this. The key reason why, despite their discomfort, the centrist establishment supports at least some of Biden's "left turn" is the need to respond to China as it becomes America's economic equal.

At the early stage of his administration, I will just focus on three issues: corruption and Afghanistan, the rise and "threat" of China, and voting rights and the Supreme Court.

Afghanistan: Corruption as Colonialism

The overall cost of the United States twenty-year war in Afghanistan was more than $2 trillion and this does not include the aid and investment from many other countries who allied with the US. As it ended, the average income in Afghanistan was less than $2 a day.[10]

When the Biden administration issued its *Interim National Security Strategic Guidance* in March 2021, "to convey President Biden's vision for how America will engage with the world", it stated that "Free societies have been challenged from within by corruption, inequality, polarization, populism, and illiberal threats to the rule of law". Corruption comes first. It went on to state: "We will take special aim at confronting corruption, which rots democracy from the inside".[11] Three months later Biden issued a detailed *Memorandum* that instructs fifteen US departments and agencies to cooperate on a full-scale review of combatting corruption and come back to him with recommendations.[12] During those months he instructed the US military to withdraw from Afghanistan.

A direct comparison of the Biden approach can be made with the British government's, which published its full National Security Review almost simultaneously. Long, detailed and "integrated", British policy only mentions corruption as a crime, not a strategic threat. As the sovereign power over most of the world's tax havens, with the City of London a hot spot for money laundering, the Johnson government simply warned those involved not to get caught. This is the usual way Western power has reproduced itself since the Sixties. By contrast, the White House recognises that a growing demand for honest government is strategic.

President Biden's decision to withdraw from Afghanistan

was not explained to the American public when it was taken, was poorly justified after it happened, was badly executed and damaged his reputation and popularity, revealing a significant weakness in his approach. Nonetheless, it was considered, it was correct in principle and part of the reason for it was to end the corruption of the American polity, not to speak of Afghanistan's. It was also a continuation of Trump's blundering approach.

In Doha, on 29 February 2020, the United States signed, at Trump's instructions, a four-page treaty with the Taliban titled *Agreement for Bringing Peace to Afghanistan*.[13] The US pledged the rapid release of five thousand Taliban prisoners, scheduled a drawdown of its own forces and their complete withdrawal by May 2021. The Taliban pledged not to attack US troops or allow to others to do so "from the soil of Afghanistan":

> The Islamic Emirate of Afghanistan which is not recognized by the United States as a state and is known as the Taliban will not allow any of its members, other individuals or groups, including al-Qa'ida, to use the soil of Afghanistan to threaten the security of the United States and its allies.

A surrender document, it allows the US to exit unharmed in return for never being attacked from Afghanistan again. There is no reference to the then Afghan government, which opposed it, only a mention of future "intra-Afghanistan negotiations". It sets out a schedule for the US withdrawing from its bases that includes its allies — it assumes in writing that the US is also negotiating their exit too. Implicitly, the US accepted that the Taliban could make treaty commitments about the whole "soil of Afghanistan" as if they were its rulers.

I recall being surprised at the time that there was little

publicity. Nor concern that *five thousand* enemy fighters were being released from captivity without the approval of the government that held them prisoner, and I wondered how much fighting it must have taken to capture them.

When Kabul fell in August 2021, I was surprised again at how many commentators said the USA should simply have ignored an agreement it had signed. Surely at least a Western power should keep its word? It seemed to me eminently reasonable, if atrociously communicated after the event, when Biden and his spokesman said that to repudiate the *Agreement for Bringing Peace to Afghanistan* would have meant launching a new war in Afghanistan. Also, that to begin a fight with the Taliban could not be done with the remaining 2,500 US troops and would demand a considerable escalation. In addition, Biden had committed the US to withdraw in his campaign for the presidency.

After he was elected "Military officials […] knew from the start that the methods they had employed with Mr. Trump were likely to no longer work", according to a short analysis in the *New York Times*. It details some of the intensive lobbying Biden was subjected to and provides a glimpse of the efforts of the military, industrial, consultancy and aid complex, as it sought to preserve "nation building" in a country few took any real interest in.[14]

Biden had a long record of opposing the US presence in Afghanistan. He also wanted to prevent the Democrats going into the mid-terms on November 2022 with coffins returning from Kabul. On 6 April 2021 Biden told the Generals their time in Afghanistan was over and they should implement Trump's Doha agreement with a four-month delay. It was publicly announced that all US and allied troops had to be out before the twentieth anniversary of 9/11. The assumption was that the Afghani government would negotiate an agreement with the Taliban — which the US pushed for.

This was the moment when the Administration should have initiated on its own terms a debate about the defeat and the significance of the withdrawal. Perhaps they feared this would have undermined the government in Kabul and precipitated an exodus. Afghanistan's civil war was taking place in the era of WhatsApp, Signal and FaceTime. Across its mountainous battlefields the two sides were talking with each other. All could read the *Agreement for Bringing Peace to Afghanistan* which is online. As agreed, the Taliban did not attack the Americans and when the US left, the Afghan army and regime, which Washington funded, simply folded, handing over to the Taliban "the soil of Afghanistan".

Twenty years and billions upon billions had created in Kabul an interventionist's capital with "Western values". An evacuation from the rooftop of the world had to be scrambled together, under the gun and with the agreement of the Taliban, to bring out Westerners, their local translators, protectors and helpers liable to Taliban punishment; while the operation was attacked by ISIS suicide jihadists opposed to any peace with the United States.

When he explained his decision in the face of media criticism of the humiliation, Biden was unapologetic and sounded exasperated — as well he might. He had listened carefully, he had been decisive, he told America straight that Afghanistan is known as "the graveyard of empires". He was doing what he promised when he ran for President; he wanted to focus on China and domestic priorities not pour more billions and lives into the Hindu Kush. It was "the logical, rational and right decision to make".

Yet it turned into a presentational and humanitarian disaster.

The US was taken in by its own billion-dollar Potemkin regime and did not prepare for its overnight collapse, or engage with allies who had lost hundreds of their own forces, or explain to the US public that this was the conclusion of a strategic defeat not just a wrap. Instead of his being lauded as the far-sighted opponent of a misconceived strategy, Biden was seen as rash and hasty. The scramble to respond to the regime's collapse made him look irresolute. The need to bring out refugees, to whom the US had a moral obligation, made him seem responsible for the disaster. That many were left behind was a more immediate defeat than 20 years of terrible bloodshed and the deaths of much larger numbers of Afghans. Abandoning women to the Islamic Caliphate of Afghanistan undermined Biden's role as an advocate of human rights and democracy and made him appear to be without empathy. It wasn't fair. As vice president he'd defied the military-Washington consensus to demand an end to the Afghan folly.[15] Now those responsible for it rolled out across the airwaves, hosted by media also implicated in it, to scapegoat Biden for *their* failure — because of the way he put an end to it.[16]

For the educated civilians in Kabul it was a genuine tragedy in the full sense of a disaster all could see was coming. Sarah Chayes published a short, extraordinary account when Kabul fell. She had covered the invasion in 2001 as a journalist for National Public Radio, and decided to live in Kandahar. She learnt Pushtu and ran two non-profits for ten years. You could not get a more liberal interventionist, and after she left she went to work for Chairman of the Joint Chiefs of Staff, Mike Mullen. As the US-backed government collapsed, she wrote:

I was there. Afghans did not reject us. They looked to us as exemplars of democracy and the rule of law. They thought that's what we stood for. And what did we stand for? What flourished on our watch? Cronyism, rampant corruption, a Ponzi scheme disguised as a banking system, designed by U.S. finance specialists during the very years that other U.S. finance specialists were incubating the crash of 2008. A government system where billionaires get to write the rules.

In an additional passage of her riveting account, she writes "in 2011, an interagency process reached the decision that the U.S. would not address corruption in Afghanistan. It was now explicit policy to ignore one of the two factors that would determine the fate of all our efforts. That's when I knew today was inevitable." Note the date: 2011. Chayes grasped the truth ten years ago and asked, what does America stand for?[17]

Yet the massive lobbying effort mounted to change Biden's election pledge to withdraw was not countered by any expert interest that demanded the President keep his word. There are hundreds of Congressional caucuses. (The *Atlantic* once ran an article on how "Congress Has a Caucus for Everything. If you have an interest, legislators have a group for it. Even bourbon and beer brewing".[18]) But there is not one on Afghanistan. So while Biden's decision was democratic — because it was an election pledge and because it was supported by a cross-party majority of voters — it was also lonely, backed by his close advisors but not by any significant bodies of interest or influence. There could hardly be a greater indictment of the country's institutions sunk in a miasma of military contracts, corruption and short-termism.

Biden's aim is to pull the US out of nation-building abroad in favour of nation-building at home. He wants to become a "new" Roosevelt leading the country out of its ruinous economic inequality while leading the world in a democratic defiance of authoritarianism led by Beijing. Instead, the Kabul evacuation signals that he could be branded, before he has really begun, as not even a transitional figure but rather a mere go-between. To avoid this image, Vice President Kamala Harris was dispatched to South East Asia to try and change "the narrative" and she denounced China for its "coercion" and "intimidation" in the South China Sea.

The China Challenge

In January 1992, George Bush senior gave the first presidential State of the Union address to respond to the collapse of the Soviet Union. He expressed the "joy that was in my heart". "America won the Cold War", Bush trilled, "A world once divided into two armed camps now recognises one sole and pre-eminent power, the United States of America." Washington ruled the roost. No enemy could be blamed for how it behaved. The true character of unrestrained American power was about to be revealed. A wise president would have called for the cooperation of other countries. Instead, Bush spoke about them as if they were domestic servants. He claimed that they "regard US pre-eminence with no dread. For the world trusts us with power, and the world is right. They trust us to be fair, and restrained. They trust us to be on the side of decency. They trust us to do what's right."

Dread was much the wisest reaction. A catalogue of blunders followed: the humiliation of Russia, the refusal to secure Palestine, the encouragement of tax havens, his son's ultimate folly of "Mission Accomplished" in Iraq, and the betrayal of the world's environment.

The underlying purpose of the Biden administration is to reverse the long humiliation of US global power and prestige brought on by its greed and stupidity since that speech, and rescue what it can of American distinction and global influence. It is an organising ambition, at once ideological, military and economic, that binds the administration's policies together.

For one country had the capacity and judgment not just to dread Washington but take its own course: China. When Bush issued his triumphalist announcement Beijing had already decided against an embrace of America's market first doctrine. After it, Beijing's leaders were appalled at the treatment of what had been the Soviet Union. They saw that they should never put their trust in a world economy governed solely by the United States.

In a fascinating new study, *How China Escaped Shock Therapy*, Isabella Weber has traced China's distinct road to capitalism. From 1980 there was a shared agreement among party leaders and experts that they needed to break from "Maoism". Weber writes that they "replaced the standpoint of class with the standpoint of the nation as a whole and turned the revolution into a national development project in which 'backward' China would aim to 'catch up' with the industrialized countries".[19] To achieve this, the Chinese Communist Party embraced the market but refused to relinquish state oversight of the economy. It didn't privatise its core industries and banks. Instead, "China drew into global capitalism without losing control over its domestic economy" using a dual-track price system, "a process of market creation and regulation through state participation".[20] It got there partly through trial and error, partly thanks to an ideological *commitment* to trial and error.

China's decision to retain a politically governed economy was of lasting importance for the world. Efforts were made to persuade it not to. Milton Friedman lectured in China in

1980 to advocate neoliberal market reform. He went again in 1988 for a Cato Institute conference in Shanghai, where "A considerable number of the speakers [...] were either Friedman's fellow Mont Pelerin Society members or closely linked to the society's work". (The Society was the original source and debating ground of neoliberal thinking.) Friedman himself met with General Secretary Zhao Ziyang "for a two-hour conversation on China's reforms". Ziyang summed up China's approach as, "the state adjusts the market, and the market guides the enterprise". Friedman repudiated this: "The state is organized from the top down; the market, from the bottom up. The two principles are incompatible [...] the combination Zhao describes is not feasible".[21]

China showed that they were compatible and Friedman was wrong. The Party integrated China into the global division of labour, and hence into globalisation shaped by Western neoliberalism, but refused to be subordinated to it. "This integration is based on the premise of being controllable and controlled by the [...] primacy of the state and not of private property". It was governed marketisation — the opposite of neoliberal ideology.

What happened can be divided into roughly four decade-long periods. From 1980 to 1990, China showed that the development model of what became known as the Washington Consensus was misconceived, or rather it worked all too well as a replacement of colonialism — a regime of extraction that saw Africa suffer negative growth and Latin America stymied in corruption, which China escaped.

From 1990 to 2000, the crippling impact of neoliberalism on developing countries was overshadowed by the success of the US in ensuring the collapse of communism. The Soviet Union broke into its constituent nations, Russia was bankrupted by reckless privatisations, and the East European satellite countries were recruited into the European Union as Germany was unified. China, by contrast, crushed its pro-Western democratic movement in Tiananmen Square at the end of 1989 and continued its historic rate of growth to become a member of the World Trade Organisation in 2001. By then its economy was the eighth largest in the world, behind that of Italy.

In the first decade of the new century, the US gave priority to the "War on Terror" rather than investing in its domestic infrastructure, as China was doing. US policy was not without a global motivation, as we've seen. When Blair told the US president that the larger purpose of the Iraq invasion was to "construct a global agenda around which we can unite the world", he was describing an American decision to assert by force the "pre-eminence" that it had proclaimed by default in 1992. Millions of us around the world were wiser than the idiots in the White House and Downing Street. For the first time mass protests *preceded* a war of aggression. We did not prevent it but were vindicated. Meanwhile, China's exports boomed. It utilised the WTO like a healthy youngster on a trampoline and hollowed out US industries. Then the 2008 financial crash threatened China's exceptional growth rate, which was 13% in 2007. It fell to 6.5% at the end of 2009. Beijing went for a domestic stimulus as it shifted away from export-driven growth.

Across the next decade, from 2010 to 2020, as the US sought to recover from the crash, China ceased to be a developing country and became a full-scale competitor, now the world's second largest economy. In forty years, the Chinese had achieved the greatest single transformation from rural to urban life in history and did so to a high level — in 2000, it had around thirty million university graduates; in 2010, it was 100 million; by 2020, according to the latest census the country had 218 million graduates.[22]

Xi Jinping Thought

China's is a staggering achievement, but it should not be exaggerated. It has chronic problems and weaknesses not reflected in the rhetoric of its president, Xi Jinping. He became General Secretary of the Party in 2012 and President in 2013 (removing term limits to his supremacy in 2018). He combines hardline control domestically with an ambitious assertion of China's strength internationally including the massive Belt and Road Initiative that seeks to embed China's economic influence. To reinforce his loathsome authoritarianism he is now crushing democracy in Hong Kong and the Uyghurs as a people.

In 2013, when Xi became leader, a set of ideological instructions was circulated. Known as "Document Number 9", it listed the seven political perils cadres and party members had to guard against. They are constitutionalism, universal values, civil society, freedom of the media, historical nihilism, questioning the socialist nature of China's socialism with Chinese characteristics, and, significantly, the promotion of neoliberalism. Warning against its economic threat to China, the document states:

> Neoliberalism advocates unrestrained economic liberalization, complete privatization, and total marketization and it opposes any kind of interference or regulation by the state. Western countries, led by the United States, carry out their Neoliberal agendas under the guise of 'globalization,' visiting

catastrophic consequences upon Latin America, the Soviet Union, and Eastern Europe, and have also dragged themselves into the international financial crisis from which they have yet to recover. [Neoliberalism's advocates] actively promote the 'market omnipotence theory.' They claim our country's macroeconomic control is strangling the market's efficiency and vitality and they oppose public ownership, arguing that China's state-owned enterprises are 'national monopolies,' inefficient, and disruptive of the market economy, and should undergo 'comprehensive privatization.' These arguments aim to change our country's basic economic infrastructure and weaken the government's control of the national economy.[23]

In his history of neoliberalism as a global project, Quinn Slobodian, describes how theoretically it projected a global capitalist class operating beyond nations in a "world economy that did not have a demos". The aim: "a world of people but a world without a people", a formulation that draws on the work of Wendy Brown.[24] The Chinese saw through the scam. It wasn't just that the shock therapy of neoliberalism would wreck their development, leaving them exposed to predatory finance, laying people's incomes to waste, as happened in Russia. It was also that this world without "a" people nonetheless had "a" ruling class: the USA's political and financial elite. They were right to see neoliberalism as an American policy to control China. It meant, as Anatol Lieven scornfully puts it, "China accepting a so-called 'rules-based' international order in which the US set the rules while also being free to break them whenever it wished".[25]

Trump the realist obliged Washington's elite to face up to the consequences of China's refusal to be subordinated to the

US's world order. In November 2018, Ivan Krastev, a shrewd European commentator, reported on a three-month stay in Washington. Despite the desire of the policy elite to see Trump disappear like a bad dream, his presidency, Krastev predicted, would be seen as ushering in "two significant changes that are likely to have staying power". The first was that Americans had ceased to believe in the United States as an "indispensable nation" with a moral obligation to make the world safe for democracy. The second, that across all parties, "rivalry with China has become the organizing principle of American foreign policy […] and that if America fails to contain China's geopolitical reach now, tomorrow it will be impossible […] a realization of the fact that China's market-friendly, big-data authoritarianism is a much more dangerous adversary for liberal democracies than Soviet Communism ever was".[26] Krastev was wrong on the first count; the Biden administration does see securing democracy for the world as its calling. He is vindicated on the second because, for this very reason, rivalry with China has become an organising principle for American policy, foreign and domestic.

US Views of China

I'll take a quick look at three post-Trump assessments of how the US should respond to the rise of China, to illustrate the breadth of agreement in Washington. The first is anonymous and stems from the traditional Republican establishment, the second is by Brian Deese who heads Biden's economic team, the third comes from his National Security advisor and likely author of the administration's strategic review, Jake Sullivan.

Between Trump's defeat in November and Biden's January

inauguration someone drafted *The Longer Telegram*, published in early February by the Atlantic Council. It was an act of homage to George Kennan's famous 1946 *Long Telegram* sent from Moscow in 1946, where he was the US chargé d'affaires, in which he set out the US Cold War policy of Soviet containment. Today's version is a verbose, eighty-page overview. The author derides the way Trump was merely "chaotic" but congratulates him on "sounding the alarm" on China and proclaiming a state of "strategic competition".[27]

The author, an experienced China expert, emphasises that "The success of China's rise has been predicated on a *meticulous* strategy" (my emphasis), which it has "executed over thirty-five years, of identifying and addressing China's structural economic weaknesses". He sets out the shift from Deng Xiaoping's instruction, when he initiated China's modernisation, that China should "hide its strength, bide its time", to President Xi Jinping's threatening call for a "community of common destiny for mankind" — used to describe the larger outcome of its Belt and Road investment.[28]

To respond, the US needs a China strategy "anchored in both national values and national interests" which are, says "Anonymous", its military, the dollar, technological leadership (he goes into great detail on China's hi-tech challenge), and the values of individual freedom, fairness, and the rule of law. "Anonymous" struggles with how to project these US national interests in universal language so as to recruit the necessary allies. He complains that China "skillfully deploys the language of cultural nationalism", to "mask" its real aim, namely: "to replace democratic capitalism with authoritarian capitalism as the accepted norm in the developing world". His fear, that "if US-China strategic competition simply becomes a contest between US and Chinese power, where the objective is to protect each state's core national interests against the other, ultimately it will be seen by the rest of the world for what it is: an atavistic national, cultural, racial, and even civilizational contest for global supremacy". It is essential, therefore, for the US to present it as something else. For example, an "appeal to defend the ideas and the ideals of the liberal international order". This can be called: "Defending Our Democracies". The inclusion of "our", "Anonymous" writes, to show his cunning, will do the trick and allow other countries to see "that this is not just a US enterprise".

The attempt to weaponise "democracy" for Washington is argued with less conviction than the demand that the US defend Taiwan. The US military-industrial complex thrives on such confrontation. It was already lobbying for expenditure in the Pacific before Xi became leader, when expenditure in Afghanistan and the Middle East began to drop, as the far-sighted Paul Rogers spotted at the time.[29] Today, the Pentagon is demanding huge increases to fund its capacity to "contain China".[30]

Brian Deese also sees the US as competing with China from his perspective as Director of the National Economic Council: China "has been *meticulously* thinking about making [...] investments with a deliberate focus on trying to build its own industrial base and its own intellectual and innovation base. And we have, for the better part of a decade, ignored or derogated those levers." That word (and my emphasis) again which so impresses the powerful, as it recognises intelligent purpose in government (and undermines neoliberal nostrums). Deese says, "among our allies and among our global counterparts, there is a big question about, can the United States deliver for its own citizens? Can the United States competently govern and invest in things that are obviously beneficial to its own welfare, its economic strength, its economic resilience?" This, continues Deese, "is really the dominant question. I think now more than any time in modern history, the world is watching U.S. domestic policy […] the world is asking this question: If the U.S. is going to lead again internationally […] first and foremost, the question is, can the U.S. get its house in order? And that question is inevitably framed vis-à-vis China". And he makes it clear, "There's not a market-based solution to try to address some of the big weaknesses that we're seeing". [31]

When Boushey, a member of Deese's Council, talks about the priority of support for working people, she motivates this in terms of need and fairness. When Deese does, he also motivates it in terms of strategic necessity for the American state.

Biden's National Security Advisor, Jake Sullivan, focused on US-China relations before his appointment. With Hal Brands in May 2020, he figured China "has two plausible paths to pre-eminence". Either by gaining supremacy in the Pacific region and then turning to the world (as the US did by first imposing the Monroe Doctrine on the Americas in the nineteenth century, they point out), or by a direct bid for global hegemony via the deployment of its economic heft and technological superiority, the Belt and Road approach. The Soviet Union, by contrast, "never had the ability, or the sophistication, to shape global norms and institutions in the way that Beijing may be able to do". [32] Also, because its "democratic centralism" is not socialist, it can grow in symbiosis with world capitalism — an unprecedented challenge. (A recent example: even as the US escalates opposition to Beijing, the titans of Wall Street — Goldman Sachs, BlackRock, JP Morgan — "lust" after China's massive savings market and are simply unable to resist piling in to try and take advantage of it.[33])

A previous article by Sullivan, written with Jennifer Harris, lays out the shift US foreign policy needs. "The growing competition with China", means that "Today's national security experts need to move beyond the prevailing neoliberal economic philosophy of the past 40 years." That couldn't be clearer. "Underinvestment is a bigger threat to national security than the U.S. national debt […] a new grand strategy for today's world will only be as good as the economic philosophy behind it […] The foreign-policy community should actively reach for a new economic model. America's national security depends on it."[34]

This perspective — that the US needs government-led domestic economic growth that benefits the whole population as a *national security* priority — now has the imprimatur of the White House. In March, the president endorsed an "Interim National Security Strategic Guidance". It needs to be quoted at length as it reveals a thoroughness that is poorly projected. Biden's introduction states: "Our world is at an inflection point." America's response must begin with:

> the revitalization of our most fundamental advantage: our democracy. I believe we are in the midst of an historic and fundamental debate about the future direction of our world. There are those who argue that, given all the challenges we face, autocracy is the best way forward. And there are those who understand that democracy is essential to meeting all the challenges of our changing world.
>
> I firmly believe that democracy holds the key to freedom, prosperity, peace, and dignity. We must now demonstrate — with a clarity that dispels any doubt — that democracy can

still deliver for our people and for people around the world. We must prove that our model isn't a relic of history; it's the single best way to realize the promise of our future.

"We must prove that our model isn't a relic of history [...] I direct departments and agencies to align their actions with this guidance". The overview communicates the core imperative of the Biden administration and provides a "unified theory" of its approach:

Democracies across the globe, including our own, are increasingly under siege. Free societies have been challenged from within by corruption, inequality, polarization, populism, and illiberal threats to the rule of law. Nationalist and nativist trends — accelerated by the COVID-19 crisis — produce an every-country-for-itself mentality that leaves us all more isolated, less prosperous, and less safe. Democratic nations are also increasingly challenged from outside by antagonistic authoritarian powers. Anti-democratic forces use misinformation, disinformation, and weaponized corruption to exploit perceived weaknesses and sow division within and among free nations, erode existing international rules, and promote alternative models of authoritarian governance. Reversing these trends is essential to our national security [...] China, in particular, has rapidly become more assertive. It is the only competitor potentially capable of combining its economic, diplomatic, military, and technological power to mount a sustained challenge to a stable and open international system.

Trade policy, the document insists, must benefit "the American middle class [...] not just the privileged few". It also:

requires us to commit ourselves to revitalizing our own democracy [...] We will combat voter suppression and institutional disenfranchisement. We will require transparency and accountability in our government, root out corruption, and confront the distorting role of money in our politics. [...]

Our work defending democracy does not end at our shores. Authoritarianism is on the global march, and we must join with likeminded allies and partners to revitalize democracy the world over [...] We will take special aim at confronting corruption, which rots democracy from the inside and is increasingly weaponized by authoritarian states to undermine democratic institutions [...] The most effective way for America to out-compete a more assertive and authoritarian China over the long-term is to invest in our people, our economy, and our democracy.

You can see how China frames everything while opposition to corruption is seen as part of opposing Beijing. It explains the mystery of how a circumspect campaign led by an aging, middle-of-the-road officeholder, who chose a transition team that would be experienced, calm and predictable, has unleashed a reconfiguration of Western capitalism. One that seeks to improve the wages of working Americans, raise tax rates, close down corruption, build infrastructure, prevent a climate catastrophe, ensure child support, end discrimination, secure voting rights for all, rescue democracy for the future, and appoints as its National Security Advisor a critic of neoliberalism as well as — by no means a small addition — a Treasury Secretary, Janet Yellen, who is intent on using US international heft to "increase the focus on inequality, including for vulnerable populations and women and girls".[35]

American Nationalism

The core of the explanation is nationalism. The process triggered in the US echoes the inner mobilisations of society familiar to those who have studied the rise of nations. Nationalism is intrinsically regressive as well as progressive, a product of uneven development as people in societies seek to find their own meaning rather than having it imposed upon them. Each nationalism justifies itself in terms of its own inner necessity and values. But it is the external forest that "explains the trees".[36] Within the ecosystem it is usually the dominant country that arouses the nationalism of others, as America did China's. Now it is the United States that seeks to *catch up* — and raise the educational, social and economic level of US society as a whole.

There is no need for a tortuous debate with the shades of the Mont Pelerin Society. Neoliberalism failed to deliver when it mattered. After four decades of hyper-capitalist profiteering and despoliation it turns out that there *was* an alternative, one that would have provided better, more sustainable growth. The course China took to lift hundreds of millions of families from poverty represses democracy and is authoritarian. But thanks to its success the American state must abandon Friedmanite market authoritarianism so that it too can govern with competence. This is an enormous tribute to China. Without conceding a centimetre to its dictatorship, the rest of the world should express our gratitude to the Chinese who have saved the possibility of democratic politics, even while they themselves have yet to enjoy it.

"Bidenism" is not the cynical deployment of patriotic tropes to extinguish rebellion against its own avarice; that was a description of Trump's hollow, tub-thumping. Nor was the problem with him that he lied, was a sexist, supported a racist incarceration and lifted regulations from Wall Street— for this is also a description of Bill Clinton's presidency. What the American governing class found stomach-churningly intolerable was that Trump openly threw in the towel on US pre-eminence. It was unforgivable that he told Putin it was "okay" to be Putin, agreed Xi could do whatever was best for China in China, that Modi was his man in India because he put on the biggest rallies, and the only real "foe" Trump denounced as such was the European Union because it sought law-based international regulation. What made Trump utterly repugnant was that his incessant bellyaching about making America Great was a cover-up for a retreat from world primacy that they revered and are committed to restoring.

In a striking phrase, US nationalism under Biden is pledged to make sure that democracy is not discarded as "a relic" by modernised authoritarianism. As a democrat, I applaud this aim. The good thing about democracy, however, is that you can't appoint yourself to be in charge of it. It poses a problem therefore if your intention is also to be the pre-eminent country in a world of nearly two hundred sovereign states.

Adam Tooze nailed the issue with respect to the climate emergency:

> in his first speech as Secretary of State, Antony Blinken had this mind-blowing line. He said, 'Like it or not, the world does not organize itself.' And then proceeds from there to explain that if America does not organize the world system there are two possibilities: chaos, or something worse than chaos, which is 'Someone else takes our place.' Of course, the idea that the world waits for America to organize it on climate policy could hardly be more remote from the truth.

The world, in fact, has to consistently organize around the problems that America has contributed, and which America's political system prevents it from seriously addressing. So people of goodwill who are pursuing climate policy in America should start by recognizing that, when it comes to international negotiations, they must not project America's hobbled, stunted discourse about climate onto everyone else, and constrain other people's choices.[37]

A crucial insight is that the world "has to consistently organize around the problems that America has contributed, and which America's political system prevents it from seriously addressing". From the point of view of humanity as a whole the way the USA is governed is a problem not a solution. It is very welcome that America is now learning from China how to develop its capacity, plan its development and improve life for its citizens. But when it comes to confronting the rise of China it is essential the US does not make matters worse.

How Not to Respond to a Threat

We have a recent example of the US creating a contrived global enemy out of a manageable challenge: its declaration of "The War on Terror". It led to the invasion and occupation of Iraq and, just as critics warned, a massive expansion of terrorism followed. As we still live with this catastrophe, Blinken felt obliged to promise the US wouldn't make a similar mistake with China.

Then as now the engine that drives US folly is a military sector consuming a gargantuan $750 billion a year, which demands a consensus about who is "the enemy" to secure funding for its lethal cornucopia. In 2002 when Middle East experts warned against occupying Iraq, they were denigrated as pointy-heads. When people marched in protest, they were scorned as powerless hence irrelevant. The leaders of American primacy felt globalisation was speaking through them, the creators of a new reality. Two months after President Bush made his "Mission Accomplished" speech from the deck of the carrier Abraham Lincoln, and declared that the US had "prevailed", Tony Blair was presented with a Congressional gold medal in July 2003 as a reward for his role. He told the joint houses of Congress, "There never has been a time when the power of America was so necessary or so misunderstood, or when, except in the most general sense, a study of history provides so little instruction for our present day."[38] History itself was dismissed to the stormy applause of Washington legislators. To claim this having just occupied Mesopotamia took the delusion of untouchability to a new level, as few parts of the world have so instructive a history when it comes to invasions. A month later, the jihad began that scholars predicted would humiliate the Anglo-Saxon powers. "History" proved instructive. It wasn't the rest of the world that "misunderstood" the nature of American power.

At the time, John le Carré said the war was "mad".[39] When this was proved to be the case, did the media interview him to ask how he knew? Not at all. Millions of us took to the streets. Has anyone in power said we were right? *This* is the point that needs to be made. Twenty years on and Blair is still being taken seriously as a "winner" in the UK, sharing a platform with John Kerry, Biden's climate spokesman, after declaring that the Greens are his political enemy. Authority marginalises those who challenge its privileges, especially when they are proved right.[40] If those in power then change their minds this shows "wisdom" — but they continue to barely tolerate those who questioned their judgment in the first place: those who were foolish enough to be right when it was wrong to be right.

This syndrome matters now because it tests the Biden administration's commitment to actual, uncomfortable democracy. The Secretary of State agreed that invading other countries has "given democracy promotion a bad name". He promised "We will do things differently." He emphasised that America must show "humility because we aren't perfect". Blinken's intention is to be reassuring. So it may seem ungrateful to point out that his formulations are alarming if not stunted. The world is no longer the USA's oyster, as it was after 1989; it is no longer possible for it to behave as it did. Blinken's pledge that it won't implies a belief that it could; whereas the US cannot but "do things differently". That "America is back" is a relief, after four years when even its development agencies were forbidden to refer to "climate change". But it has not returned to a world that will ever, or should ever, accept American direction in the way that it once did. To embrace democracy now, as it claims to be doing, the US government needs to recognise that its invasions were not acts of "democracy promotion". On the contrary, the democrats were those who opposed its historic embrace of neoliberal economics (including distinguished figures like Joe Stiglitz) and the millions who opposed its neoconservative "War on Terror" and Iraq invasion (like le Carré). The opposition to so-called "democracy promotion" *was* democracy. The same spirit of opposition to unbridled use of power remains democracy's foundation. If America is to build on the spirit of democracy that it has in plenty, it is here that it should turn and not to the cynical manipulators of polarisation.

A new version of the "War on Terror" will make things

worse. Adamantine opposition to Xi's authoritarianism in China does not demand a polarisation that will only further militarise not democratise America. For all its tremendous achievements, China has huge numbers of poor, is intensely unequal, suffers chronic problems of the environment and is in no position to claim global "pre-eminence". Xi's bellicose language is evidence of weakness and fear of opposition. Blinken's formula, now used across the administration is: "Our relationship with China will be competitive when it should be, collaborative when it can be, and adversarial when it must be". It places the emphasis on aggression. It takes at face value China's vainglorious claims to be laying down the guiderails to "the common destiny for mankind", and prefigures a confrontation whose consequences will be even vaster military expenditures. The danger is real: "I am going to be exclusively focused on the China threat and exclusively focused in moving our maritime strategy forward in order to protect Taiwan and all of our national security interests in the Indo-Pacific theater". This was the pledge Biden's new Secretary of the Navy, Carlos Del Toro, gave at his confirmation hearing.[41]

China Will Not Take Over

It's tragic that America embraced neoliberalism. It's ironic that Communist Beijing's success showed it that there are better forms of capitalism. It's a relief that, with respect to the welfare of its own people, the US will become more like China in order to compete with China. The shift from a claim to lead the "Free World" to a desire to head an "Alliance of Democracies" could signal a transition from the globalist claims of neoliberal "pre-eminence". But such a collaboration cannot simply have China as its opponent. It is true that China has a hideously authoritarian government that supports repression in Myanmar/Burma and Zimbabwe. But China is not going to take over the world. It would be daft even to attempt to conquer Taiwan, which has the right to exercise self-determination. A seaborne invasion against intelligent mines and automated kamikaze drones? Beijing lives in fear of its population and is not likely to risk the domestic response to the massive economic disruption of military sanctions.

More important is the spirit of democracy in China itself. Xi Jinping is closing the country off from the rest of the world, preventing parents from having their children taught outside of government schools, restricting learning English, making masculinity patriotic to stop boys being sissy,[42] and clamping down on pop fans as well as breaking the autonomous power of would be internet platform oligarchs. At the moment such neo-Maoist nationalism is "Confident, vocal, and performative".[43] It should not be inflamed. America must not legitimise a bellicose Chinese nationalism or repeat the insanity of the "War on Terror".

The Chinese will not take to being controlled so tightly by Xi. There was opposition within the Communist Party three years ago when Deng Xiaoping's son, Deng Pufang, cautioned Xi against being "overbearing", telling him to "stick to the direction of peace and development."[44] At some point there will be a Chinese Gorbachev committed to democratic socialism who builds on the depth of self-belief in China, as well as its economic, cultural and technological achievement, all of which was missing in 1980s USSR. We can look forward to China challenging the United States as a democracy.

Meanwhile, when it comes to democracy around the world, Washington's ally Saudi Arabia is more repressive and the US funds the suppression of the Palestinians. While, as Edward Snowden points out, the targeted surveillance of opponents, especially bloggers and investigative journalists and their sources, with the pinpoint software of the Israeli-owned Pegasus programme and the complicity of the big US platforms, is a world-wide danger.[45] Peter Geoghegan, investigating the role of dark money, concludes that the rules of democracy "are not fit for purpose" and must be rethought or they will be taken over by internet platforms.[46] Steve Coll's dry conclusion in the *New Yorker* stands: "In this gathering age of digital autocracy, it is hard to avoid the impression that the dictators are winning."[47] This, and the corruption that supports it, which is a strong theme of Biden's national security analysis, are the two greatest threats to democracy world wide — not China.

Vote and Race

Perhaps the most striking aspect of the Biden government's presentation of its national security strategy is the inclusion of commitments to end voter suppression in the US itself and to combat the corruption of its own political system. Both are articulated with a sense of genuine urgency, as it sets out its priorities for the rest of the world. A battle has been joined to make America a rule-based electoral democracy in which all its citizens have an equal opportunity to vote and dark money is brought into daylight. It is a momentous, ongoing confrontation to end the country's caste system, endemic racism and economic exclusion when it comes to voting — and therefore when it comes to more than voting.[48]

We've seen how the Republicans launched an exceptional effort to suppress the vote of the poor and minorities in a coordinated multi-state effort immediately after the 2020 election. For this to be defeated, there has to be a fight back. When it began, my fear was that the media and Democrat establishment would put up only feeble resistance and that the long permissiveness of racial injustice would be reproduced. Instead, Biden declared, "We're facing the most significant test of our democracy since the Civil War." The Supreme Court Justice Elana Kagan denounced her colleagues with a blistering, authoritative minority opinion. A ground and legislative campaign has been announced to reverse Republican efforts to rig the political system even more in their favour.

This is America. Minoritarians have launched widespread attacks on the 8,000 election officers across the US. One in six have received threats of violence; one in three say they feel unsafe. According to a report in August, "Election workers had their homes broken into. Their private information was maliciously posted online. Some fled with their families into hiding. Others faced down armed crowds outside their workplaces and homes. And nearly nine months after Election Day, the threats persist."[49] Many may leave their jobs. Some Republican states are seeking to impose political control over returning officers. In the background, half of Republicans are reported to agree that force may be necessary to "save" America's way of life. The right is laying siege to the other side of America and its thorough and in the best sense bureaucratic administration that plays by the rules.

Securing the vote across this battleground will be decisive for American democracy. The issue has outstanding advocates like the Brennan Centre, Ari Berman's coverage in *Mother Jones*, reports on the *Daily Poster*, investigations by Greg Palast and others, and above all by the many on-the-ground campaigners now symbolised by Stacey Abrams in Georgia. Today, all such advocates of democratic reform confront a modern problem. The historic demand for the vote dramatised by the suffragettes was a fight for inclusion in a system of representation that seemed to matter. The neoliberal era has been so successful in eviscerating elections from making a difference it is harder to persuade people to concern themselves with the right to vote. In January 2021, 69% of Americans agreed "that American democracy serves the interests of only the wealthy and powerful". Seventy percent of Democrats believed this, as did 66% of Republicans. They think this for the simple reason that it does serve the interests of the wealthy and powerful.[50]

The undermining of American democracy has been substantial not just procedural. To convince people who don't want to participate in what they see as a farce, voting needs to make a difference in term of welfare, health, inclusion, security and redistribution — it has to be an effective means of empowering those who are not wealthy and powerful; otherwise, what is the point? A double-helix of change is essential. Unless voters believe that voting will make a real difference to their lives, they won't care enough to fight for the right to vote. Equally, unless they are able to vote, plutocracy will not be reversed and Trumpism will win the day. It is imperative that social, economic and environmental programmes are combined with political reform; unless they are wrapped around each other, neither will prove lasting.

Reluctance to vote also has causes that often relate to the internalisation of the consequences of neoliberalism. Afro-pessimism, for example, is right to challenge Marxist arguments that don't respect the autonomy of racial conflict and see it as a mere function of class struggle. But no group, however oppressed, is the single definition of oppression;

whites have the right to refuse to participate in racist structures, just as Brahmins can repudiate the caste system. Also, voting cannot "make a difference" overnight, as it is about having a voice in your lifetime and the way your society reproduces itself. This is one reason why young people have the lowest turnout even though they have the most to lose. Precarity, debt and the prospect of climate annihilation, the sheer nihilism of hyper-capitalism, have made voting almost a leap of faith, rather than a basic claim of right. The political objective of neoliberalism is to disaggregate citizens into forever marginalised, decentred receptacles of market choice instead of politicised communities of interest. In part it has succeeded and one form of resistance is to insist there is no escape from its fate.[51] But as I have tried to show, there are deep currents of human resistance which have persisted and grown, even while deprived of a creative political expression.

With the filibuster protected by right-wing Democrats like Senator Manchin, progress on voting reform will at best be partial, considering the full extent of what is needed. In July 2020, as the election was under way, Barack Obama spoke to the memorial service for the Georgia Congressman and civil rights veteran John Lewis. He spelt out a large part of the constitutional revolution America requires with his usual eloquence; except that he did not include expunging the role of secretive money and limits to election expenditures. "But even as we sit here," Obama said in his eulogy for Lewis, "there are those in power who are doing their darndest to discourage people from voting — by closing polling locations, and targeting minorities and students with restrictive ID laws, and attacking our voting rights with surgical precision, even undermining the postal service in the run-up to an election that is going to be dependent on mailed-in ballots so people don't get sick."

He listed what was needed: automatically registering every US citizen to vote, including former prison inmates; creating polling stations voters can get to, expanding early voting; making election day a national holiday; giving full statehood to Washington DC and Puerto Rico (important for rectifying the built-in white advantage in the Senate); ending gerrymandering; and abolishing the "filibuster" rule in Congress, which he called a "Jim Crow relic".[52]

Obama showed no regret that his own presidency is not identified with this agenda. There is something unsatisfactory about hearing the demands made by him now in the favourable atmosphere of a church memorial meeting. The urgency of Stacey Abrams, writing in the *Washington Post* after the assault on the Capitol, is more appropriate: "Time is short. The forces standing against a democracy agenda seek to preserve and expand paths to power by shrinking the voting pool […] We don't know how many chances we will get to reverse our democracy's near-death experience. We must not waste this one. We must go big — the future of democracy demands it."[53] It's a spirit that is echoed in Congress. The House majority whip, Jim Clyburn, who swung Black support behind Biden for the Democratic nomination, told the *Guardian*: "There's no way under the sun that in 2021 that we are going to allow the filibuster to be used to deny voting rights. That just ain't gonna happen. That would be catastrophic."[54]

He was referring to the *For The People Act*. Passed by the Democratic majority in the House of Representatives, it would have secured improved voter access, imposed Federal safeguards on voting rights, limited the role of money and reined in gerrymandering. Mike Lee, a Republican Senator from Utah, told Fox News: "This is a bill as if written in Hell by the Devil himself".[55] The filibuster was indeed used to prevent it from proceeding in the Senate. As I write, a weaker version based on a redraft by the right-wing Senator Joe Manchin is also undergoing trial by filibuster.

There are three underlying democratic issues: the US tradition of *rigging* elections, which wasn't always but is now squarely an issue of *racism*, and the role of the *Supreme Court* and the US constitution in this.

Rigging and Racism

Historically, Europeans witnessed an expanded franchise introduced from above by the state and reliably administered. In contrast, the US had a rough and tumble history captured by the phrase "Vote early, vote often", that goes back to the nineteenth century, as control over seats in congress and state legislatures were fought over. Stealing presidential elections was rare and the result has to be close for the allegation to be plausible. As it was in 1960, when out of 68 million votes cast, Kennedy got only 112,827 more than Nixon. Officially, that is. Nixon always held it was stolen from him thanks to vote rigging in Chicago and Texas.[56] His response was the "Southern Strategy" that made the Republican party the opponent of civil rights and brought him the presidency in 1968. His chief of staff, H.R. Haldeman, recalled that Nixon told him, "the whole problem is really the blacks". Or the whites, only 51% of whom today say voting is a fundamental right. Most will be Democrats or Democratic leaners, 78% of whom say they view voting as a "fundamental right" for every US citizen, whereas only 32% of Republican and Republican leaners feel the same, a chilling index of minoritarianism.[57]

There is no tradition of an independent, non-partisan commission to ensure voting is fair. The gerrymandering of constituencies, especially for the House of Representatives, is blatant, has historically been exercised by both parties, and is clearly discriminatory. Today's gerrymandering and voter suppression is scandalous because it is so overt. But Republican efforts to exclude those likely to vote against them builds on familiar practices. This does not make it any the less scandalous but it does help explain why they think they can get away with it — it isn't "un-American".

An eloquent picture of voter suppression can be found in "Never a Real Democracy", a short chapter in Heather McGhee's *The Sum of Us*, backed up with seventeen pages of detailed references. She stresses the adverse impact on whites, as well as Blacks and Latinos, of the gerrymander mentality of American politics.

The Supreme Court

Gerrymandering and voter suppression have been institutionalised by the Supreme Court, which has become one of the most dangerous opponents of democracy in America. It is worth looking at this more closely as it seems specialist and technical but takes us to the heart of the struggle over the future of America — as the monstrous Hyde dons the black gowns of jurisprudence and masquerades as Dr Jekyll.

Arizona passed ballot restrictions that were tested in the Supreme Court, which issued its verdict on 1 July 2021.[58] It provides a close-up of the whole process. Two sets of restrictions were objected to as discriminatory. One concerned invalidating legitimate votes cast in the wrong precinct, the other invalidated postal ballots delivered by anyone apart from the voter or his or her immediate relatives. The majority of the Court upheld these restrictions by six to three. To read the judgments is to enter the front line of a dirty war fought in courteous phrases.

That a legal ballot should only be cast in a voter's precinct seems reasonable, until on reading the minority opinion you learn in graphic detail how the locations of precincts are constantly being altered in Arizona, which alone of all the states has disqualified thousands of such votes in a discriminatory pattern. The lengthy minority opinion was written by Justice Elena Kagan and is a bracing read. To understand what the Supreme Court is doing, I quote from two sections written with power and precision. First, from her introduction:

If a single statute represents the best of America, it is the [1965] Voting Rights Act. It marries two great ideals: democracy and racial equality. And it dedicates our country to carrying them out. Section 2, the provision at issue here, guarantees that members of every racial group will have equal voting opportunities. Citizens of every race will have the same shot to participate in the political process and to elect representatives of their choice. They will all own our democracy together—no one more and no one less than any other.

If a single statute reminds us of the worst of America, it is the Voting Rights Act. Because it was—and remains—so necessary. Because a century after the Civil War was fought, at the time of the Act's passage, the promise of political equality remained a distant dream for African American citizens. Because States and localities continually 'contrived new rules,' mostly neutral on their face but discriminatory in operation, to keep minority voters from the polls. [...]

Today, the Court undermines Section 2 and the right it

provides. The majority fears that the statute Congress wrote is too 'radical'—that it will invalidate too many state voting laws […] I could say—and will in the following pages—that this is not how the Court is supposed to interpret and apply statutes. But that ordinary critique woefully undersells the problem. What is tragic here is that the Court has (yet again) rewritten—in order to weaken—a statute that stands as a monument to America's greatness, and protects against its basest impulses. What is tragic is that the Court has damaged a statute designed to bring about 'the end of discrimination in voting.' I respectfully dissent.

Justice Kagan is charging a majority of her fellow justices with rewriting statute law passed by Congress. I'll come back to the significance of this. But in a long judgment, one passage communicates what it is they have done. It concerns the question of who is allowed to collect and deliver a mail-in ballot and why confining this to close relatives and forbidding "third-party" delivery discriminates against a minority, in this case the Native American communities that live in Arizona:

The critical facts for evaluating the ballot-collection rule have to do with mail service. Most Arizonans vote by mail, but many rural Native American voters lack access to mail service, to a degree hard for most of us to fathom. Only 18% of Native voters in rural counties receive home mail delivery, compared to 86% of white voters living in those counties. And for many or most, there is no nearby post office. Native Americans in rural Arizona 'often must travel 45 minutes to 2 hours just to get to a mailbox' ('Ready access to reliable and secure mail service is non-existent' in some Native American communities). And between a quarter to a half of households in these Native communities do not have a car. So getting ballots by mail and sending them back poses a serious challenge for Arizona's rural Native Americans.

For that reason, an unusually high rate of Native Americans used to 'return their early ballots with the assistance of third parties.' The majority faults the plaintiffs for failing to provide 'concrete' statistical evidence on this point. But no evidence of that kind exists: Arizona has never compiled data on third-party ballot collection. And the witness testimony the plaintiffs offered in its stead allowed the District Court to conclude that minority voters, and especially Native Americans, disproportionately needed third-party assistance to vote [...] voting 'is an activity that requires the active assistance of friends and neighbors.' So in some Native communities, third-party collection of ballots—mostly by fellow clan members—became 'standard practice.' And stopping it, as one tribal election official testified, 'would be a huge devastation.'

The majority decided the "devastation" was constitutional as it was of only marginal significance that some would be so deprived of their right to vote. After the majority and minority opinions are drafted, they are shared with each other for comments. Justice Alito, who delivered "the opinion of the court" for the majority, responded that "the Postal Service is required by law to 'provide a maximum degree of effective and regular postal services to rural areas'". To which Kagan replied that "the record shows what the record shows", and went on to add, "That kind of background circumstance is central to Section 2's totality-of-circumstances analysis—and here produces a significant racial disparity in the opportunity to vote."

Legal judgments are often hard to follow and dangerous

to simplify as judgments combine multiple factors. To take just one in this case: the absence of a local postal service means that some Native Americans use members of their clan to deliver their fully legal and registered postal votes. They apparently tend to vote Democrat. The Republican state of Arizona has passed a law saying that postal votes can only be delivered by a close family member. No one is disputing that the vote itself is valid. The Voting Rights Act states that no rules on voting procedures should produce a significant racial disparity. But by banning the delivery of postal ballots by clan members the Arizona law does just that. The Supreme Court majority suggests that the Native Americans who are affected can seek redress in other ways because — wait for it — the law stipulates that there ought to be a postal service available for them, even when there isn't. The purpose of the 1965 Voting Rights Act was to address actual realities taking place despite the law. By casting its gaze away from what is taking place the Supreme Court majority endorses new forms of racist gerrymandering.

The Supreme Court is now widely regarded as an instrument of unjust discrimination. In an extraordinary, detailed and sweeping summary in the *New York Times*, Donald Ayer, deputy solicitor general in the Reagan administration and deputy attorney general in the George H.W. Bush administration, upbraided the Court's conservative majority for dishonest judicial meddling and in effect supported Justice Kagan's charge against a majority of her fellow justices that they are so rewriting the law as to make the court a branch of the legislature.[59] One key example occurred in 2013, in a case called Shelby County v. Holder. The court decided by five to four to eliminate a key part of the 1965 Voting Rights Act that called for the "preclearance" of new State regulations on voting with the Federal government. The purpose: to prevent discrimination. The Court ruled that because the law was forty years old and the situation had changed it could be cast aside. The late Justice Ginsberg, in her minority opinion, pointed out the reason the situation had changed was because preclearance *was working* to prevent gerrymandering: "Throwing out preclearance when it has worked and is continuing to work to stop discriminatory changes is like throwing away your umbrella in a rainstorm because you are not getting wet." The rain followed immediately.

Ten years later, and it has become a storm. The latest report from the Harvard Electoral Integrity Project found Wisconsin's voting system to be at the same level as Jordan, Bahrain and the Congo. Autocracy is being "built into democracy deserts" across America.[60] The reason for the storm is that, finally, there is vigorous resistance. In 2013, the Supreme Court decision that opened the way to modern gerrymandering was denounced by President Obama, but did not generate widespread opposition. It was a period of low turnout and demobilisation. If voting didn't really matter, why should its gerrymandering? The 2020 election has changed this. Turnout is rising massively. White supremacy is no longer the natural presumption of a majority and has become the aging prejudice of a minority. Gerrymandering itself is intensely unpopular with Republicans and Democrats alike (88% of Republicans and 90% of Democrats oppose partisan gerrymandering[61]). The Trumpite accusation of a rigged system has become a blatant projection of its own methods, the last chance for the dark money that backs Trumpism to uphold a chronically undemocratic polity. Its chosen instrument to secure its sway is the Supreme Court.

When this became an issue in the election, Biden chose to

avoid committing himself to the reform of the Supreme Court. Instead, he promised to establish a Commission to consider its role, which was promptly established. In a magnificent submission, Nikolas Bowie, an Assistant Professor of Law at Harvard, exposed the undemocratic nature of the Court in its composition, role and history. Drawing especially on the work of political philosopher Elizabeth Anderson, Bowie shows that the only minority consistently assisted by the Court has been the wealthy. He calls for constitutional oversight to be carried out by a body selected by sortition (i.e. at random like a jury).[62]

Reading Bowie's paper is refreshing. It is free of the dreadful American vanity about the superiority of its Constitution compared to all others. Even if he takes too rosy a view of the laughable quality of debate in the House of Commons, Bowie brings out the backwardness of the US's arrangements compared to other countries. His paper left Maximilian Steinbeis, the editor of Europe's main website on constitutional developments, *Verfassungsblog*, almost speechless at the US failure to have a "well-functioning constitutional court".[63]

The "Crisis Crisis"

As Joe Biden headed into his first autumn as president, he was losing the voter support essential for him to win the mid-terms and defeat Trumpism. The immediate reason was a mixture of crises: Afghanistan, immigration, the Delta variant of COVID, and legislative gridlock in Congress. The larger reason was the combination of two challenges: the brutal realities of US politics and the limited extent of Biden's opposition to them.

Far from having the large majorities in Congress enjoyed by Roosevelt and Johnson, the Democrats won by the narrowest of margins in 2020. This exposes Biden to the merciless hostility of Republicans, along with the peculiar mercies of two right-wing Democrats, Manchin and Sinema, essential to securing outcomes in the Senate.

While Biden wants to restore the activist approach of Roosevelt and Johnson, they built their way out of a crash and a crisis. He confronts a different threat: a rampant, popular movement. Many things could go wrong: COVID may resurrect itself; Biden could fall ill, die or be assassinated; high inflation or a financial crash or immigration surge could deliver a knock-out in the mid-terms or 2024. At least a climate catastrophe is unlikely to benefit the Republicans. The fundamental vulnerability of the Biden administration, however, is its relationship to Trumpism.

In 2020, Biden secured a choice for the USA and hence the world. This alone is a historic achievement. But the ferocity of Republican opposition confirms the ongoing civil-war-like polarisation. When Biden's vaccination programme began to work and started to bring Americans together, the Red States under Republican control initiated anti-vaccination policies that have led to thousands of deaths, kept the economy off-balance and ensured the continued prevalence of the disease. Republican leaders will burn the country to protect the profits of their backers. I track their messages. I've just had one from Donald Trump. "Anthony", he writes, "The largest number of illegal aliens in the history of our Country are pouring in by the millions. They are totally unchecked and unvetted. They can do whatever they want, and go wherever they want. **Our Country is rapidly becoming unrecognizable**". The message continues: "This is not just a Border Crisis, this is a Crisis Crisis, and I need your help".

Trump added to his falsehoods that among "the millions" pouring into the US are "murderers, drug dealers, and criminals of all shapes and sizes". This merely added a further frisson of alarmism to his core, dramatic, bigoted message: that "Our Country" was becoming "unrecognisable" and needs him to rescue it. Daily emails like this are not the racist puke of a deranged sect, they come from the leader of the party of Abraham Lincoln, determined to regain control of the White House.

Against such Trumpite assaults, Biden's plan is to deliver policies that break from neoliberalism. In this he comes up against two further forms of opposition. First, from the pre-Trump management, now that it seems Biden means it. When he split his programme into two, he ensured that the "American Jobs Plan", that budgets $1 trillion over ten years on traditional infrastructure, gained enough Republican support to pass the Senate on a bi-partisan basis. The "Reconciliation Bill" is for soft but just as critical infrastructure, such as pre-kindergarten and family and medical leave and measures to limit the climate emergency that Republicans won't touch. Originally budgeted at $3.5 trillion over a decade, it is hardly left-wing and is being halved and filleted by right-wing Democrats as I write.

The traditional centre-right and mainstream media assumed that Biden divided his programme so as to dump the more redistributive "reconciliation" package. Instead, Biden went to Congress on 1 October and confirmed he wanted both Bills. The *New York Times* reported this as an ill-advised turn to "the left":

> Given the range of the party's suburbanites-to-socialists coalition, it may have been inevitable that Mr. Biden would eventually anger one wing of his party. What was striking, and perhaps equally surprising to both blocs, was that he alienated

the moderates who had propelled him to the nomination while delighting the progressives who vociferously opposed him in the primary.[64]

Outside the meeting, Biden told the press he didn't mind if it took "six minutes, six days or six weeks", he would get his legislation, however modified by compromise. Simultaneously he must also secure voting rights from the predations of Republican state administrations. But having wrecked his initial momentum, the neoliberals will do all they can to demobilise his support.

The additional form of opposition to Biden's programme is the relentless and massive corporate lobbying effort, by big pharma especially, to scupper it. Efforts now scrupulously documented in the *Daily Poster*. From the beginning, as we've seen, the Biden administration identified corruption as democracy's enemy. Legal corruption and secrecy are perhaps the most corrosive.

In these circumstances, forced to make concessions, the best, perhaps the only way, to do so and expand your public support is to be clear and inspiring about the destination you want to achieve. This is Biden's weakness. You can see his problem. To end corruption, he needs support from corrupt politicians. To preserve America as an open society, he must close down Trumpism. In order to overcome polarisation, he needs to polarize — to define why he is different and not let others do it to him.

Can Biden spell out "the change of paradigm" he seeks? I've emphasised the importance of the "double-helix" combination of democratic reform to secure voting rights and economic reform for social betterment. Progressive change needs both, if it is to be sustained. In addition, Biden needs a larger sense of purpose: what kind of America will the "double-helix" secure? How will it *empower* the lives of regular Americans? In his brutal, reactionary and racist manner, Trump offers a sense of agency. It may not seem like dignity and respect to those who find him abhorrent. His supporters feel he gives them meaning, if only in the negative sense of defying those who would patronise them. Biden needs to offer a better form of empowerment.

Writing in the *Atlantic*, David Frum foresaw support for Biden slipping away unless he dealt with prices, borders, and crime.[65] Such traditional issues matter but no longer determine support. Voters forgive failures provided they approve of the larger sense of direction. It is when this is lacking that they punish leaders by condensing anger onto unresolved problems. Biden's weakness here is palpable. At the start of this chapter, I quote his press secretary on how there has been a "60-year battle to make voting more accessible, more available" which Biden intends to continue. She does not say he regards voting as a "fundamental right". Rather than go on the offensive, she describes his commitment in terms of process not principle, and as a continuation of an old battle not a determination to defeat racism in its new guise. Or take Biden's Reconciliation Bill which is so important to him. Its policy proposals can score over 80% public support. Yet backing for the Bill itself among voters is only half that.[66] A striking measure of the absence of a unified, compelling project.

The progressives have their answer, in the sweeping narrative of the Green New Deal. Biden has yet to embrace it and with Manchin crouched in the corner you can see why he judged it to be not politically viable. Instead, the Biden team may have hoped to use the threat of China to justify their ambitious efforts to improve America.

For some, the lure of a new Cold War is that it can be used to mobilise US society in an active fashion from above, without the need for activists. Fortunately, unless China actually declares war on Taiwan's autonomy, this option is not available. The capitalist world needs China, which is now crucial to it. It is too late for Washington to contain it, as it did the USSR. In addition, unlike the threat of Communism, which a Red Scare can big-up into a domestic enemy, "Xi Jinping thought" has no ideological attraction whatsoever. It is atheist and state-centred and thus doubly abhorrent to the Christian libertarian right; it is capitalist and authoritarian and so twice repugnant to the democratic, progressive left.

In a further twist, Biden wishes to secure the constitution against Trump, when the "deep constitution" and Supreme Court have been captured by the divisive forces he needs to confront. In every country, democracy and nationalism are linked to its constitution. The US is no exception. Its constitutional framework is now being defined by the Supreme Court as a license to gerrymander and a permission for elections to be bought by corporate power. Reversing this is an opportunity to rethink the US Constitution itself in the age of the internet, given the need for voice and participation.

Such are the challenges when, as I tried to describe, a historic failure of the political order forces political leaders to "back into" a transformation. Later, I also noted how Biden's National Security Advisor, Jake Sullivan, observed that a key lesson of Trump's success was the need for simple, telling slogans, which in fact were missing from Biden's election. As president, Biden cannot now escape the need to be clear about the direction America needs to take. It won't shift Manchin or Sinema, but it is essential to secure the future votes of the millions, who supported him as the alternative to Trump. He has to show them that he has a credible, inclusive vision.

Should he fail to hold off Trumpism, it will be because Biden never did create Biden*ism* and never told US voters in clear, compelling language what the new "paradigm" is that he wants to see, or how it will secure their future as citizens of an America all of them can be proud to recognise. You can't just move on from neoliberalism as if it was a mere policy error to have believed in "trickle-down" and not invested in child-care. The core function of market fundamentalism is to extinguish popular engagement, and it is this that must be reversed.

7.   The Argument Resumed

I have sketched the nature of Trump's support that makes it an ongoing threat; how Trumpism is a minoritarian and nativist response to defeat in the Middle East and Afghanistan and the failure of market fundamentalism; how it reversed the political fatalism that neoliberalism had seeded and grown inside voters, and the globalisation that undermined nationalism; how it did so by redoubling the cult of winners and losers, supporting corrupt elements of the wealthy, and making explicit the repression of democracy that is central to market fundamentalism.

I have described seven forces of humanisation (there may be more) that resisted neoliberal fatalism. Since the Seventies they have been counter-currents below the surface of the massive, incoming tide of hyper-capitalism, even as they picked up energy from it. I've tried to show how they fed the ground campaigns that ensured Biden's election success that brought Trumpism to a halt, even if temporarily.

I've looked at how the early Biden government shaped up to the task of trying to ensure that the defeat of Trumpism is permanent. I've shown how this has created a potentially historic, progressive opening not because of the strength of "the left", but because of the internal, financial breakdown of market-dominated politics in 2008, followed by its external humbling by a more successful China, culminating in Trump's political humiliation in failing to deal with COVID-19.

Thanks to the stupidity, financial venality and military overreach of the bipartisan Washington power elite, since it had literally ruled the world after 1989, the United States nearly fell before Trump's authoritarian sway. Thanks to the way the forces of the counter-currents reinforced the strengths and vitality of America, it didn't — at least it didn't in 2020.

The epoch of neoliberalism now has two defining dates to mark its formal beginning and end: 1980 and 2020 — from Reagan to Trump. It started life in the Seventies under Nixon, it will twitch on, doing great damage, as in my own country under Johnson. But in its homeland of America, it is being replaced. This uncertain and contested process creates an opportunity for democrats, to think afresh, act anew and create a sustainable, possibly "socialist" (a term I'll come back to) outcome before the century's end.

How can we do this? This is the question. The "we" being everyone, whoever we are in the world, who identifies as being human and is open to the realisation that they are not inherently superior to any other fellow human.

An answer demands a reassessment of what it means to be a democrat. Too often arguments for political change are either removed from reality or obsessively focused on the immediate. They need to be rooted in a strategic understanding of the present conjuncture: the here and now understood as a combined set of processes that are unpredictable because how they are combined is reflexive, feeds back on itself, and is therefore open and alters. This is why I try to root my argument in a history of the present embracing its uncertainties.

What Is at Stake

A good way to clarify what is at stake is to ask, "What is the question to which the Biden administration is the answer?" It should be: "How do we save the human planet from environmental catastrophe?" Biden is committed to a carbon neutral strategy but is still licensing oil extraction. What ought to be every government's top priority isn't his yet.

Some in Washington would like the Biden administration to be the answer to, "How can the USA return to being the world's pre-eminent power?" If this does become the question, then whatever the answer it will be bad news.

The question the Biden administration itself says that it must answer is, "How can we prevent America from becoming neo-fascist?"

This is a good question. Since 1945, never until now has there been a serious threat of fascism across the West. Despite all the horrors it inflicted on the rest of the world, the West's liberal order remained a constitutional one at home. Relatively speaking, we have enjoyed freedom of speech and belief, the right to organise, contested elections and the rule of law, within a shared framework in each nation. When countries like Spain emerged from fascism, this was what they became. There are also the beginnings of international institutions capable of treating small and large countries equally and assisting the development of the poorer ones. It is a class-based system of power. Speak too freely and you are ignored. Even if you are not ignored it makes little difference: the media is integrated into the overarching, capitalist regime. Organise too well and it will try to break you. But for the most part, you are not jailed arbitrarily or assassinated by hitmen. Within democratic capitalist countries there is still an overarching degree of consent that allows powerful differences to work themselves out and governments to change without violence.

Or there was.

Trump was obviously an authoritarian individual. Writers, notably Timothy Snyder, warned immediately of the danger of fascism.[1] At the time I was not convinced. That he would enjoy — if he could — smashing the checks and balances of the American settlement and the "deep state" of functionaries and lawyers that oversee it, was not in doubt. But what kind of ruling class is reckless enough to throw away such assets? Initially I believed that Trump was only a master of self-promotion, genuinely significant as a symptom of the failure of the neoliberal order, which voters had understandably turned against, who exploited the deep veins of America's racism. I didn't see him as having the support necessary to terminate the constitution of the United States, which was surely not going to be toppled by a property tycoon, even if he has an exceptional talent for money laundering and "reality" television.

The opposite is the case. Trump may well burn himself out. But Trumpism is alive, entrenched within the USA's gerrymandered system, and it aims to recapture the White House and not allow itself to be ejected. Trumpism deploys administrative power to ensure minoritarian rule and confine the effective political community to its supporters. It will end the broader consent essential to representative democracy. It is a project that has begun to hold sway in nearly half the legislatures and governors' mansions of the fifty states, as it redraws districts and suppresses voter access while preparing its police for any blowback. The aim: to capture the state.

The success of the Biden administration stands between us and them and, were they to win, a world of modern neofascism. This is how Biden himself seemed to present it when he decided to run in August 2017. In a furious condemnation of

Trump's response to a grotesque, torchlight march of death at Charlottesville, he wrote

> Today we have an American president who has publicly proclaimed a moral equivalency between neo-Nazis and Klansmen and those who would oppose their venom and hate.
>
> We have an American president who has emboldened white supremacists with messages of comfort and support.
>
> This is a moment for this nation to declare what the president can't with any clarity, consistency, or conviction: There is no place for these hate groups in America. Hatred of blacks, Jews, immigrants—all who are seen as 'the other'—won't be accepted or tolerated or given safe harbor anywhere in this nation.[2]

But Biden ran against a racist president not a racist party. He hoped that when Trump was defeated his support would fade away and he would be perceived by Republicans as a one-off disaster. Normality would be then be restored. Instead, Trump turned out not to be eccentric and there *is* a place for such hate groups in America. The depth and solidity of Republican support for Trump's post-election defiance of a peaceful transfer of executive power according to the majority of votes cast, means that hateful Trump*ism* is an ongoing threat. Furthermore, because the depth of its opposition to traditional American constitutionalism has only just been confirmed in 2020, we have to recognise it as a new force that is just beginning to cultivate its strength and purpose.

A successful return of Trumpism would be a tragedy for those of us who enjoy the United States and have benefited from its generous culture. But the consequences will not be limited to the USA. A world order is at stake. The fate of democracy in the USA would not matter so much if Brazil was a thriving, well-governed society, protecting the Amazon, its cities and beaches safe and egalitarian as well as beautiful; and if India was true to its constitution and ensured the toleration of all faiths, did not discriminate against Muslims and Dalits and was relaxed about self-determination in Kashmir, so that it was indeed the world's greatest democracy; or if South Africa, instead of pledging in its constitution that everyone had the right to work, actually ensured there was full employment and decent education, creating a dynamic, multiracial example of *ubuntu* — of people thriving thanks to the wellbeing of others — for the whole of Africa; and also if Russia was the home of culture and human development we all know it could be. Perhaps *then,* even if China was still constricted to so-called "democratic centralism", and Europe to arguing with itself, and the Middle East continued its wars of religion, a white racist authoritarian USA would be terrible for America but not irreversible. We could be confident that it would eventually catch up with the other continents of democracy.

Should Trumpism return to power in Washington as a durable form of government it will be as a lynchpin for our existing world. It will join the Russian, Chinese, Indian and other states now developing hi-tech surveillance absolutism, where protests by majorities have been crushed in cold blood, supported by a swathe of smaller dictatorships and populist regimes from Belarus and Turkey to Burma and the Philippines. The liberal, multilateral world will be terminated, if a lasting rather than temporary American authoritarian takes over in Washington. As Martin Wolf argues in the *Financial Times*:

Biden is playing for huge stakes — and knows it […] It is not just about proving that the US government is capable of doing important things. It is now about protecting the core of democracy — peaceful acceptance of electoral outcomes.

If that were to go in the US, would-be autocrats everywhere would have carte blanche to do as they pleased. The danger is great, since the Republicans are no longer a normal democratic party. They are increasingly an anti-democratic cult with a would-be despot as their leader.

I desperately hope Biden succeeds […] The future of democracy is at stake.[3]

The future of democracy is of more immediate importance than the climate emergency if only because it will determine the response to the climate emergency. Environmental disasters are coming; it is already too late to prevent them. But authoritarian, carbon-based regimes will use extreme weather shocks to double-down on their supremacy as climate activists are rounded up like so many Cassandras punished for their foresight. No enlightened, environmentalist despot can emerge from a collectivity of crooked, malevolent hi-tech kleptocrats and chauvinists. To avert climate catastrophe there has to be wide support to pay for the costs. This demands intelligent democracy and there is no shortcut around its development.

Part of the danger is that Trump beat the liberals to the democratic draw, as he abandoned neoliberalism first. For forty years, popular political agency was hollowed out by marketisation and many came to regard voting as a humiliating expression of their own pointlessness. Trump's astonishing contribution to democracy has been to show that voting can deliver change. In 2020 he smashed the hex of neoliberal fatalism twice over. First, by defying conventions in office so that white power intransigents, who felt that administration after administration justified their loathing of Washington and refusal to vote, backed him in their millions. Second, because he also broke the spell of resignation felt by millions more who found him so loathsome they voted against him in even larger, record numbers.

The Democrats have to retain these voters and transform their rejection of Trump into an affirmation of a Biden "paradigm shift" in 2024. Hence the significance of the "double helix" that secures voting rights alongside social and economic gains and reinforces an inclusive national story.

The difficulty is that this involves a showdown with the historic nature of America. It was uniquely the land of the free. It was also uniquely the land of industrial scale slavery and Jim Crow. There has always been a fascist side to the USA. This was externalised in 1945 with the double use of nuclear weapons on Hiroshima and Nagasaki, and after with the atrocities of Vietnam, the massacre in Indonesia, the use of torture after 9/11. And domestically there are nearly one and a half million incarcerated in prison in today's America, Black men being nearly six times more likely to be imprisoned than whites.[4] The country that pioneered law-based liberty did so in a historic compromise between rights-based politics and racialised subordination.

Obama's project was to undo this — and effect a soft-landing for whites to accept that the days of bigotry were over and they had no need to be alarmed. Instead, Trump cashed their fears, and won in 2016 thanks to the complacencies of Hillary Clinton. What followed was the transformation of the Republican party under his presidency. This has generated a confrontation of a different order. By denouncing the 2020 result, assaulting the integrity of election officers and implanting coordinated voter suppression in the State governments that they control, the Republican party of Donald Trump has repudiated the founding compromise. The fundamental settlement of the United States is coming apart. The continued coexistence of "Jekyll and Hyde" in the singular polity of America has been rendered inoperable. The choice is now one or the other: either minoritarian nativism or multi-racial democracy.

Biden's battle with a fascistic individual, who he saw as usurping the role of president, has become a showdown with the dark side of the United States. It is a civil war. To win the Democrats not only need to secure voting rights and ensure that the childhood, education, family life and prospects of regular Americans improves and are made sustainable, they also have to redefine what it means to be American.

As if this wasn't hard enough they have an added difficulty. Trump has set them a negative example of how to attempt such a redefinition. As a populist he seeks a dramatic, exclusive singularity which is exciting — to oppose as well as support. Whereas the democratic national-popular is pluralist and inclusive and must reach out to Trump supporters not demonise them. Wisdom and consideration *has* to lack the thrill of huckster demagogy. Biden needs time to prove its benefits, time the other side won't give him.

Across the board intelligent progressives share the fear of the "doomsters" that Biden will fail as Trumpite nativists rig the ballot in plain sight to ensure their minoritarian supremacy and the Democrats fail to stop them.[5] Familiarity with years of concessions, complacency and capitulation to Wall Street leads many to believe that real change comes only from the right and far-right.

My fear is that Biden will start to succeed when no one seems to be prepared for this. Everyone I know on the progressive left is braced for defeat. All the familiar mental muscles developed over forty years of confinement are clenched in preparation for disappointment. Instead of thinking long-term, most remain consumed by a profound anxiety; reinforced by the gathering strength of corporate interests demanding a return to the corruption of Clintonism.

Yet, despite its decades of depoliticisation, neoliberalism was unable to squelch the desire to put humanity before the market. A desire expressed in our reactions to COVID and in the roar of protest over the manner of the murder of George Floyd. It now needs a politics. It is called democracy — an open, republican democracy that gives us each a voice and rights and a way to share control. Biden claims to have summoned up the spirit of intelligent self-government. Like the sorcerer's apprentice we need it to take on a life of its own. The future of humanity depends upon our achieving this, within and outside the United States.

But is the US capable of becoming a real democracy and, if so, are progressives capable of playing a part in this?

8. Can Actually-Existing Democracies become Democracies?

President Biden has declared that there is a contest between democratic capitalism — represented by his America — and authoritarian capitalism — represented by President Xi's China. It is also a contest on two fronts given the threat of authoritarian capitalism at home.

Clearly, Xi's China is not a democracy and Trump is a danger to American democracy. But is the US a capitalist democracy? Can there be such a thing? This is a double question. First, with its Supreme Court, a Senate with a baked-in racist imbalance, and a House that is gerrymandered, is the United States constitutionally capable of being a democracy of justice (to draw on the language of Martin Luther King)? Second, even if it is possible for the USA to transition to government *by* the people, will its capitalism permit it to do so? Is it possible for a real democracy to be capitalist?

Can the US Become a Real Democracy?

Between the 1770s and the 1860s, the rulers of both the Anglo-Saxon countries, Britain and the USA, developed their form of representative government with a limited male property-owning franchise. It provided strong government with one positive and three negative — in the sense of preventative — outcomes. The positive was that it developed an independent judiciary, administration and a professional military. The preventative outcomes were: that it prevented dictatorship, prevented revolution and prevented democracy. By achieving these ends it ensured the ownership of property and capital secure from the arbitrary potential of both the state and the mob. It thus permitted those in command to enjoy legal security and political freedom at home while exercising a cruel imperial expansion abroad. With this framework, industrial capitalism was unleashed on the world. In order to pull it off, the Anglo-Saxon powers achieved something else: helped by elections, they organised domestic consent.

Both the founders of the US, with their 1776 Declaration of Independence and the 1789 Constitution, and the ideologists of Britain's uncodified parliamentary rule, were clear about what they were attempting. James Madison, one of the chief drafters of the US Constitution and later president, put the problem that they collectively solved as follows: "you must first enable the government to control the governed; and in the next place oblige it to control itself". They wanted powerful states that could control the population, prevent dangerous uprisings and raise the forces to fight wars, while ensuring they did not turn into an arbitrary monarchy or dictatorship. The ascendency of Napoleon showed the foresight of such concern. In the US, Madison and his colleagues created a republic as opposed to a democracy. The same process was worked through in London, where the famous historian Lord Macaulay defended the Great Reform Bill of 1832 as a way of preventing democracy — this being "fatal to the purposes for which government exists".[1]

On both sides of the Atlantic, a hard-edged government

of laws was achieved with as broad a support as possible across all property holders — who felt secure enough in their own rights, religious belief and speech, that they gave their government their assent whether their faction was on top or not. Slaves were left outside the pale, while the poor and the female, most of whom were illiterate, would have no direct say at first, but their loyalty was desirable and largely achieved. In fits and starts, over a long period, the franchise was extended, especially after wars when the proven loyalty of the larger population meant the core principles had been maintained.

In the US, however, in 1861, the Southern states withdrew their consent. A four-year civil war followed. The price of their subsequent reintegration by conquest was, after a period of reconstruction, the long pushback of Jim Crow racism as Blacks were violently excluded from equal participation in the body politic and social and economic life.

When he wrote *The English Constitution* in 1867, just after the US Civil War, it did not occur to Walter Bagehot to consider the political integration of all citizens as political actors. Instead, he compared what he regarded as England's version of top-down republican government to America's. He boasted that the informal fusing of legislative and executive power in the Cabinet was more efficient than America's separation of powers, and the monarchy's decorative orchestration of public loyalty was more effective at ensuring consent.

Consent was the key. Power was not democratic. On the contrary, wealth and privilege ruled and regarded the unwashed as a menace. The Declaration of Independence says that to secure life, liberty and the pursuit of happiness, government gets its legitimate power "from the Consent of the Governed". The Constitution itself does not even go that far. It states that its purpose is a "more perfect union".[2]

Neither document mentions "democracy", even if, famously, the Constitution speaks of "We the People". During the Civil War, Lincoln referred to "government of the people, by the people, for the people". In terms of what today we think of as "the people", it was an aspiration.

There is something important and difficult to accept about the American process. By creating from nothing a new government of men that did not claim its legitimacy from monarchy or God, it contained an unmistakable kernel of democratic agency, namely a claim to joint self-government. The constitution sets out the lawmaking machinery and the rights and freedoms of "We the People". But ever since, a ferocious clash has ensued — sometimes volcanic, sometimes smouldering — over who the "we" is. Who is included to enjoy the self-proclaimed privileges of the constitution and who is not, became a battleground of class and race. It both fundamentally is, and at the same time never was, a democratic constitution.

Representative democracy everywhere reproduces this tension in different ways according to the specific national circumstances. It creates a zone of contest between classes, between the rural and the city, between nation and region (and in some countries, oppressed nations) and with neighbours, with shifting borders and frontiers impacting on who is counted as a citizen (or still, in the UK, a subject).

The United States has three peculiarities compared to the now many other representative democracies. It was very early, which meant that, from the start, America's political and economic rulers sought to constrain the democratic potential they were the first to draft into existence. This made their constitution both radical as a claim for liberty and independence and today among the most undemocratic constitutions of its kind.

Second, from the outset the US Constitution was both the most human and inhuman of documents of its time. This was soon recognised. Elizur Wright in 1833: "While this nation held up its declaration of independence — its noble bill of human rights, before an admiring world, in one hand; it mortified the friends of humanity, by oppressing the poor and defenceless with the other. The progress of time has not lessened the evil. There are now held in involuntary and perpetual slavery […] more than 2,000,000 of men, women and children".[3] Over the course of the nineteenth and early twentieth century, the US became the destination of mass trans-Atlantic immigration. The new arrivals immediately became Americans. The millions who had preceded them crossed the Atlantic in chains. They had a prior claim yet were excluded from full citizenship. Racism and its violence and paranoia penetrated the entire culture, not just the South. The outpouring of protest over George Floyd's de facto lynching was a multiracial repudiation of the legacy, still regenerating itself in voter suppression and gerrymandering, in today's contest over who is included in "We the People".

Third, the US has another particular twist. That the constitution permitted the reproduction of slavery mattered less to many of its drafters than that it enabled a coordinated expansion of the western frontier, with a continental army that could defeat the Indian nations, whose lands it seized and whose societies it then sought to exterminate. You can read the debate over the constitution as a parochial argument over how to hold sovereign power to account with "checks and balances" to prevent tyranny, by people who were familiar with Aristotle's definitions. Their purpose was also to raise and deploy an early modern army and navy which would be an instrument for tyranny over others. The same colonies that won liberty from Britain expanded America with genocidal intent. This additional duality, an external expression of internal white supremacy, went global with victory in the Second World War. Nowhere was its Dr Jekyll and Mr Hyde nature to be more starkly illuminated than in Vietnam:

> 'All people are created equal; they are endowed by their Creator with certain unalienable Rights; among these are Life, Liberty, and the pursuit of Happiness.' This immortal statement was made in the Declaration of Independence of the United States of America in 1776. In a broader sense, this means: All the peoples on the earth are equal from birth, all the peoples have a right to live, to be happy and free. [...]
>
> We are convinced that the Allied nations, which at Tehran and San Francisco have acknowledged the principles of self-determination and equality of nations, will not refuse to acknowledge the independence of Vietnam.

This was from the Vietnamese Declaration of Independence made in Hanoi in 1945 to the acclaim of the country's younger generation. But the allied nations did refuse. The United States killed two million Vietnamese in its attempt to overthrow a declaration of independence that was a successor to its own — made by "natives" who had the impudence to claim autonomy. The impact of this on the anti-Vietnam War movement, that grew in the United States from the late 1960s, prefigured divisions that have roiled America since. Much of its activist leadership concluded that the US was inherently imperialist, while most of their followers felt the US had betrayed its core values. At the time, the pressures generated by the war made it impossible to articulate how both were true simultaneously. Arguably, the division broke the American left's ability to develop a credible, national politics.

The meaning of a constitution is defined less by its words than the process and motivations of its drafting. In the United States these were two-faced: a government of laws was created within so as to better exercise lawlessness without. Beyond the windows of some of the world's finest libraries, whips lashed without mercy. After 1945, when confident of its world role, Washington reproduced this legacy in a new way. The need for white supremacy at home diminished thanks to American superiority abroad. It did not disappear. If you were to call the Supreme Court majority racist, they would object vociferously. Yet somehow, as we have seen, they fail to treat the Native Americans of Arizona as Americans like themselves.

In his immediate response to the Trumpite insurrection on the Capitol, Nikolas Bowie (whose critique of the Supreme Court I've mentioned) evokes and confronts the duplicitous inheritance: "Protections of racial subordination pervade the Constitution", he writes, which "the Supreme Court condoned" repeatedly. Yet, he continues, "this story need not end in tragedy [...] An antiquated document that enabled so much that was wrong has also protected so much that is right [...] new principles are necessary for the Constitution to live up to its own words and 'establish Justice'".[4]

That the US institutionalises evil and good is not an original insight. Bowie's phrase, "this story need not end in tragedy", indicates something different. An ending is in sight for the United States. The military and financial implosion of America's post-1989 global supremacy has drained away the external superiority that was a crucial support for its permissive domestic racism. It is becoming impossible for the US to hold both the civilised and the barbaric sides of its character in tension any longer. Either the governing system of the USA becomes exclusionary and abandons justice, as the Supreme Court has so often done in the past and has just done again in Arizona, and this is institutionalised by the return of Trumpism; or it embraces the justice that is democracy for all its races, for which it has a unique capacity, as Bowie believes it can. That it could be captured by Trumpite minoritarians is not in doubt, but Bowie asserts that constitutionally America is also open to becoming a democracy of justice. I want to probe this claim.

From Consent to Democracy

On both sides of the Atlantic after 1945, economic growth benefited all classes. Along with elections that provided a useful safety valve, even opposition that expressed class differences became a form of allegiance stronger than mere consent. It was a model for what became known as "The Free World".

Those for whom the post-1945 period is distant history may find it hard to realise how palpable and almost physical the culture of "consent" was. The term makes it seem merely intellectual. Its roots went back to the experience of a "good war". In January 1941, President Roosevelt delivered his address to Congress after being newly elected for an unprecedented third term. Japan had not yet attacked Pearl Harbour and the US was not at war, but he committed his country to unequivocal support of the conflict being fought against the dictatorships. He ended by looking forward to a world "founded upon four essential human freedoms" — these were freedom of speech and worship and freedom from fear and want. The speech is famous for them. But what he set out as the domestic objectives for American society would today make him seem like someone on the far-left:

> For there is nothing mysterious about the foundations of a healthy and strong democracy. The basic things expected by our people of their political and economic systems are simple. They are:
>
>> Equality of opportunity for youth and for others.
>> Jobs for those who can work.
>> Security for those who need it.
>> The ending of special privilege for the few.
>> The preservation of civil liberties for all.
>> The enjoyment of the fruits of scientific progress in a wider and constantly rising standard of living.
>
> These are the simple, the basic things that must never be lost sight of in the turmoil and unbelievable complexity of our modern world. The inner and abiding strength of our economic and political systems is dependent upon the degree to which they fulfill these expectations.

What today seems a utopian prospectus and not at all simple to achieve was delivered for white Americans after 1945. There were jobs, there was security, the privileged were taxed, the standard of living and education levels did indeed rise constantly. There was not equality of opportunity but there was opportunity for youth and for others. Political consent rested on the lived experience of this set of material foundations.

I don't need to repeat how this world was undone by market fundamentalism except to note that insecurity replaced security as a positive value for ensuring high returns for investors. Instead of delivering *freedom from fear and want* for "our people", the role of the government was to make sure corporations could *impose* fear and want on the employees and communities dependent upon them.

The Biden administration would like to transport the United States back to those halcyon days of Roosevelt, however idealised, only this time with the full consent of minorities. The claim that the 2020 election was "stolen" expresses a white minority's withdrawal of consent at this prospect. Bowie's legal perspective can stand as a judgment that extends across the nature of US society as a whole. It need not end in tragedy, but there will need to be an ending.

Either this will take the form of populist authoritarianism, or consent will be replaced by genuine constitutional democracy. The difference can be described in terms of Madison's challenge ("you must first enable the government to control the governed; and in the next place oblige it to control itself"). With authoritarianism, the governed remain under control — but by a government that is uncontrolled. With genuine constitutional democracy, government "of the people" becomes government "by the people" — and the governed take control of government.

Such a democratisation of existing representative democracy will be a process, not a replacement. For democracy here means a democracy of justice: of rules, deliberation, inclusion, participation and the protection of minorities. It isn't populism. It is a route to achieving a humanisation of how we govern ourselves that needs a material foundation of security, health and education. If the state cannot be trusted to deliver the four freedoms then "We the People" will have to. The existing constitutional structures designed for a republic and not a democracy will need to be changed, I'll discuss how in the conclusion. But the most important asset the USA has is a constitutional culture that will permit and even encourage such radicalism – and it has it at the level of the different States more than at the Federal level.

Given the entrenched nature of arbitrary power, corrupt and extremely unequal wealth and privilege, bigotry, racism, religious zealotry and sincerely held fundamentalism, even to suggest such an aim seems naïve and "utopian". Surely a return to the old form of top-down form of government based on "consent" is preferable? There are two reasons that make this almost impossible.

It can't be achieved by the behaviour of one side. "Consent" belongs to the system, not a party. Today it would require a cross-spectrum majority to believe, for example, that the Supreme Court is fair and judicious, not partisan; that if the Republicans win the House on gerrymandered seats and a minority of the votes it's OK because it's always been the American way; that the party you oppose nonetheless offers a legitimate leadership, which will ensure that the regular administration is fair and non-partisan. Such shared beliefs are not sustainable any longer.

There is also a change in the political culture due to the way marketisation has made people feel responsible as well as powerless. It generates an uncanny form of life sentence as we become accountable for ourselves alone — how we appeal to others, our debts, our unemployment, the cost of our rent. Each of us generates our own neoliberal inner policeman, forced to treat our identity entrepreneurially as an asset. This leads to many pathologies. One is an often bitter acquiescence, expressed in high rates of abstention from voting, another is defiance. It led many people, often those with some property, privilege, or pride to express their fear of dispossession by voting for Trump as a kind of talismanic protection. The surprise — and they are as surprised as anyone — is that they did indeed make history: they *have* given the elite a good kicking! They are now political agents. Millions experienced this delight and will never again accept a "consensus" on how they should be ruled "for their own good". In turn, the outrage aroused the others from absentionism and they too are now empowered by achievement. On neither side will this new sense of agency be lightly surrendered — why should it be?

Meanwhile, younger generations never knew a time of deferential consensus. Especially for those born after 9/11, who are beginning to become old enough to vote and have known only futile wars and climate reckoning and the manipulations of platformed internet, the idea of putting one's trust in the system is absurd.

America is a different country from the 1950s when Biden was a boy and the US had just won the Second World War and enjoyed government *of* the people. To replace it with government *by* the people will be complicated and demanding and will take at least half a century. In America it has a chance thanks to its energy and self-confidence; especially as the conservative veneration of the American constitution as an indispensable gift to human kind is coming to an end.[5]

Capitalism and Democracy

The US constitution and others may permit a transformation into genuine democracy, but will capitalism? Can the existing economic system survive the active empowerment of voters? In the US, 93% of financial assets are held by 10% of the population; it is hardly an economic democracy. Within the top 10%, the ultra-wealthy control an even more unequal proportion of wealth and this is translated into control over the media and influence over political agenda, policies and personnel. As Branko Milanović points out, in the 2016 US election the top 1% of the top 1% of the wealthy made "40 percent of total campaign donations".[6] One can imagine a capitalism governed by democratic, rule-based self-government, but will the rich allow it?

Some of them don't want to. The proposed *For the People Act*, designed to ensure the integrity of US elections, limits secret campaign spending — there is overwhelming support for this across the political spectrum. The *New Yorker* investigative reporter Jane Meyer, author of *The Dark Side*, on the Bush-Cheney presidency's cult of torture, and *Dark Money*, on the role of secret political funding, obtained a recording of a conference call about the proposed legislation. It was between staff of "prominent conservative groups including a policy advisor to Mitch McConnell" and Kyle McKenzie, a research director for the billionaire Koch group which presumably helps to fund the staff. McKenzie reported to the group that "polling shows that no message they can devise effectively counters the argument that billionaires should be prevented from buying elections".

Meyer writes, "The speakers on the call expressed alarm at the broad popularity of the bill's provision calling for more public disclosure about secret political donors". But McKenzie told them, "When presented with a very neutral description" of the bill, "people were generally supportive [...] the most worrisome part [...] is that conservatives were actually as supportive as the general public was when they read the neutral description." Conservatives, here means right-wingers, and "neutral description" means factually accurate. In other words, even far-right members of the public support legislation that "stops billionaires from buying elections"! McKenzie warned that "the worst thing conservatives could do would be to try to "engage with the other side" on the argument. He explained that the Koch-founded group had invested substantial resources "to see if we could find any message that would activate and persuade conservatives on this issue" — and failed. He also warned that they tested arguments in support of the bill as a whole and the one condemning billionaires buying elections was the most persuasive — people "found that to be most convincing, and it riled them up the most".[7]

This vivid cameo of full-time minoritarians, the staffers of hard-right Republicans in Congress, confronting the revulsion expressed by their own voters at the secret funding that pays their salaries, is worth more than a laugh. A trademark complaint of the Trumpite right is that the system is rigged, and here are their leaders' functionaries discussing how to rig the system. In the past, thoroughgoing racists would delight in the idea that billionaires are making sure they win. But today, the de facto racist supporters of the right are "riled" by the loss of agency involved. No messaging could be found to convert them to support secret funding, even for instrumental purposes such as stopping Alexandria Ocasio-Cortez. The conclusion of the telephone conclave was that only "under-the-dome-type strategies" will work to stop the bill. The "dome" refers to the great dome of the Capitol building. The advice: use only procedural manoeuvres such as the filibuster.

So, claims that the rich fear and seek to subvert democracy are well founded and can be documented. And the one percent can no longer rely on mystifications to mask their role, only secrecy. There is cross-spectrum support for transparency as a democratic principle. Here is a bipartisan issue, so far as the public is concerned, to test Biden's metal, up against that other form of "bipartisanship" — the collaboration of elected Republicans and Democrats, who benefit from often identical corporate and ultra-wealthy donors.

We know for sure that neoliberal capitalism is anti-democratic and secures the rule of the rich. Now that it has failed, the Biden administration seeks a "democratic capitalism" where government frames and directs the market. "I'm a capitalist," Biden said, and added, "But here's the deal [...] My sole measure of economic success is how working families are doing, whether they have jobs that deliver dignity." Wall Street executives and business owners, the president continued, "should be rewarded for their success and the risk they take. I just think after decades of workers getting a raw deal, it's time they be given a fair shake."[8] Many in Biden's core team have served and been paid by corporate America, especially through WestExec Advisors, and the investment fund, Pine Island Capital Partners.[9] Biden's domestic policy advisor Susan Rice was ordered to divest $34 million of holdings, including investments in a US oil pipeline.[10]

It does not follow that Biden's team won't crackdown on corruption and ensure that the very wealthy pay more tax. Not all capitalists are neoliberals who favour profit maximisation before everything; some loathe bankers and despise Milton Friedman.[11] Others can stop believing in Friedman and embrace a wider view of the need to support "stakeholders" and save the climate.[12] Pete Buttigieg, Biden's Secretary for Transport, a young centre-right advocate of both deficit reduction and democratic capitalism tweeted, "I'd say neoliberalism is the political-economic consensus that has governed the last forty years of policy in the US and UK. Its failure helped to produce the Trump moment. Now we have to replace it with something better".[13] He told CNN, "Capitalism has let a lot of people down", and "at the end of the day we prioritize democracy".[14]

When running for the nomination, Biden told the Poor People's Campaign Presidential Forum that poverty was "the one thing that can bring this country down"; he listed several new programmes to help the poor that he would fund if elected, and told them, "We have all the money we need to do it." Then he pitched his campaign to wealthy donors in New York, saying, "The truth of the matter is, you all know in your gut what has to be done. We can disagree in the margins, but the truth of the matter is it's all within our wheelhouse and nobody has to be punished. No one's standard of living will change, nothing would fundamentally change."[15]

But when a direction changes, those who initiate it look backwards and can't know for sure where they are going. A US government that raises pay and ends voter suppression points to the possible emergence of a new stage in the history of capitalism. Branko Milanović is confident only of capitalism's continued suzerainty. His tone is one of realism not enthusiasm. In his *Capitalism, Alone: The Future of the System That Rules the World*, he is clear about the amoral character of what he calls hyper-commercialised capitalism and the inevitability of corruption associated with it. He is authoritative about the systemic inequalities it generates, within societies and on a world scale, on which he has published pathbreaking research. He is frank about the nature of life under capitalism and the "reign of half-truths in our private lives". He asks, could we not "ditch the world of hyper-commercialized capitalism in favor of an alternative system?" His answer: "the problem with this otherwise sensible argument is that we lack any viable alternative". "The domination of capitalism as the best, or rather the only common way to organize production and distribution, seems absolute. No challenger appears in sight." He also observes: "The capitalist spirit, a testimony to the generalized success of capitalism, penetrated deeply into people's individual lives [...] Capitalism has successfully transformed humans into calculating machines endowed with limitless needs [...] To live in capitalism, we do not need the capitalist mode of production in factories if we have all become capitalistic centers ourselves."[16]

Exactly this aspect of capitalism convinces Albena Azmanova it will be "subverted" from within: "we stand at a tipping point in history when acute dissatisfaction with capitalism is rising, not on account of its poor economic performance or the unfair distribution of its wealth, but rather its excellent economic performance, its intensity [...] exploitation is no longer the key engine of social injustice. Instead it is the competitive production of profit—the key dynamic of capitalism—that is felt as harmful by all participants [...] What is being challenged is not simply the unfair distribution of wealth, but, importantly, the very process through which wealth is generated and the impact this has on individuals, communities, and nature."[17]

These arguments are part of an ongoing literature that revolves around the question of whether capitalism will permit us to organise society in the interests of humanity rather than the priorities of capital. The answer depends on whether we can organise ourselves to create the democratic institutions that can achieve this.

Revolution or Else?

Some claim it is simply impossible within capitalism to develop a democratic politics that might threaten to displace its domination. Dylan Riley, a California professor and an editor of *New Left Review* writing in the *Jacobin*, set out a warning to those attracted to the rising interest in democratic socialism. He explains that the "fundamental *class* interests" of capitalists means they do not have to "control government directly" because uniquely, capitalism "is compatible with formal electoral democracy" (as well as fascism and authoritarianism). Indeed, because different branches of capital compete, "they also have a *positive* interest in electoral democracy". Only up to a point, however. As soon as "a self-conscious working-class movement struggling for socialism appears to be anywhere near achieving victory", any such interest in democracy becomes "residual". A transition to socialism, "cannot occur within the framework of electoral democracy". Instead it must be "vastly more democratic in a *participatory* sense" — the italics being a coded formulation for some form of insurrection. Furthermore, when economic growth slows as it must, it will be "profoundly damaging to the liberal-democratic mechanism, which requires 'tolerance' and a willingness to accept the aleatory results of elections as legitimate" (aleatory means uncertain, as in gambling). Indeed, "There are no historical cases of capitalists tolerating the outcome of elections that might threaten capitalist property relations." The establishment of socialist democracy, therefore, will only take place "beyond capitalism".[18]

My first reaction on reading Riley is that the prose is cold. It permits no disagreement and reads as if he is fulfilling an instruction from the ideological rectification subcommittee of an inter-planetary politburo. Some potential cadres on planet earth have had their hopes aroused by talk of "democratic socialism" — his instruction is to put such nonsense to rest. But isn't such a response just what "they" want? If there is a collective capitalist interest, as Riley supposes, wouldn't it nod its hydra-head in unanimous and satisfied agreement with him? *Jacobin* has thousands of highly educated readers influential with their friends. The last thing the capitalist class can desire is to see them energetically organising to get additional Alexandria Ocasio-Cortezes elected to Congress, it much prefers them to be sitting on their hands.

My second reaction is "How does the politburo *know?*" What does capitalism do when the coming crisis hits China, for example, with 300 million graduates and the authoritarians *already* in charge? What do the capitalist elites do in the US if a climate catastrophe hits North America and its educated population has a better idea of what is happening than they do? Rounding up Mexicans, seeking *Lebensraum* on Mars, regimenting Facebook entries? What solutions will there be to prevent a majority that wants a democratic resolution? How will this not be "tolerated"?

Also there is the tone of voice, the ideological ukase, the threatening vibe of implacable impersonality. The sterility of such theoretical rectitude feels so unhealthy. No one should be asked to accept the promise of a "socialist democracy", always tomorrow, *mañana*. People know enough history to know that there can't be a sudden, tyrannical breakthrough to freedom; after a hundred years they know that the 1917 Russian revolution was misconceived not betrayed. Workers won't become part of Riley's "vast participatory democratic challenge" without the practical experience of making a claim on politics through politics itself.

My experience of demanding democracy is limited and met with overall defeat. But it's fair to say that I engaged in hand-to-hand combat with the British government at the end of the last century. A campaign based on the twelve demands of Charter 88, which I coordinated for seven years, sought to create a sufficiently democratic state to have the chance to build the kind of movement now developing in the United States. Partial successes, such as a Scottish Parliament, the Human Rights Act, and Freedom of Information, were doomed by a strategic failure which I did my best to warn against. Finally, I sent Tony Blair a blunt memo. His Chief of Staff, Jonathan Powell, wrote back on 26 February 1998 to tell me the prime minister "found it extremely helpful and we will give the issue some thought"; he then phoned and summed up my view as "After us, the deluge". Just so — today we in Britain are living in the deluge because New Labour refused to forge a new democratic settlement when this was possible. Were we wrong? Was it mistaken to have worked for the UK to have a democratic constitution because, without it, one could no more get democratic socialism from the British state than milk from a vulture? We wilfully defied the odds, I grant, and were brought short. But what campaign for change doesn't start as an act of defiance? Such efforts should not be sneered at as naïve pointless "reformism". All politics is a gamble. Or "aleatory", as Riley puts it. The choice of language, the chilly style itself *de haut en bas,* as from on high to those down below, suggests a fastidious desire of campus Leninism not to be contaminated by error — an attitude that is itself mistaken and a negation of the political. Riley is right to warn that capitalists will be ruthless in seeking to shut down a democratic challenge. It doesn't follow that they have to win.

So if the American president wants to replace hyper-commercialised capitalism with democratic capitalism, then let's roll! His prime interest may well be to secure capitalism. It is up to democrats to secure democracy. Even if it will take a generation or more, there can't be a better time to start, it may be the only chance we have.

From Outsiders to Allies?

Out of force of necessity, the US political elite has gambled on a new direction. After 245 years of confining democracy, a majority including many in the military, the Democratic Party, the foreign policy establishment, the police, trade unions, churches and the global corporations, want to prevent Trumpite tyranny. This demands they enfranchise everyone, insist on racial fairness, provide basic welfare such as child care, tax wealth and prevent climate change. The imperative divides every class including America's wealthiest families (oddly personified by the split between Murdoch's two sons). While its motivation is defensive, it sets in train a process that has its own dynamic and relies on progressive forces to register voters and get them to the polls. America's institutional racism can't be terminated, nor the staggering mistreatment of America's working classes recuperated, without the collaboration of North America's exceptionally able and practical movements for much wider forms of change. An opening has therefore occurred for those who want real democracy. The threat of self-government is no longer being snuffed out at the first smell of danger.

In a forceful conclusion to his essays collected in *This Is Not*

Normal, which is mainly about Britain, Will Davies examines the fatal nature of a division between the left and the centre that needs to be overcome in the face of authoritarianism.

> Liberal ideals, of constitutional process and the 'separation of powers', have played a fundamental role in legitimating and sustaining capitalism since the eighteenth century, which renders them suspicious in the eyes of the left. But [...] it's no longer clear that contemporary capitalism has need of a norm-based, legal model of the state, indeed platform capitalism prospers by defying it. Companies such as Facebook and Google thrive by attacking existing norms around ownership and privacy; code acquires the sovereignty once reserved for law. This is where the 'disruptors' of Silicon Valley find a common cause with those of the new conservative insurgency.
>
> Moreover, there is much to gain from diverting liberal ideals (of restraint on executive power) towards democratic socialism, and against the overbearing power of contemporary capital [...] It seems too often that, while the left is willing to defend key liberal planks of political modernity such as human rights and attention to facts, this is not reciprocated with support for economic democracy and wholesale redistribution of wealth and income. A crisis ushered in by coronavirus has accelerated the need to find this common ground between the defenders of institutional norms and those who agitate for economic justice.[19]

There seems zero expectation of such an alliance soon in Davies's England, where it would need the Labour Party to call for a progressive alliance. In Scotland, the centrist governing SNP tolerates an arms-length alliance with the left in the larger independence movement, but keeps it at bay in government. Neither it, nor Labour under its present leader Keir Starmer, have woken up to the end of neoliberalism. They simply think it is now fashionable for governments to spend money, while assuming they can rely upon twentieth-century manipulation. In the USA, however, left and centre are exploring the common ground Davies describes. Centrists are easy to mock as they resist the fact that their policies led to the success of Trumpism. It does not follow that those of us on the left do not need to raise our game.

9.　The Left from 1968 to Occupy

Whatever it is that Biden has started, to succeed he needs the energies of activists and progressives who have been sidelined from official politics since the 1960s. To prevent the victory of Trumpism, Black, Hispanic and white activists have to become the allies of a democratic liberalism, to forge a renewal of the United States. Before we can conclude by probing the issues this raises, we need to look back at the defeats, foresight and frustrations of the protest movements.

The American (and British) system of elite rule was put to the test in the Second World War. In Europe, the Anglo-Saxon alliance benefited from the Soviet Union's decisive contribution. In Asia, the US moved to prevent a Soviet share in victory and dropped a "Little Boy" and a "Fat Man" on Hiroshima and Nagasaki, took Japan's surrender alone and emerged triumphant as the foremost global power.

In the twenty years that followed, its consumer capitalism became a model for the world and the US Marshall Plan invested in a European recovery. The long boom generated a transformation within the US and across Western Europe. Beneath the old, now self-satisfied patriarchal framework, teenagers came into existence — a form of humanity that had never previously existed — television intensified collective awareness, Black music entered white souls via rock and roll, contraception transformed sexual relations and mass higher education began. Three processes then combined to explode in the Sixties, which led in the decade that followed to the birth of neoliberalism as a world system.

The Sixties Trinity

First of all, the Sixties rode the tiger of the "Great Acceleration" mentioned in Chapter 4. The exponential growth which began in 1950 with GATT, the General Agreement on Tariffs and Trade, altered what it means to be a human. 1968 witnessed a striking intensification. The dimensions for a universal system of containerisation across ships, rail and road transport was defined by "ISO 668" (in part thanks to the US army wanting to secure its massive shipments from "Viet Cong pilfering") and world trade took off. The first Boeing 747 Jumbo Jet emerged from its hangar; it was to go into commercial flight in 1970, transforming global tourism. In December, the so-called "Mother of all Demos took place" to signal the development of the personal computer and mouse, while the foundation of Intel initiated the coming era of the microchip; and in 1969, ARPANET, "the precursor of the internet", sent its first message.[1] Colour television became ubiquitous, internationalising the possibility of a "shared experience". The most striking image of the totality of changes brought about by applied, postwar science was taken on 24 December 1968: the first colour photograph of Earthrise over the Moon. It symbolised the way we were now holding our planet in our hands and helped initiate environmentalism.[2]

Second, as this qualitative transformation of consumer capitalism began, the alternative to it, Soviet Communism, began its implosion. Starting with the French Communist Party's opposition to the student revolt of May 1968 it intensified to the point of irreversibility with the Soviet invasion of Czechoslovakia in August 1968, that snuffed out "the Prague Spring" of the reformers seeking a democratic socialism. At the same time, the Chinese communists were consuming themselves in the so-called "cultural revolution", that was so bitterly unfair to the Vietnamese seeking to make good their August Revolution of 1945, arguably the only democratic revolution to be led by Communists.

Vietnamese resistance to the American effort to crush their national independence fed into the third defining aspect of 1968 — it became a year of worldwide revolution. There was a revolt of the young — especially, but not only the student young — against paternalism, traditional authority and the fetters of the imagination. We could be free in a way no previous generation had been because we were the first to grow up without scarcity. We did not have to toil for the necessities of life, or constrict our sexual behaviour for fear of pregnancy; travel was easy, music was original and cheap, skirts were short, emotions and identities could be expressed in radical ways. What previously had been the privilege of a tiny elite was now for the taking. No generation gap has been as great, and we were not going to be confined by the rules, the bureaucracy, hypocrisy and authority of our parents and their deference to hierarchy. It was a wonderful emancipation. It was also painful and deeply ambivalent. The demand to stop the war divided America: calls for peace, love, civil rights, participation and an end to the horrors of Vietnam, were met with an abundance of violence, assassinations, massacres and censoriousness.

What can be called the "long 1968", a worldwide year of revolution, began in June 1967 with demonstrations in what was then West Germany against the visit of the Shah of Iran, and Black riots against police abuse in the US.[3] There were many different '68s. To note just two in Europe: the French '68 saw: "the biggest strike in the history of the French workers' movement, and the only 'general' insurrection the overdeveloped world has known since World War II. It was the first general strike that extended beyond the traditional centers of industrial production to include workers in the service industries, the communication and cultural industries — the whole sphere of social reproduction".[4] It was a unified strike that failed and it traumatised French politics and culture thereafter. In Germany, by contrast, while the extreme leftist edge was captured by the Red Army Faction, a terrorist network supported by East Germany, a generational shift took place. A "revolution" (that in Britain was almost entirely cultural) had a massive impact in West Germany with what was known as the "anti-authoritarian movement". It led an entire generation, right as well as left, to take up the reckoning with their parents' Nazi past, known as the *Vergangenheitsbewältigung* (the dealing with the past) — it civilised the country thereafter.[5]

If the Sixties revolution unified Germany and traumatised France, it divided the USA. Today the strength of Trumpism has forced the Democratic Party into an alliance with the progressive and activist left in a shift, still in its earliest, most vulnerable stage, symbolised by Bernie Sanders and his supporters taking part in the 2020 convention process as allies of the winning candidate to ensure he broke from the neoliberal legacy of the Clintons. By contrast, at the Democratic Convention in 1968, progressives were clubbed down on the pavements outside the venue in Chicago on the orders of the Democrat Mayor Daley.

The Two Sides of the Sixties

In the previous chapter, I mentioned the way the anti-Vietnam war activists divided over their understanding of the nature of the USA. They also divided the country at large. Millions of Americans served in Vietnam and regretted only that the US lost. Richard Nixon won the presidency in November 1968 on a pro-war ticket. His cynical deployment of a "Southern", racist strategy to beat the Democrats, who under Lyndon Johnson had passed the Civil Rights Act, was an early expression of a new reactionary pushback. Returning veterans embittered by defeat created the white power movement, as we've seen. In the UK, Enoch Powell launched white English nationalism with his "Rivers of Blood" speech.

There was another aspect to the reactionary side of the Sixties. Alongside a collectivist, humanitarian empathy and calls for the liberation of the oppressed, there was a different kind of liberation in the opposite direction. A permissive, rule-breaking, fame-fucking irresponsibility also meant that Sixties transgression embraced extreme individualism and fortune-hunting. The unrestrained, individualist libertarian-racist side of the Sixties was to find its ultimate personification in Donald Trump.

The reaction *against* the initial, macho-sexism of the musical and political radicalism of the Sixties, and its sexual libertarianism, generated its most lasting and genuinely transformative influence: feminism. It was passionate about reversing a ubiquitous, unjust inequality. It was intellectually audacious and prolific. It was decentralised and attempted different tactics. It pioneered consciousness raising. It helped inspire gay rights. Today, the inheritor of decades of arduous efforts is #MeToo, which took off in 2017, a year after millions of women had marched against the election of a misogynist to the White House. The clash between feminists and Trump reworks the confrontation that burst into the open in the late Sixties. Implicitly, #MeToo reprimands the limitations of the early movement, demonstrates the unstoppable demand for fundamental equality and human dignity, and signals how long real change takes.

David Graeber, who was from a later generation, captures the dual nature of the Sixties revolution and its legacy:

It's fashionable nowadays to view the social movements of the late 1960s as an embarrassing failure. A case can surely be made for that view. It's certainly true that in the political sphere [...] a prioritizing of ideals of individual liberty, imagination, and desire, a hatred of bureaucracy, and suspicions over the role of government [benefited] the political right. Above all, the movements of the 1960s allowed for the mass revival of free market doctrines that had largely been abandoned since the nineteenth century [...] In retrospect, though, I think that later historians will conclude that the legacy of the 1960s revolution was deeper

He asks how financialized capitalism managed to convince the world it was the only viable economic system and answers:

The pre-emptive attitude toward social movements is clearly a part of it; under no conditions can alternatives, or anyone proposing alternatives, be seen to experience success. This helps explain the almost unimaginable investment in 'security systems'.[6]

His account is subtle and compelling. The challenge of the Sixties upsurge gave the ruling authorities the fright of their lives, trade union leaders and left-of-centre politicians as much as bankers, presidents and industrialists. To put it in its full historic context: the system of consent which had delivered their privileges was contested for the first time by a credible, educated, passionate demand for direct democracy and participation. Modern and contagious, it was quite different from the authoritarian Stalinist challenge they had known since 1945. Capitalist societies set about repressing it.

The Sixties Repressed

Since 1968, you could write a history up to the present in terms of how different ruling systems around the world did everything possible to prevent real democracy: through repression, marginalisation, modernisation, globalisation, corruption, public relations, medicalisation, religion, wars, game shows, censorship, consumerism, fatalism, monetarism and marketisation. Until we arrive at the world of the pandemic, when billionaires are free to make added billions in an era of mass death. While the cultural difference between the polished patriarch of the 1950s and oligarch geek of the 2020s is immense, there is a similar desire to control and exploit consumers and workers and to head-off any empowerment of citizens that would hold them to account.

Political, financial and religious masters had always been aware of the danger that insurrection posed to their privileges. Notoriously they were willing to update themselves so that things could stay the same. But the challenge of the Sixties was different. It threatened an expansive democracy that questioned the way power was exercised with demands to participate in decision-making in a transparent fashion. The shock to the ruling elite was that the modern world had given birth to people capable of governing themselves.

The challenge this posed went on well into the Seventies. In 1970 itself, the National Guard shot students at Kent State University as they protested the invasion of Cambodia. It took the whole of 1973 before the Watergate scandal ensured Nixon would be impeached in 1974, and he resigned. The Vietnamese finally drove the US from Saigon in 1975. In the UK, as Andy Beckett writes, the Seventies was when "the great Sixties party actually started", with a victorious miners strike in 1972, and another that saw the government itself voted out in 1974.[7] The popularity of Allende's government in Chile, overthrown by the US in September 1973, symbolises the global nature of the upsurge.

How to reconfigure consent and thereby restore rule from above when you have lost deference and people want self-government? This was the question posed by the Sixties and early Seventies. It was explicitly investigated by the 1975 quasi-official Trilateral Commission in *Crisis of Democracy* — subtitled: *A Report On The Governability Of Democracies*. The Commission was founded in 1973 by David Rockefeller and organised by Zbigniew Brzeziński, who became President Carter's National Security Advisor. Paul Volcker, who headed the Federal Reserve for both Carter and Reagan and ramped up interest rates and unemployment, and Alan Greenspan, who followed him, were both founder members.[8]

The report diagnosed "A general drift toward alienation, irresponsibility, and breakdown of consensus". The latter being a key term. "The late sixties have been a major turning point," its authors wrote, "The amount of underlying change was dramatically revealed in the political turmoil of the period which forced a sort of moral showdown over a certain form of traditional authority [...] a marked upswing in other forms of citizen participation, in the form of marches, demonstrations, protest movements, and 'cause' organizations". There was, it continued, "an excess of democracy". This now demanded "moderation" so that it would give way "in many situations [to] the claims of expertise, seniority, experience, and special talents".[9]

How to go about achieving this? The Commission's authors referenced Madison on the need to "control the governed" while keeping government itself in check. They felt that "the effective operation of a democratic political system usually requires some measure of apathy and non-involvement", and continued, "The vulnerability of democratic government in the United States thus comes not primarily from external threats [...] but rather from the internal dynamics of democracy itself in a highly educated, mobilized, and participant society". The conclusion: "There are also potentially desirable limits to the indefinite extension of political democracy. Democracy will have a longer life if it has a more balanced existence."[10]

America's governing class had concluded there was too much democracy for America's own good. They defined the problem; Milton Friedman, among others, offered them an answer. In the year following the Trilateral Commission Report he lectured in South Africa and issued, "an unremitting diatribe against political democracy—an explicit rejection of, in Friedman's words, 'one person, one vote' [...] Voting, Friedman declared, was inescapably corrupt, a distorted 'market' in which 'special interests' inevitably dictated the course of public life [...] True democracy, Friedman insisted, was to be found not through the franchise, but the free market, where consumers could express their preferences with their unencumbered wallets."[11]

The Neoliberal Resolution

Friedman's answer, neoliberalism, fitted requirements. Certainly, it was worth a try. As Mark Fisher put it, "Neoliberalism is best understood as a project aimed at destroying — to the point of making them unthinkable — the experiments in democratic socialism and libertarian communism that were efflorescing at the end of the Sixties and the beginning of the Seventies".[12] I'm repeating myself deliberately. Neoliberalism had economic priorities: to deepen the market, engorge corporate power, privatise public services and financialise globalisation, but it was primarily a political strategy — its function was to head off the growth of popular self-government. It provided a way to tell people who now felt capable of governing themselves not to want this, or even better, to believe that it was in fact impossible.

Ironically, the anti-authoritarian claims of the Sixties offered a way to achieve this. Collective claims to self-rule would be diverted into the individual demands of the "democracy" of the marketplace. Meanwhile, surveillance was essential, in case people were not convinced. It is a paradox that one aspect of the Sixties was used against the other. The experience of, and desire for, collective agency could be dissolved by the freeing of individual desire, which was commercialised and politically disempowered by hypostasising "the market" as natural — an absurd claim, as markets are the creation of states and legal systems, but never mind. Government then became the problem. Looking back, we can see that there was a particularly important aspect to the way the dark side of the Sixties provided the energies to contain its non-violent, humanist desires for transparency and to chill and have a say. It allowed the challenge to be met not with old-fashioned repression that restored command to "expertise, seniority, experience, and special talents". Instead, it was out with seniority and experience (if not "special talents"). To displace political democracy with hyper-marketisation was *modern*. It out-played the radicalism of the Sixties at its own game and enabled rulers to stay in charge and lay claim to the future — but at a price: they had to abandon their conservatism.

The freshness of neoliberalism was an aspect of its genuine appeal. Margaret Thatcher saw herself as "progressive", or at least was willing to use the term, and her sale of council houses at below market price created a new strata of working-class property owners. "Right to Buy" remains embedded in popular imagination in the UK as a consciousness-shaping moment when neoliberalism was genuinely empowering while the collectivism of council ownership was not — and claims to solidarity were torn apart. In the old country of the UK, its novelty was combined with a shout-out to "Victorian values", no less, by Thatcher when she initiated it as a culture of government. Stuart Hall nailed this as "regressive modernisation". The latter was the aspect that mattered. It gave Thatcherism a competitive and substantial emancipatory quality compared to Fabian centralisation. It's good to own a home. It's great to have a choice of attractive furniture. It makes one more human. It generated a way of life at once daring and confined: "Neoliberal culture works specifically to *enhance* our creative capacities while inhibiting any attempt to put them to work in a collective, political, democratic fashion", Jeremy Gilbert observes (my emphasis).[13]

Neoliberalism was unconvincing as an economic project for the general good but it was a cold-blooded way to reproduce the crucial twin attributes of the historic tradition that dates back to the founding of the US constitution: it rejuvenated the elite's ability to control the governed while ensuring their consent. The method was to transform consent into political fatalism — with personal economic success as the reward. For some this meant a high-energy embrace of market opportunities, for most a stoical acceptance, for everyone an increase in insecurity in an age of unprecedented abundance. What followed was an anaemic version of consent, to ensure "good enough" turnout for elections and the flexibility and legitimacy they provided. Politics itself was relentlessly pilloried as a compromised activity, while the public realm was defunded and denigrated. As "choice" was glorified by tabloid consumerism, elections were emptied of the capacity — that danger whose touch-paper was lit in 1968 — of filling the political arena with meaning and life and therefore the ability to challenge class relations.

The outcome was a form of closed democracy. There was no conscious plot. It was not the result of a mastermind but a pragmatic exploration of what worked. It's wrong to see neoliberalism as the clever instrument of unchanged ruling classes. Conservatism, with its sense of honour and integrity, perhaps its only worthwhile values, became a victim too, suborned by the attractions of money. Aware that their paternalism was doomed, Western rulers chose the cool of the marketplace over tradition, to ensure they retained the privileges of wealth. And they broke the democratic challenges that threatened them from the left.

Resistance Crushed

Marketisation was also resisted. From the start, deliberate coercion, of the kind we witness today in Hong Kong, was part of the mix. There always was an alternative — but in the West it was repressed. Two examples signal how the democratic potential of the time was snuffed out. In 1970, Salvador Allende became the elected left-wing president of Chile. Nixon and Kissinger mobilised the resources of the US against him and ensured his bloody overthrow in 1973, before he could call a plebiscite to legitimate his policies.[14] Much less dramatic, in the UK, the left under Ken Livingstone won the leadership of the Greater London Council — the GLC — in 1979 and it became a base for radical municipal government, pioneering popular anti-racist and feminist programmes. For a short blast of time, political power, freedom to experiment, open-minded radicalism, popular planning and anti-racism came together in England's capital. It was a formative moment for a cluster of talent, including Hilary Wainwright, whose books and the magazine *Red Pepper* keep its spirit alive; John McDonnell, the most serious and intelligent of the Corbyn group, who became Shadow Chancellor from 2015–20; and Robin Murray, the developmental economist whose London Plan, had it been implemented, would have made London a centre of modern craft and design. Instead, the GLC was simply abolished by Thatcher in 1986. In both Chile and the GLC efforts were made at experimentation, at investing in worker's participation, and in open forms of planning, within a market context. It was only after they proved popular, despite vicious media opposition, that they were physically eliminated; Chile then became a test bed for the first implementation of rigorous neoliberal monetarism.

A much later example of the coercion of Western electorates not usually understood as such, perhaps because it failed, is the Iraq War. Its intended role needs to be recognised as a reminder of how the external projection of the state shapes its domestic hegemony. The justification for the need to conquer Iraq was a set of lies: that Saddam Hussein was an international threat, had weapons of mass destruction, and was involved in 9/11, when he wasn't — taken together, the greatest falsehood of the twenty-first century. Its apparent purpose was to triumph in the oil fields of the Middle East. But there was another aspect too. The UN had overseen the destruction of Iraq's actual chemical weapons after the 1993 war, when his conquest of Kuwait was reversed. The US (and the UK) then imposed punishing sanctions on Hussein's appalling regime and operated a no-fly zone over most of Iraq, keeping it closely surveilled. They knew he posed no threat and his army could be swept aside. They wanted an easy military triumph to prove their domination. The protests and popular opposition in their own countries and around the world may have been stronger than expected. In Britain, 1.5 million filled London on 15 February 2003 — the UK's largest demonstration ever. Nonetheless, Washington went ahead, confident that this would reinforce the aura of supremacy it desired in order to entrench its "global order". The powerlessness of citizens to prevent this was grist to the mill. The pinpoint ballistic missile attack on Baghdad that launched the war was named "Shock and Awe". And the populations in the US, Europe and around the world watching it on their TV screens were the political targets to be awestruck. If there is a defining *military* expression of the hateful and odious creed of Milton Friedman's neoliberalism, its claim that the sole purpose of economic life is profit, that democracy is the "free market" which the population must be subdued into accepting, this was it. Shock and Awe was its slogan, a despicable war of choice was its method, Baghdad was to be its finest example, greater even than bankrupting Russia, "Mission Accomplished" would be its name. There would be no alternative.

At the time, most of those I knew were profoundly depressed by the defeat of our opposition; some withdrew from engagement with politics or adopted melancholia. There seemed to be no other option than fatalism. In 2005, with Isabel Hilton, then the main site editor at *openDemocracy*, I took the view that a long term "democratic warming" was underway. We argued that the beginning of deliberative democracy, along with the rule of law, had to be defended from both fundamentalism and the "War on Terror". We claimed that the opposition to the Iraq war had been "historic", because for the first time in history the people on the streets had been proven more far-sighted than their leaders in the US and UK in "an argument over the coming use of power" by demanding "a wise, well-judged refusal of a war of choice and its likely consequences". The tables of democracy had been turned. The wisdom of the pavement had been vindicated while the elite clearly no longer knew what was best.[15]

Although it took ten years, longer than I expected, and was initially led from the right, a possibility that had not occurred to me, the full-scale collapse of consent and the eruption of anti-elite anger can be dated back to 2003. Only it didn't grow out of the wisdom of the pavement but rather the fury and disappointment, mixed with economic vulnerability, of those who had saluted the flag, supported the war, felt betrayed and recycled hatred of Muslims.

Today, a left radicalism that can trace its roots back to opposition to the Iraq invasion is now part of the heritage of the movement that installed Biden in the White House. One of its characteristics is a cultural conservatism that resists internet-boosted marketisation. After 9/11, it was the left that defended due process and, increasingly, liberty itself — as new web giants penetrated into our privacy and the state rolled the taste of internet surveillance between its lips. In Britain, Henry Porter fought a long and often lonely battle against government surveillance and a database state.[16] As Amazon, Facebook and Google exploited unregulated sovereignty of our data and metadata Shoshana Zuboff called out "surveillance capitalism". The left criticised "neo-illiberalism" and sought to defend the separation of powers. After the pandemic struck, it was Naomi Klein writing in *The Intercept* who swiftly rang the alarm as Eric Schmidt, on behalf of Silicon Valley, sought a surveillance "Covid-Capitalism", with state-funded data-sets on everyone's activities, so as to catch up with China's "advantage".[17]

A good way to bring into focus the far-sighted nature of the opposition to US-led globalisation is through the work of Naomi Klein and her relationship to the political storms and left-wing strategies since the mid-1990s. She is the finest and most original critic of neoliberalism. Her book *No Logo*, published in 1999, achieved two things for wide readerships. She explained the transformation of capitalism from its "Fordist" model of mass production towards its "platform" model, where corporations outsource and globalise production while controlling their brands, freeing capital from unionised workforces. The brand is then marketed with intense investment which aims to manipulate people's desires (she is very funny on their "quest for cool"). In effect, brands create consumers, who are the true object of its production lines. She set this out in a way that demystified people's everyday experience — and so empowered their resistance with understanding.

Then, in her 2007 *The Shock Doctrine*, Klein exposed a fundamental aspect of neoliberalism. Hitherto, capitalism had grown by participating in existing authority structures. While it always had slumps as well as booms, to reproduce itself it entered into a symbiotic relationship with official national regimes which recharged their religious, educational, legal, media and military orders. It was the combination of tradition with the market that gave hegemonic authority to the system of production. In response, the left desired not just economic transformation but also the downfall of stifling hierarchies. Now, as neoliberal capitalism globalised itself and put the market above nations, it undermined those traditions and institutions rooted in historic values other than moneymaking. In well-researched accounts, Klein laid bare how global finance made cynical use of local satraps and took advantage of the weakness of developing and post-communist countries to implant itself. Market fundamentalism created and then exploited instability. Disruption was its name. Real tradition its enemy. Shock therapy became a means of intensifying inequity as constraints were broken. It created today's unequal world.[18]

If this seems like stating the obvious, it is in good part thanks to Klein.

From the Crash to Occupy

The Shock Doctrine's subtitle is "The rise of disaster capitalism". It came out in 2007. In September of that year, Lehman Brothers — then the world's fourth largest investment bank — collapsed, taking the financial system with it. Few authors have been so grimly vindicated. The banks were bailed out while millions in the US lost their homes, and the system became even more unequal. Klein's book, with its research, insight and clarity, was a publishing success. But there were no political parties capable of turning such analysis into a call for change. Instead, in response to the impotence of official left of centre parties, the new decade opened with occupations known as the "Movement of the Squares" that filled central plazas in nearly a thousand towns and cities worldwide and became a generational turning point.

The initial inspiration was the Egyptian revolution, whose aim was to create a parliamentary democracy of the kind failing in the West. In January 2011, Cairo's Tahrir Square became the epicentre of an exemplary effort to mount a peaceful yet forceful protest against dictatorship that was livestreamed around the globe. On 15 May the *indignados* took off in Spain, starting in Madrid's Puerta del Sol, its central plaza, which was occupied without violence from 15 May to 12 June. The 15-M movement spread to eighty cities across Spain. According to one Spanish RTVE poll, up to seven million participated in some way: 20% of the population.[19] In July, the *Economist* reported 80% approval among the Spanish public, while it accused the protestors of being "earnest".[20] I was one of the earnest ones and found it inspiring. The theorist of the networked society, Manuel Castells, addressed the throng in Barcelona's Plaça de Catalunya and said,

Nobody is in a hurry, we have to make history, there is no need to rush. Others can run, we don't, because we are advancing systematically […] My long experience in social movements, starting with the May of 68 in Paris, where I participated actively, tells me that what we are living here, and […] around the world, has substance, has roots, and whatever forms it takes and whatever will happen, this movement will continue […] But [it] is not going to be easy. When the powers that be realise what is going on is serious (because for the moment they don't believe this is serious), they will react. And they will react probably violently because there are too many interests at stake. That is why it is essential that this process be slow and profound to reconstruct democracy. It must also have non-violence as a fundamental principle, which is already expressed and put into practice.[21]

This is a strange political declaration, with no programme, manifesto, or sense of urgency but great self-assurance (and he was right about the powers that be). I got to Puerta del Sol on 25 May — ten days after it began. As you approached, a tent city, shielded from the sun by plastic sheeting, emerged with narrow entrances. The passages were congested with people moving in all directions, there were stalls everywhere with temporary desktops, across which earnest conversations took place, some were working spaces, such as the library or kindergarten. The atmosphere everywhere was businesslike and purposive. It felt familiar yet strange. It was like entering an Eastern bazaar or souk, with the same dreamlike suddenness of going from outside into an enclosed but public space: intensely busy, crowded with its own rhythm that assaults your senses. Only it was the opposite of a bazaar, which is packed with commodities for sale, spices laid out to tempt you, carpets, watches and leather goods of dubious quality hanging on display for you to bargain over. In the bazaar, every friendly gesture is also instrumental: aimed at getting a good price or striking a bargain. In the huge souk of Occupy, it was the opposite. Instead of commodities to be sold, words are shared — not sold, offered freely as part of a common learning and collective exchange. Words are everywhere: notices, slogans, banners, jokes, announcements, leaflets, marker-scrawled schedules, maps of the current layout of stalls and services, in notebooks, on notices, in suggestion boxes and on screen and especially and continuously on everyone's lips. Everywhere there are conversations, enquiries, discussion, people meeting in small circles. In the communications tent, laptops cover wobbly tables, running thanks to a noisy generator that powers the lights and the excellent speaker system that is strung throughout the encampment. And a torrent of words in the general assemblies and different commissions, livestreamed, with occupations in other cities, signalled in sign language in an effort to communicate to everyone, especially those usually excluded. And everywhere people were listening.

Like many, I had assumed that mutualism and cooperation might work on a small scale. What I learnt in Madrid is they work best on a large scale. An extraordinary construction, being built, mended, cleaned, fed, secured, was looking after itself — no alcohol was allowed within — it was a collective gift.

I interviewed a young spokeswoman who had joined on the 16th, the day after it began, when it was still tiny. By now, its scale, seriousness and intensity was mind-blowing. "We have broken the silence," she told me, "We need change. And we are also changing the way that we ask for change [...] We just want to have what we deserve. That's why we want it now.

But we have no rush in achieving real democracy because, as it is something that I deserve I don't need to be in a hurry [...] I know it sounds a little bit of a contradiction, but I think it makes sense."[22] What was taking place there, and, shortly afterwards on an international scale, was that young people, who unlike my generation experienced unemployment, high rents and debts and indeed often had to live with their parents, put down a marker. They abjured violence and were not seeking "a revolution", instead they insisted on "real change", confident that the world could be organised differently — and would be.

Frustrated Opposition

To understand the originality of what will prove to be the starting point of twenty-first century democracy we need to glance back at the previous forms of organised opposition to neoliberal globalisation. There have been four kinds of overall resistance to its model of political economy. From the beginning of the 1980s, there was a human rights-inspired challenge, often supported by churches and religious associations. Over the decades, some had an influence: a few egregious torturers were jailed, blatant forms of pollution banned, many more young girls were educated, some extremes of inequality reduced, cluster bombs disarmed and more. But campaigners for rights have never been able to shake off the complicity of being the street-sweepers of marketisation. Funded by skilled foundations and often well run by dedicated organisers from small NGOs to international agencies, humanitarian resistance was unable to challenge the power structures that caused the problems.

I witnessed an amusing illustration of the conundrum this

provoked in what had become an amelioration industry when, as a founder of *openDemocracy*, I was invited to a UNDP — the United Nations Development Programme — conference in Oslo in 2011. Officially the UNDP mission is to "advocate change to help people build a better life for themselves". It is a classic human rights endeavour of the broadest kind and it does important work. Its annual reports rank how well countries in the Global South are managing their development. Now it had a problem. Its method of scoring had listed Tunisia as a top ranking success. Then its population rose up to trigger the Arab Spring! The UNDP had accepted that the market was the way people bettered themselves; it had collaborated with depoliticisation and was unable to build real democracy into its criteria of "development". A correction was needed. The conference was about whether the UNDP would see Tunisia as a slip or should from now on encourage development that strengthened self-government so as to resist market globalisation.

Back in 1991, a far-sighted effort had been made to build democracy into globalisation after the collapse of communism, and create a "social democratic" model of equitable development: the Helsinki Citizens' Assembly. While anti-nationalist, the aim was to enhance popular agency, oppose corruption, support good government and democracy, to ensure that the end of the Cold War would initiate an era of social progress. They would never have made the Tunisian mistake of the UNDP. The success of such an unofficial, people-oriented organisation depended upon persuading left governing parties to support it. Instead, following the lead of the Clinton Democrats, Europe's social democrats embraced "shock therapy" as the route to embed the triumph of capitalism around the world. The process exemplified the way that Washington, the right-wing media and lack of funding, drove into irrelevance those who worked to give civil society the capacity and agency needed to resist corporate power. Today the valiant Turkish branch of the Helsinki Citizens' Assembly is a heroic reminder of what was lost.[23]

In its place, a militant, leftist challenge to "the whole system" emerged. The alt-globalisation movement opposed the World Trade Organisation's efforts to turn the nation into the "shell institution" as Tony Giddens identified it in 1999. Giddens, a Blair intellectual, in charge of the London School of Economics and a New Labour life peer, asserted that the "era of the nation state is over".[24] But it remained the only arena for democracy to assert itself. Thus a movement led by those inspired by classic Marxist internationalism found itself raging against the efforts to establish global overlordship. Policed and pushed to the margins, the far-left often self-marginalised as it issued "demands" for an entirely different world order. But the arguments associated with its radical criticism were well researched and damning. The pioneering Amsterdam-based Transnational Institute (of which I was an early Fellow) produced a critique of neoliberalism *avant la lettre* in Susan George's *How the Other Half Dies* in 1976, and continues to do so to the present.[25] Its foresight led into the later anger at official indifference. The G8 summit at Genoa in July 2001 drew over 200,000 demonstrators and saw vicious police repression and collective punishment of protestors, one of whom was shot.[26]

The alt-globalisation's most impressive achievement was the WSF — the World Social Forum, an anti-Davos that brought activists together from around the world. It began in 2001 with tremendous acclaim as 60,000 gathered in Brazil's Porto Alegre. Had the WSF remained an open space exploring alternatives to neoliberalism and sharing experience — a "world fair" was how Susan Richards described this in 2003[27] — it could have had a lasting influence. Instead it succumbed to traditional leftism. In 2005, a *Porto Alegre Manifesto* was drawn up with a list of right-on calls to create "another world".[28] It was signed by eighteen men: half had been born in the early 1940s; the other half came from even further back, in the 1930s and 1920s. And only one woman, who was also the youngest signatory, born in 1947.[29] Few took any notice of the self-important gerontocrats. What mattered was the absence of a counterblast in the Forum's name. The new generation it inspired had not yet found its voice or sense of direction, despite the hundreds of local causes in which younger people resisted the impacts of global capitalism. No generational handover took place and as a gathering of resistance the WSF folded. When the financial crash of 2008 vindicated its claims it had disappeared into irrelevance. Klein, an early participant, was among the first to see the likely outcome, writing in 2003:

> For some, the hijacking of the World Social Forum by political parties and powerful men is proof that the movements against corporate globalisation are finally maturing and 'getting serious'. But is it really so mature, amidst the graveyard of failed left political projects, to believe that change will come by casting your ballot for the latest charismatic leader, then crossing your fingers and hoping for the best? Get serious.[30]

There is nothing dishonourable about being defeated. From Allende's Chile onwards, neoliberalism took down its opponents. With the full power of the media behind it and no enemy in sight after 1989, it could marginalise opposition, as happened with the Helsinki Citizens' Assemblies. But the

World Social Forum had got market fundamentalism bang to rights, which is why 60,000 gathered in Brazil in 2001. Support for it was hugely increased by the worldwide opposition to the Iraq war, when even a *New York Times* report said, "there may still be two superpowers on the planet: the United States and world public opinion".[31] Yet as a movement it flopped. It wasn't defeated, it failed. Had those running it been open and democratic, it would have become an arena for the "Movement of the Squares" after 2011, to come together to debate and draw strength from each other. Instead, those who initiated the World Social Forum were unable to hand it on and were even unable to integrate it with the internet, and the opportunity it created was thrown away.

Occupy

The result was that when the fourth wave of opposition made its Madrid breakthrough and Occupy took off, the "Movement of the Squares" was like an orphan with no sense of being part of a strong tradition of resistance and no international framework to share experience. Instead, its older activists were determined to break from the withered frustrations of the past. This gave it a freshness and a heady self-belief, similar to 1968, as a youthful generation made a breakout on its own.

In the US, perhaps 300,000 participated in various Occupy encampments. "At its core, it was a movement constrained by its own contradictions: filled with leaders who declared themselves leaderless, governed by a consensus-based structure that failed to reach consensus, seeking to transform politics while refusing to become political." The description is by Michael Levitin, who is an enthusiast.[32] It was a key moment because neoliberalism's class nature had been exposed by the crash and was now made explicit. Molly Crabapple, one of the artists of the protest, was asked by Matt Seaton about its later relationship to the rise of Bernie Sanders, AOC and the mass sales of books on capitalism. Her answer:

> Occupy broke the American taboo on talking about class. Even better, it named a clear enemy: a corrupt, rapacious, and frankly none-too-bright financial elite that they called the one percent, which had bought off the politicians and was sucking all the life and money out of everyone else. This was bracing stuff and, I'd argue, did much to make everything you mention possible.[33]

Before Occupy there was an earlier response to the crash, from the right in the form of the Tea Party. A precursor of Trumpism, its supporters' revulsion at the bailout of Wall Street was stoked by the existence of a Black, Democratic president with an exquisite style. Now Occupy Wall Street assaulted the same citadel of racketeering. It was a watershed moment. Two wild, gushing streams of antagonism to the elites moved in opposite directions, becoming rivers as they were fed by their separate political ecologies, divided by the mountainous heights of the American super-rich.

Both were fast-flowing. The media talked up the Tea Party after Romney, himself a multi-millionaire, failed to restore Republican control of the White House in 2012 — and Trump registered the slogan "Make America Great Again". Obama's success in holding the presidency misled the Democrat leadership. The impetus of Occupy went into a wide number of civil disobedience and direct actions such as blocking pipelines and, above all, into the Sanders camp.

A contemptuous Clinton operation and Democratic party machine regarded their activism as electoral disaster, only for Clinton to be bulldozed by Trump's ability to see the way the waters on his side of the mountain flowed. His triumph confirmed the call of the Occupy generation. Traumatised by Trump's success, the Democrat leadership had to go down their side of the mountain to partake in and draw upon the energy of the Occupy revolt, now multiplied by #MeToo and then Black Lives Matter. There is a continuity from Occupy Wall Street through Sanders to Biden. Meanwhile Trump personifies the violence that Castells foresaw when he spoke to the *indignados* in Barcelona about what would happen when "the powers that be" understood their call for real democracy was "serious".

The Occupy generation is international. Despite the size of Spain's 15-M movement it inspired almost no immediate solidarity apart from Greece. It was Occupy Wall Street in September 2011 that precipitated a global avalanche of similar actions in over eighty countries and nine hundred cities, from Santiago and Tel Aviv to New Delhi. Equivalent generational events had already preceded it, and greater ones followed: the umbrella movement in Hong Kong, the occupation of Istanbul's Gezi Park, the *nuit debout* in France (even aspects of the *Gilets Jaunes* with their call for citizens' assemblies). In Italy, the "sardine" mobilisations filled the squares to frustrate Matteo Salvini's right-wing ambitions in Emilia-Romagna at the end of 2019. In the early 2020s, in Belarus, Burma/Myanmar and Cuba, protest movements are ongoing. Usually, they fail; often, they are ruthlessly defeated. Sometimes they succeeded, as in Slovakia, where leaders were installed who backed democracy and were less corrupt;[34] or in Chile, where the protestors forced a referendum that will now create a constitutional convention in which independents are the majority. In England, students "broke the silence" early in October 2010. The pattern of England's 1968 was reproduced, in that it had an immense influence on those who were politicised but did not reach out in a lasting fashion to the wider public. The difference was that they did influence the Labour Party, thanks to the rise of the Corbyn leadership, and as this collapsed a social media intelligentsia has found a voice and hopefully a future.[35]

Global in scale, the occupations and mobilisations were national in their appeal. This is another, distinctive strength. A comparative study by Paolo Gerbaudo of the Occupy movements in Spain, Greece and the USA, shows how they broke from the "self-ghettoising" of previous alt-globalisation protest and the fragmentation of identity politics. Unlike their predecessors they no longer "considered the notion of the sovereign people as part of an authoritarian past" and sought to represent the people as a whole.[36] Occupy Wall Street expressed this with its unforgettable slogan "We are the 99%" — which dramatised the super-fortunes of the US oligarchy and punctured the myth, which survived the neoliberal decades, that the United States offered a good life to all who worked hard, as it pointed the finger at the 1% and how the system was rigged. More important, its message was heard. The left had been complaining about such inequity for decades; this time it broke through into the media.

The outstanding theorist and one of the key initiators of Occupy Wall Street was David Graeber, whose book *The Democracy Project* describes its history, analyses its impact (and sets out how to self-organise). He asks, "Why was the USA media coverage so different from virtually all previous coverage of left-wing protest movements since the 1960s?" At first, it wasn't. The *New York Times* didn't cover OWS for five days and then ran a piece mocking it as "a pantomime of progressivism with no discernible purpose". But, accelerated by the internet, similar actions were taking place across the US; there was international coverage in *Al Jazeera* and the *Guardian*, which broke the monopoly grip of the established media. Also, in Graeber's view, the main media had given such immense coverage to rise of the Tea Party that it could not but report on the upsurge from the left. For the first time since the 1960s, he felt, what protestors were actually saying was covered, rather than disparaged and distorted.

Occupy Wall Street achieved its impact, Graeber insists, because it made no demands and issued no manifesto. This was the anarchist reprimand to the gerontocratic Leninistas of the World Social Forum. His argument stresses the political conjunction. In contrast, Judith Butler later presented a pure defence of the tactic. Demands can only legitimise the oppression of existing institutions which are designed not to deliver them, she argued. Therefore, to make demands "would defeat itself in the course of its articulation".[37] Butler aestheticised the refusal into a form of purism free from contamination by any association with power. Graeber's analysis highlighted a different aspect. In 2008, Obama, an ex-community organiser, had skilfully raised the hopes of the young, offering an anti-racist movement and a slogan, "Yes We Can", drawn from César Chávez's United Farm Workers. It was a brilliant campaign, that pioneered use of the internet and raised hope of real change — only for him to then support the power elite. Even though he shifted the dial on race, Obama's slogan confirmed the powerlessness inflicted by neoliberalism. In these circumstances, no one who was young and radical would rally to "demands" for reform, whereas they would symbolically "occupy" Wall Street itself on behalf of the 99%, to repudiate the imposition of the bankers' victory and to defy the ongoing humiliation. Occupy Wall Street was a stronger, better way of saying "Yes We Can" — itself an utterly demand-free slogan — to what had become, by 2011, Obama's "No, we can't at the moment, but give me a break."

Over the course of 2012, OWS "shrivelled" away and was terminated by a ferocious police action. Graeber was contemptuous of left-of-centre organisations that saw its impact as a way of galvanising the Democratic Party. He and the others who initiated it were committed to horizontal organisation as such. They had identified the problem: "the fusion of finance with government". Their solution was "a genuinely democratic culture" which, "if it succeeds, is likely to take a very long time".[38] The wisdom of the Occupy crowd was to support Bernie Sanders rather than Graeber's approach.

Nor was the Graeber approach good enough for Naomi Klein. She liked the "dual power" aspect of "practicing a participatory democracy [...] a staging ground for struggle outwards". But thought, "of course we have demands, of course we want things". For her, "the greatest possibility lies in bringing together the ecological crisis and the economic crisis". She told an interviewer at the time,

There is more possibility right now than I could have ever imagined. I think in the not-so-distant future, we can win a lot of things that actually improve people's lives [...] and we can grow into a mass movement with the strength to propose another kind of world and also fight for it [...] I think it's totally possible to have a political and economic system that we have a genuine say in, that we democratically control, that we participate in, that is equitable and liberating, where we have autonomy for ourselves and our communities and our families, but are also in solidarity with one another.[39]

That was in early in 2012, when the vibes from the squares could still be felt. Eight years later, looking back, she was less complimentary,

With any luck, we learn from our mistakes, and I think that the limits of the movements of the squares, one of them was that a lot of them didn't put forward alternatives to this failed system. There was a kind of fetish for not having demands — it was a no, but it wasn't a strong yes for what we want instead […] The shout in the streets was, 'We won't pay for your crisis,' and it was this incredible, powerful uprising […] in country after country, and people were resisting and they were naming it. It was already clear that just 'no' was not going to stop it […] that's when I decided to write *This Changes Everything*, because I made this concerted decision to keep my distance a little bit. I felt really strongly that we needed to have a sweeping 'yes,' a really transformational vision of what kind of world we wanted.[40]

In that interview, Klein reports something both shocking and revealing. She went to Europe as part of her research for *This Changes Everything* and met with Alexis Tsipras and Pablo Iglesias. Tsipras was then the prime minister of Greece. He had created a new left-wing party, Syriza. Iglesias led the creation of Podemos, which became a high profile opposition party to the Spanish government and was a political expression of the *indignados*, but with an explicitly national-populist strategy.

He had a background in the Leninist left and was a successful television interviewer. They became the two most successful political representatives of the squares. Klein reports that, "Literally, Tsipras said to me, 'Nobody cares about the environment anymore. All they care about is the economy'". And Iglesias told her, "People can't care about climate when they have to put food on the table". Klein was appalled at their failure to lead and see that "We can create family-supporting jobs that heal our planet simultaneously and get us off fossil fuels." Their shared indifference to the climate emergency was not their only misjudgement but it was telling enough. It shows that if you default from a "movement", however popular, into a zero-sum, leader-centric electoral contest where the rules of "popularity" have already been fixed, it is likely to be disastrous. Within a few years both Tsipras and Iglesias were humiliated for their arrogance.

The Green New Deal

Klein took a different route: "So what I was doing in that period was working away on what ultimately became our blueprint, which we launched first in Canada, the LEAP Manifesto, exactly five years ago," she said in 2020.[41] With an impressive list of individual signatories and thirty initiating organisations, followed by hundreds more and over fifty thousand signatories in Canada, the manifesto was launched just before the 2015 Canadian elections. Its demands — a stop to fossil fuel subsidies to the country's powerful extractive industries, assist local democracy and put an end to austerity — ensured that the political parties disliked it. Politicians and corporate media hate high-energy, intelligent, agenda-setting coming from outside their official processes. It is hard work to turn manifestos from a shout into something that is heard and shifts thinking. The LEAP Manifesto made an impressive difference and influenced the development of "The Green New Deal" internationally. In *No Is Not Enough*, Klein gives an account of LEAP's development and launch and concludes, "The peoples' platforms are starting to lead — and the politicians will have to follow."[42]

Will they? In 1970, millions filled the streets across America to mark the first "Earth Day". It was the first major expression of popular environmental consciousness. The generation who mobilised then invented the modern NGO. The environmental ones made the greatest media impact: Greenpeace, especially, and Friends of the Earth, as well as Médecins Sans Frontières, while Oxfam and Amnesty were revitalised. The aim, to affect real change whatever party was in power. Their professional culture learnt from corporate effectiveness in marketing and branding. Their activist aims were the opposite of neoliberal, accepting responsibility for outcomes, opposing profit maximisation, demanding good government for all. They wanted to set a lead that politicians would follow. But for all their efforts and their attractive combination of reasonableness, practicality and radicalism, the politicians didn't follow them — they followed the money. In Canada, during the COVID downturn, the LEAP organisation shut down, as it took the decision not to become yet another NGO. Politics, it seems, can only be really changed by politics.

Looking Back, Looking Forward

Some of the key figures from the Sixties went into politics. A tragic symbol was Ralph Nader's attempt on the presidency as the Green Party candidate in 2000. He got nearly 100,000 votes in Florida and thereby gave the White House to George W. Bush, who won the state by a dodgy six hundred votes from the environmentally conscious Al Gore. Others include Bernard Kouchner, who cofounded Médecins Sans Frontières and became Sarkozy's Foreign Minister; Danny Cohn-Bendit, a leader of the French May, a Green member of the European parliament; Tom Hayden, one of the Chicago 7, was a state senator in California; Joschka Fischer became German Foreign Minister. Each made an individual impact, none left a legacy that can be built upon. Instead, a new generation has burst into overdue protest thanks to Greta Thunberg and the Extinction Rebellion, which draws inspiration from Occupy, the Suffragettes and the uprising in Hong Kong where leaderless protests were "like water".

I've looked back briefly at radical opposition to neoliberalism since the Sixties in a very partial account. I've not discussed the crushing of trade unions and the dissolution of their influence by globalisation which deflated class resistance to hyper-inequality and stopped the accumulation of experience. The green movements tried to get elected as well as to protest. Brazil's Lula escaped the limits of social democracy. In the Nineties, the break-up of Yugoslavia and the wars in the Balkans became a dress rehearsal for liberal interventionism and the demoralisation of democracy. In this long complex story two things stand out. That people wanted a different world and, second, the failure of leadership on all sides to provide a route to this. In 2005, Fred Halliday, who with his many books and speaking 14 languages was like a one-person international, saw only the "three dustbins of history": Soviet Communism, Washington's war on terror and the global protest movement, all three were all doomed cul de sacs. He died in 2010, before the Occupy movement. The novelist Ece Temelkuran describes the hopes of those who wanted change:

> During the first decade of the twenty-first century people around the world filled city squares demanding the same thing: dignity. From the Seattle protests in 1999, to the Arab uprisings, to the large scale protests in Europe and the US, millions of people shared the same cry [...] that the value of humankind cannot and must not be translated into a market price. They demanded to be recognised as human beings and to be treated accordingly, with dignity [...] And they performed the joy of this new life even amid tear gas and police violence. Coming from a range of different social classes, they also showed us that everyone could help to build the world and nobody is too powerless to act like a person with dignity.[43]

A stubborn, defensive refusal, rooted in the seven (or perhaps more) processes of humanisation, persisted through an epoch of capitalist triumph whose media relentlessly pulverised belief in non-market traditions and cultivated the immediate, the aggressive and the profitable. Resistance persisted, but the foundations for a positive politics could not be laid. These include a shared sense of history without which we are fragmented and individualised; a scientific uncertainty, demanding refutability, verification, well-argued disagreement and not "correctness", with its associated paranoias; love of the modern with its technology and engineering and capacity for enhancement; a confident embrace of pluralism and effective democracy.

Then, a Seismic Moment

On 25 May 2020, police officer Derek Chauvin knelt on the neck of the handcuffed George Floyd for nine minutes. Assisted by two other officers, he killed him as Floyd cried out, "I can't breathe", while a fourth police officer kept onlookers from intervening as they shouted in protest. One of them, the 17-year-old Darnella Frazier, steadily videoed what was a ritual slaughter. The world observed Chauvin's indifferent demeanour, his look of barely concealed contempt at those calling out for him to stop in the name of humanity, his presumption that the person below his knee wasn't a person like himself, the businesslike way his police colleagues assisted him as he carried on disposing... of us. Until this moment the dehumanisation, the indifference, the contempt which the neoliberal order has for regular people, the refusal to accord us the dignity of being equally human, had never been filmed for what it is. There were no fine words, no pretence, no anger. It was effortless. Below Chauvin, humanity itself, already cuffed and deprived of agency, was being refused the right to breathe.

Veterans who had protested at the Iraq War, many now working for corporate employers; everyone opposed to the way the climate is being throttled and poor countries exploited; the many whose mortgages are at risk, or whose student debt had been indifferently compounded until they feel they can't breathe financially; the many who delighted in the Occupy movement's demands for dignity; many who had rightfully and powerlessly resisted what is being done to us; we all said "Enough!".

Yes, we said "Black Lives Matter". Yes, we said it would not have happened had Floyd been white. Yes, it had a relationship to the history of lynching. But it was not the racial injustice alone that was being protested around the world, when unprecedented numbers took to the streets in solidarity, while even corporations were appalled at what was now undeniable, and raced to rectify policies of exclusion and indifference. It was a protest against what racism does to all of us. In the US, "95 percent of the counties where Black Lives Matters demonstrations were held were majority white".[44] It was the moment neoliberalism began to be ended from below. Because, by mobilising against a systemic inheritance, BLM brought the importance of history into the present, exemplified by arguments about statues and monuments that can't be resolved by market demand.

Steve McQueen, the Oscar-winning film director of *12 Years A Slave*, put it well. "George Floyd didn't die in vain. COVID-19 is linked to climate change, to how we treat each other, how we look at health, wellbeing, morality, human rights, not to mention the outcome of the US election. I think this has been a seismic point in the history of the world [...] We have the power now to demand, to recognise and to voice things [...] For the first time, people have felt that they could say what they feel and be listened to [...] We have come to a point in the history of the world that, with our moral conscience and recognition of the challenges we face with climate change, things can never go back."[45]

How, then, do we go forward?

10. America's Multilayered Crisis

If there are grounds to hope that the early 2020s are a turning point when the activist left can move on from its defeats, we have to remember that systems of government are almost never changed just by the strength and intelligence of opposition to them. Power beats the powerless irrespective of who is right. System change comes about when demand for it from below coincides with the need for it from above.

Comparison may be helpful as a way of illustration. I have witnessed two moments of transition that promised more democracy and failed. Gorbachev became head of the Communist Party of the Soviet Union in 1985 and launched *Perestroika* and *Glasnost* (reconstruction and openness). He demanded that democracy replace bureaucracy under the conditions of Communism. I went to Russia in 1987, guided by Nella Bielski, to assess the credibility of this official commitment to freedom in the Soviet Union. Nella was John Berger's partner, a Russian citizen who had lived in Paris since the early Sixties, and we had long debated what Russia was like. She and Berger had written about the Gulag, the Siberian system of concentration camps. They knew in a way few did what had gone wrong with the revolution — but believed in the Russian soul. I set out my reflections in a book of reportage, *Soviet Freedom*, published in 1988 (with two additional chapters by Nella). A Dutch journalist interviewed me about it and asked why I concluded Russia would change, given that every conversation I reported showed that Russians themselves were convinced nothing would and were consumed with pessimism after decades of stasis. There were two reasons. First, I had met and interviewed Vietnam's Gorbachev, Nguyễn Cơ Thạch, who was confined to being his country's Foreign Minister. I had witnessed how communist regimes could produce genuine figures of the world, who wanted socialism to be an expression of freedom and intelligence. When Gorbachev and his supporters said they would replace bureaucracy, I was confident they meant it. Second, as I describe in the book, "the Sixties had arrived in the Soviet Union". The combination meant the society would not default back to the long epoch of bureaucratic sclerosis.

Gorbachev's revolution was still "dramatically unresolved". I did not understand the sheer demoralisation of Communist Party members or the corruption of its functionaries and how they resented and rejected him. They had stopped believing in Socialism, were defeated in Afghanistan, from which Gorbachev initiated the Russian withdrawal, and felt broken by the West. They had no interest in a democratisation likely to strip them of their privileges.

The dynamism of China demonstrates that stasis is not a necessary product of one-party rule. Perhaps something else took place. The great test of the Soviet Union had been the German invasion of 1941. Although the twenty-four years that separated it from the revolution of 1917 saw the disasters of collectivisation, a new society had been built. The Soviet generation that fought back against Hitler was a revolutionary one, toughened by survival. Its equivalent in China was a generation led by Deng that emerged from the Cultural Revolution a quarter-century after the People's Republic was founded in 1949. They too were still believers, despite everything. By the mid-Eighties in Russia, however, a *post* post-revolutionary generation had taken over. It had been indelibly compromised by long collaboration with administrative Stalinism. The great Russian novelist Vasily Grossman's final book, *Everything Flows*, was written between1955–63, at the beginning of what he calls the "third stage of a state without freedom". He had been a star reporter for the Red Army at Stalingrad, wrote about the discovery of the Treblinka extermination centre and witnessed the liberation of Berlin, only to find that his truthfulness made him untrustworthy and have his writing confiscated. His hero asks what went wrong with the revolution in which he had believed. As he approaches his death, he looks back with a painful ambivalence and concludes that the experience of Lenin's revolution, of Stalin and then the third stage of a "state without freedom", was haunted by an inescapable Russian culture embedded in the experience of serfdom.

A second encounter with a historic transition was less significant in the scale of history but consumed a portion of my life: when I tried to convince Britain to adopt a democratic constitution. As New Labour headed for office in 1997, I wrote *This Time: Our Constitutional Revolution*. I looked at the weird way the Blair government was undertaking what it called "the most ambitious and extensive programme of constitutional reform and modernisation this century" yet desired it to remain "incremental". What was being initiated was not going to be contained within the traditional guiderails of the British state. A "free-market populism" could be one consequence, I predicted, but I projected my desires onto reality and said the country could embrace another: the democratic constitution it obviously needed.

In a less dramatic way than the Soviet Union, the old order of the UK was doomed by incomplete reform. Blair's efforts at modernisation humiliated the English, which I've argued eventually paved the way to Brexit. If the long shadow of serfdom cast its pall over Russia, in England the deadly cultural pull was and still is "restoration". This is far more benign and has a longer pedigree. It was forged after the regicide and revolution of the 1640s by a restoration of the Crown in tandem with a property-owning parliament. The result was early capitalist modernisation in a traditional frame. It enabled the creation of Britain after the union with Scotland in 1707 and then a global Empire that was pitiless and intelligent. It was culturally inventive: England produced Darwin and Keynes; Scotland gave us James Clerk Maxwell and Tom Nairn — who discerned the fundamental duality of electromagnetism and nationalism respectively. But restoration was built into English energies. This created a society exceptionally capable of change provided it was wrapped in monarchical camouflage. By the end of the twentieth century, it became a debilitating formula as the Empire closed down. Many of us called for an honest democracy.[1] The camouflage won. The result today is a government that boasts that it has revived our ancient sovereignty when this has become preposterous — a system breakdown, not as sudden or as catastrophic as the Soviet Union's, is underway likely to terminate the UK's multinational nature, just as Russia lost its grip on its subordinate nationalities.

America now confronts a comparable challenge to the USSR in the 1980s and the UK in the 1990s. The US emerged from the Second World War as overwhelmingly the richest and strongest economy and for a time the world's only nuclear power. It occupied both its main wartime enemies, Japan and the western, wealthiest part of Germany; subordinated its allies Britain and France along with their empires; and proceeded to define modernity not least through Hollywood. After forty-five years its only military competitor, the Soviet Union, imploded and the US became the "sole, pre-eminent power". It then committed four enormous mistakes.

Most significant was its continued commitment to financialised, market fundamentalism that culminated in the financial crash of 2008. Second, it used China as a source of cheap manufacturing to undercut its own working class, as it aimed to integrate Beijing into the dollar economy and subordinate it to Wall Street. Instead, it fed a genuine competitor. From the point of view of humanity "as a whole" this was a tremendous gain, an equalisation without precedent, despite the grim oppression of Tibet, the Uyghurs and Hong Kong. But for Washington as a great power, it was a disaster. Third, unbelievably, when it won the Cold War, instead of helping Russia in the way that it had successfully raised up yet subordinated Europe and Japan after 1945, the US humiliated Moscow, permitted its oligarchs to ship their loot to the West, and let it go bankrupt. This laid the basis for todays' dedicated, vengeful enemy that treats protests of its illegality with scorn and has allied with China. Finally, the US political class used a criminal attack made in 2001 by misbegotten fundamentalists to try and run up the stars and stripes over globalisation by declaring a "war on terror". It assumed that by demonstrating its military prowess in Iraq in 2003 (against the public advice, it should be said, of the then head of the US Army, General Eric Shinseki) it could, in the immortal words of Bush's vassal, Tony Blair, "unite the world".

What we have to try and understand is the impact

of the cumulative loss of US primacy on the American psyche, media and politics. US capitalism has survived but the four-fold catastrophe has caused a vast legacy of mental wreckage. The 2021, mid-summer trauma of American liberals and mainstream media at the enraging evacuation of Kabul illuminates what happened. They had assumed that a continued US presence meant that America had not really lost. The waves of frustration, shame, humiliation and anger that swept through the good globalists as Afghanistan folded into the hands of the Taliban, generated a painful contemplation of America's reduced place in the world. Many of Trump's supporters, however, like Ashli Babbitt, had already internalised the scale of the disgrace. They were not "soft" supporters of "nation-building" from the comforts of Washington or the privileges of a Green Sector. They gloried in the military demonstration of America's superiority not the education levels of the villages. They felt the rage and humiliation long before the final 2021 flights from Kabul. For the right, especially after 1945, US global superiority had confirmed the rule of the Christian white man. Now worldwide primacy was lost. This wasn't a technicality; it was a trauma. It became necessary to reassert what they had lost — at home.

This was Trump's calling card. He campaigned against Mexicans; his first action was a ban on Muslims; he gaslighted Obama; he described the racists of Charlottesville with their torches of hate as "fine people"; and at the first opportunity he denounced COVID as a "Chinese virus". Someone had to make America Great Again, now its role as solo hegemon is over. The domestic and global are linked. The rhetorical and psychological advantage of Trumpism as a world view is that it simultaneously boasts of America's racial and

Christian power and withdraws from claims to hegemony and expansion, making a virtue of necessity. The culture of injured defiance and heroic victimhood that radiates from Trumpism is a reaction to the loss of global pre-eminence. For all its insanity, as expressed, say, in opposition to vaccination and mask wearing, its truthfulness is a passive-aggressive acceptance of reality. Psychologically, for Trumpites the evacuation of Kabul had already happened. Russians went through a similar rage and response after they witnessed the Red Army being humiliated by the mujahideen in the 1980s.

Biden supporters may find Trumpism rebarbative and unacceptable but they too must respond to the conditions that created him, the loss of pre-eminence, and the domestic pathologies this has generated. Their answer is to withdraw from imperial over-stretch and seek to establish a moral primacy as the leader of democratic capitalism, underpinned by the continued supremacy of the dollar. To achieve this, Biden must establish voting rights at home — otherwise a claim to be the world's democratic steward will fail. His domestic equivalent of *Perestroika* and *Glasnost* is "Development and Integration", meaning economic growth that benefits all Americans and full voting rights for minorities. As I have tried to show in Chapter 8, the constitutional challenge is massive as it replaces a deep structure of the Union's creation. It is made all the harder by the weakness of left, outlined in Chapter 9, that lacks both a trade union based politics of ongoing organisation and solid public support for the radicalism of the younger generation.

In these circumstances, recent parallels tell us Biden's reforms are likely to fail. Gorbachev wanted to democratise but not replace bureaucracy. Blair limited constitutional reform. Both leaders cut a radical image but moderated their actions, in part thanks to regressive cultures. Why should the fate of Biden's call for the cessation of voter suppression and for government-led investment end differently? He has compared the battle over voting rights to the Civil War, yet he desires "bipartisanship" — code for the alliance of legality with racism. Against opponents like Trump's Republicans, who do not seek compromise, such ambiguity is usually lethal. If the totality of the Biden project is to end minoritarian rule and make the USA a genuine democracy, we can be pretty confident it will be frustrated. Far too many voters would experience it as the internalisation of global defeat, not a revival of their country.

However, there are two major reasons why, in today's US, Biden's programme can succeed. First, the United States has not been defeated. It has not seen its hopes smashed like the USSR or had its empire replaced like the United Kingdom. It has only suffered a self-inflicted if traumatic car crash, due to vainglorious overreach, predicted in 2001 and unmistakable since 2011. At the same time, it remains a country of enormous vitality and resources. Even as it threw away its international primacy it created a new form of platform capitalism by deploying the microchip with astounding élan, inventiveness and investment to alter life around the world, and created an entire new sector of the economy: Silicon Valley. However great the demoralisation, the country's "can do" confidence is intact.

More important for Biden's potential success, the US is undergoing two other simultaneous system crises: the political meltdown of neoliberalism and the imperatives of climate action. Because they bring multiple interests together that need a democratic mandate, the combination of all three makes a progressive outcome possible.

The crisis of the Soviet Union in the mid-Eighties, and the UK in the mid-Nineties, stemmed from the need to modernise in response to an energetic neoliberal order — whose aversion to democracy thwarted their internal renewal. The US suffers from the opposite development. The crash of its global pretentions is intensified by the implosion of a demoralised neoliberal politics whose hollowing out of democracy has already been reversed by Trump's mobilisation. The confrontation over the need for a democratic redefinition of who Americans are, which is demanded by the loss of planetary pre-eminence, is overdetermined by another conflict over the need to govern the economy with democratic legitimacy, and not leave this to market forces now that neoliberalism's forty-year playbook is obsolete.

Overlaying both crises is a third, the climate emergency and the imperative of decarbonisation in a coordinated global fashion, that confirms the US's necessarily diminished place in the world, yet also provides a pathway for influence if the mighty fossil-energy interests are defeated.

None constitute a crisis "of capitalism". All challenge how the leading capitalist nation is governed while its citizens are aroused and know their votes matter.

The triple-layered nature of the turning point opens the way for an alliance of left, liberals and the centre right, to put in place a democratic renewal of the United States. I've stressed that, on their own, demands for a transformation in how we are governed, however justified, are not sufficient. It is the combined determination of the explosive pressures that led to Trumpism that generates the imperative of system renewal and opens the way for the USA to become a multi-racial democracy. But nothing happens without an articulated sense of purpose either. Ideas and organisation really matter in such a context. On a positive note, while recognising that we are currently on a knife edge and that the effort will take decades, we can look at some of the challenges democrats now face.

11. Shared Empowerment and Humanisation

In 1983, Margaret Thatcher secured her re-election. It allowed her to consolidate policies that would establish the priorities and character of Britain for the next forty years, including the development of the City of London as a global bridgehead for US financial suzerainty — a step in the worldwide penetration of finance as the alleged valuer of everything. It was not a certainty that this would happen. Thatcher's first term badly damaged manufacturing, and unemployment was very high. She was unpopular including with many in her own party until her victory over Argentina in the short war in the South Atlantic over the Falklands/Malvinas in 1982. But the opposition Labour Party had split over membership of the EU. The breakaway Social Democrat Party in alliance with the Liberals got over 25% of the popular vote in 1983 — just less than Labour on 27%. Despite the Falklands boost, Thatcher got only 42%. This was slightly lower than the support she won in 1979, when she had ridden to power in protest against the chaos and drift of a Labour government. She never increased her electoral popularity. A clear majority of voters always opposed her — but were split down the middle. In a winner-takes-all electoral system, such division is fatal. Thatcher boosted her parliamentary majority in 1983 by over a hundred seats. More important, she was the voice of a new right-wing politics of privatisation and "self-reliance" (very different from "self-determination"). She personified a fresh political philosophy with a powerful sense of direction. It would be fourteen years before the Tories would lose office and then only to a Labour Party that accepted the "primacy of the market" that Thatcher had established. It was a trajectory shaped by the politics of the United States. Ronald Reagan's 1980 victory over the Democrat Jimmy Carter ensured twelve years of Republican rule. The year before, Carter had appointed as Chair of the Federal Reserve Paul Volcker, widely seen as a financial architect of market fundamentalism. Reagan reappointed him.

This was the context for a far-reaching essay the left-wing writer Raymond Williams published in 1983: "Resources for a Journey of Hope". Aware that the world was entering a historic turning point, he called on the left to "rigorously re-examine" all its ideas. Rethinking was essential because a fundamental progressive assumption had been undone. Throughout his lifetime the left had regarded the forces opposing it as conservative and reactionary and therefore as not genuinely forward-looking. This notion, that progress and the future naturally belonged to the left, went back to before the First World War. The right was dangerous. It might entrench a powerful fascism or persuade voters to indulge their traditional attachments to empire, nonetheless modernity would inevitably be progressive. Poke a Tory and you would find dead wood. In contrast, as more and more of us were lifted to a better way of life, this was bound to be collective and social.

Such a belief, Williams warned, was now worse than complacent. It was wrong. The right had conceived "a new hard line on the future: a new politics of strategic advantage". He decided to call it "Plan X". Looking back, it is chilling to see how clearly he discerned so early the overall nature of what we now call neoliberalism. He identifies the ruthlessness with which competition will be driven forward; how "Plan X people resemble the hardest kinds of revolutionary"; the way its commitment to calculation and advantage had already penetrated discourse; that it promotes narrow skills and professionalism as against a "full sense of the human purposes"; that to call it a "mere conspiracy" underestimates its seriousness as an attempt to "control the future".

Any response, he continues, has to be "*more* rational and *better* informed" to support a "mutual general interest" and wellbeing. This, he writes, "is where the real political problems start". If a successful resistance is not mounted, "there will be a long series of harshly administered checks; of deliberately organised reductions of conditions and chances; of intensively prepared emergencies of war and disorder, offering only crude programmes of rearmament, surveillance and mutually hostile controls. It is a sequence which Plan X can live with, and for which it was designed, but which no active and resilient people should be content to live with for long." The problems of any response, however, went deep. The left had to move away from its focus on industrial production to begin a "long and difficult movement beyond a market economy". It needed to challenge "monetary institutions […] oriented to short-term profit". Social control over investment could not be achieved by "older socialist methods […] of state centralisation". Instead there should be "new kinds of auditing of resources". To achieve this a "unified alternative social theory" is needed that involves "three changes of mind".

First, economic arguments must be brought together with ecological ones, so that people and the environment cease to be treated "as available raw material". Second, we must stop looking at history in terms only of modes of production. This needs to be replaced by "the new orientation of livelihood". What Williams means by this is a switch away from work and class as defining, to understanding the family, place, education, and creativity as well as employment and class as the sources of value that make a whole way of life. Third, it follows that issues the traditional left denigrate as "emotional", such as feminism in particular, need to be recognised as having "an absolute and primary significance" (Williams does not mention race). The central element, he concludes, is "the shift from 'production' to 'livelihood' [...] [to gain] confidence in *our own* energies and capacities". In effect he proposes livelihood as a replacement for socialism. Livelihood includes consumption as well as production, living conditions as well as work, all generations (this would connect to the contemporary arguments of Roman Krznaric in *The Good Ancestor*), and connected relations with others and cultural creation as an integral part of any "whole way of life". This is the way to push forward what is going to be a "long revolution".[1]

What was the response in his own country to Williams' analysis and proposal? Some of us opened files of cuttings that showed how fruitful the concept of "livelihood" is in making connections for democratic change. Variations of the concept have been developed, notably *Buen vivir* by the Latin American thinker and activist Eduardo Gudynas.[2] While Williams remains exceptionally influential since his death in 1988, the strategic direction he suggested found no political expression. The success of "Plan X" was to be complete — until the Occupy movement in the wake of the financial crash. It was so complete that for many who grew up in the Nineties and after, socialism had the attraction of a long-lost cause. In this century, Owen Hatherley has excavated architectural traditions that show socialism was part of modernism, to the astonishment of many.

Our Turn

The crisis that eventually led Williams to warn of "Plan X" started in the Seventies. Neoliberalism was never a preconceived plan and was implemented in an experimental fashion over the decades: what he grasped was the sense of purpose it had gained by the early Eighties. Today, our situation is not akin to the moment when he observed a hardening strategy for governing capitalism. Rather, we are in the equivalent of the Seventies — a period of breakdown without settled strategies of resolution.

One of the difficulties in understanding this is the deep role of economic change. The outcome will not be technologically determined; it never is. The Seventies began to witness the deconstruction of traditional industry and its proletarian organisation, and the start of new forms of production often described as post-Fordism. Neoliberalism was not the inevitable outcome of this transformation of production — the Chinese example shows that post-Fordism could be led by government, not the market. Also, as David Edgerton argues in *Shock of the Old*, the significance of the new is often exaggerated. But a sustainable political direction has to be able to express itself through and within the direction of the emerging technological and organisational change. New forms of production can ensure the *failure* of political movements, even though they do not determine what succeeds. Across the West, traditional parties of the working class, with their welfare forms of collectivist politics, discovered they were incompatible with the decline of labour-intensive mass production. Today, it is not clear what the impact of the cyberspace economy will be, as houses, vehicles and even our bodies, as well as our phones, are controlled by software licences and "rentier" capitalism is intensified. Corporate platforms like Google, Amazon and Facebook could support an oppressive surveillance capitalism that will seek to drive democracy into irrelevance; we can also imagine an open form of networked, participatory democracy that would be inconceivable without the internet. What is certain is that any resuscitation of the left will need to embrace contemporary technology: to secure our traditional liberty we need a modern liberty.

A good way to start our own "rigorous re-examination" is with a contemporary restatement of the need for a participatory socialist approach set out by Thomas Piketty. While there are other calls for a transformative strategy, his has a special authority. He is the political economist who claims to have proven that inequality will continue to grow without decisive action to reverse it. In the first of a pair of thousand-page mega-tomes, he shows that:

> When the rate of return on capital significantly exceeds the growth rate of the economy (as it did through much of history until the nineteenth century and as is likely to be the case again in the twenty-first century), then it logically follows that inherited wealth grows faster than output and income.[3]

The current growth of inequality is not exceptional — it will get worse until it is inverted by policy decisions. Piketty sets out how he believes we can achieve this in his second volume, *Capital and Ideology*. Like Williams, he disagrees with Marx and Engels, that all history can be reduced to "the history of class struggles". He holds that that "the struggle of ideologies and the quest for justice" also determine history. Unlike Williams, he only gestures to the huge cultural shift this demands and is more concerned with policies:

I am convinced that capitalism and private property can be superseded and that a just society can be established on the basis of participatory socialism and social federalism. The first step is to establish a regime of social and temporary ownership. This will require power sharing between workers and shareholders and a ceiling on the number of votes that can be cast by any one shareholder. It will also require a steeply progressive tax on property, a universal capital endowment, and permanent circulation of wealth. In addition, it implies a progressive income tax and collective regulation of carbon emissions, the proceeds from which will go to pay for social insurance and a basic income, the ecological transition, and a true educational equality. Finally, the global economy will need to be reorganized […] to be replaced by new rules based on the principles of financial transparency, fiscal cooperation, and transnational democracy […].

He then adds, "Some of these conclusions may seem radical. In reality they belong to a historical movement toward democratic socialism, which since the late nineteenth century has been working toward profound transformations of the legal, social, and fiscal system."[4]

Another example is a book I find sympathetic, *Doughnut Economics*, by Kate Raworth, who rolls up her sleeves and sets out how we should think and act as economists, now we can all see how constant growth is the equivalent of a planetary death wish: "The twenty-first-century task is clear: to create economies that promote human prosperity in a flourishing web of life, so that we can thrive in balance within [a] safe and just space."[5]

Many people would love to see the world arranged along the lines Piketty or Raworth propose, which are indeed not "radical", but rather are entirely reasonable. The problem is that they seem impossible. How do we get from here to a situation that approaches what they describe? How do we avoid readers sighing in agreement with Piketty and then putting down his book — perhaps with some relief because of its exceptional weight — just as some nodded in agreement with Raymond Williams forty years ago? Can inspiring concepts like livelihood, justice, participation, an economy that thrives rather than grows, or the need for "capability" that Amartya Sen calls for, or "the common good" that Michael Sandel wishes, be sufficient to revitalise the political process? Who is going to achieve them? Where is the party, organisation, financial interests or networks with the power to make them happen against the power of those currently in charge? It's that damn issue of "agency" again.

Without credible analysis and strategies for change, a dominant system cannot be replaced. Analysis and strategies are mere piss in the wind without a popular demand for change. But today we are fortunate to have both intense networks of opposition to the concentrations of wealth and analyses of how to supplant them. The idea of replacing oligopoly capitalism is popular, especially with the younger generation, who are experiencing a perfect storm of insecurity, debt, climate emergency, COVID inequity and have been described as a new class: "the precariat"[6]. At the same time policy proposals and analysis exist in abundance. Neoliberalism has not just failed; since the great crash of 2008 its arguments have been thoroughly rebutted. While primarily a political theory of government that disarmed democracy, neoliberalism justified itself with the claim that it expressed the fundamental, competitive character of human nature. Research shows that on the contrary, as George Monbiot puts it, of all the species, "We are [...] the supreme co-operators [...] Our extraordinary capacity for altruism and our remarkably social nature are the central, crucial facts about humankind."[7] Rutger Bregman followed up his bestseller, *Utopia for Realists*, with *Humankind A Hopeful History*, which sets out evidence of humanity's capacity for decency. When it comes to the core economic arguments about the primacy of the market, Mariana Mazzucato has shown definitively in *The Value of Everything* how governments create value. Heavyweight scholars and eloquent popularisers alike have demolished the philosophy of market fundamentalism.

The preconditions are in place: there is popular support for change; there is research on how the status quo can be superseded; the narrative that legitimates the status quo has been exposed as hooey; forces of humanisation toppled neoliberalism in the face of the pandemic. But nothing goes until it is replaced, and this applies with a vengeance to undemocratic capitalism. Here, for consideration, are five aspects that will be involved in any replacement: class, time, culture and organisation, institutional inventiveness, and the nation. I put them forward to be suggestive, not exhaustive.

Class

Only when there is majority assent for a replacement of the dominant system can such change take place democratically. Far from being a tautology, this is a massive political challenge. Both building such support and replacing the dominant system are processes that call for participation in advance. The principle is that a society of self-government has to be achieved through the actions of self-government, or tyranny will follow. The paramount factor is clear majority support. Socialists who look to the state as being the prior instrument of transformation "on behalf of the working class" are more reluctant to embrace this than, for example, those from the anarchist or republican traditions, like Noam Chomsky or Quentin Skinner.

In their internal organisation, the democracy of the classic socialist and social democratic movements was collectivist. Its premise was that because the working classes they represented were the majority, they were intrinsically democratic. It remains inconceivable that there could be an egalitarian democracy that does not have workers at its heart. But the miners, factory operatives, dockers and builders that formed the historic "proletariat" no longer constitute a majority, nor are they organised as they once were in lifetime routines. Progressives need to seek a wide cross-class majority to "supersede" capitalism, to use Piketty's term. Progressive politics has to justify itself directly as being in the interests of all, as full human beings.

Time

We are running out of time to save the planet. This is probably the final decade in which we can head off the tipping point, after which climate heating becomes self-reinforcing. Action is needed that can't wait for democratic support via participatory assemblies that have not yet been empowered. Such processes work, regular people are far-sighted. The French Citizens' Climate Convention that President Macron established, made up of 150 non-politicians, to recommend measures to reduce carbon emissions took its brief seriously. In its final vote it gave Macron a "woeful" 3.7 out of ten for delivery while right-wingers in the Senate simply vetoed the Convention's call for a referendum that would "enshrine the fight against climate change in the French constitution".[8] It is not the people or the poor who are holding us back on climate action, provided it is done fairly.

It's necessary to say something this obvious to ensure that a discussion of the "long revolution" that awaits us is not taken as procrastination or advocacy of gradualism. Time has to be built into expectations of change as a matter of basic wisdom. A long revolution is never steady. Change "pulses", as Sarah Chayes observes. Feminism shows how a sea-shift occurs, with moments of acceleration followed by absorption, reaction and then deepening progress. Patriarchy is far from overthrown. Yet feminism is a far more inspiring example of deep transforming change than the Russian revolution. Its achievements will be lasting. One of the qualities of the demands made by feminism that saved it from demoralisation is that even at points when it has been at its most militant no one thought that real change would be quick.

Time is the friend of great, progressive change. "Let our plans be big, significant, but not hasty... We can do almost anything we like, given time. We must not force the pace — that is necessary warning. In good time we can do it all. But we must work to a long-term programme".[9] This was the English economist John Maynard Keynes in April 1942. It was at a dark point in the Second World War but also the birth of hope for a new world. In January, the Soviet Union had held off Hitler's armies outside Moscow and Germany was now bogged down, deprived of an Eastern blitzkrieg victory. The

Japanese had attacked Pearl Harbour and brought America fully into the war, which would ensure success. The Japanese had also just captured Singapore and terminated the British Empire – a huge relief to far-sighted members of the elite like Keynes. Victory was certain *and* there could be no going back; the chance to build a new, much better Britain lay ahead. It was a moment to plan a genuine revolution from above and this inspired Keynes' confidence.

Today, we know better than Keynes could, how capable we are of planning and creating a much better world. But because of the climate emergency, the need is more urgent while, unlike 1942, the enemy is not heading to certain defeat — circumstances that generate a treacherous impatience. A recent negative example of the danger of short-termism in politics was when Jeremy Corbyn was elected surprise leader of the Labour Party in 2015. He gained immediate popularity as an anti-elite figure who opposed neoliberalism but his team encouraged the idea that he could become prime minister on a minority of the popular vote thanks to the electoral system — and then deploy the British state overnight on behalf of the downtrodden. For his young supporters, the promise of his socialist politics was like winning a football cup.

For various reasons, not least continued incompetence, Labour was crushed in the 2019 election. Corbyn's initial elevation had inspired an exceptional flowering of ideas as well as a creative "teach-in" style gathering — The World Transformed — at the party conferences. The wind was taken out of such initiatives. Wiser supporters of the Corbyn wave always warned that it was only the start, given the scale of the historic defeat in the 1980s, but the Corbyn leadership did not integrate this perspective into their culture.[10] A young participant shared a painfully honest description when the

2019 election results came in: "inspired and traumatised, activated and numbed. I don't yet know — I suppose I'm waiting to find out — how deeply or lastingly, and in what ways, this personal change will manifest itself in future." She acknowledges that this may hinge on what new movement happens next, one that she will "lie in wait for". The Corbyn experiment itself, that she threw her energy into, had provided no framework for the long term.[11]

I believe the attitude of "lying in wait" for the next movement is widespread in England. It lets people hold onto and protect their desire for real change privately, so as not to dissipate it. It also means that when such a moment comes there will be little preparation — whereas we dare not allow the familiar cycle to continue as there are less than ten years in which to save or lose the viability of the environment. COVID-19 has shown us how painful it is psychologically, let alone how hard it is strategically, to combine the imperatives of the immediate with the expectations and necessity of the long term. The likelihood is that "normal time" just like normal weather is now a thing of the past.

Culture and Organisation

The way forward will have to include progressive alliances, non-party campaigns, conventions that debate the issues and share the outcomes in person and online, global forums, direct action, media coverage and investigations. Such initiatives kept opposition alive when market fundamentalism was supreme. As I have tried to set out in chapter 9, they were essential but have not managed to accumulate influence and reshape politics. The first real exception is the Bernie Sanders movement — even if its supporters are eating the carpet at the slow rate of change.

There is no single reason for the blockage. A major one, however, is the nature of the political system itself. There is a general crisis of the representative system. Representation was developed, as we've seen, as a means of keeping democracy at arms-length and it has done so successfully. Now we need to work out ways of restructuring political institutions with full public support so that they work for all of us. One starting point for achieving this is our own political culture. I'll suggest a principle, a method and an inspiration that may help this process. I'm sure there will be better suggestions. Nothing works without the difficult task of trying it out.

The principle is shared empowerment; the method is to follow the examples of feminism; the inspiration, as described at the conclusion to the last chapter, is the 2020 upsurge of Black Lives Matter. I'll discuss them in reverse order.

Black Lives Matter
Black Lives Matter was an immense multiracial refusal of oppression. I'm not talking about the organisation that goes under its name but the determination behind the demonstrations. What freaked out the right was that they couldn't stereotype BLM as a minority or special interest and thus project onto it their own stunted nature — which is their usual method. The point was made so well by Steve McQueen in the quote at the end of Chapter 9 that there is no need to say anything more: we, people of all races, can make ourselves heard and demand the rejection of white supremacism — after decades when we could not, this is inspiring.

Feminism

Feminism has shown us how deep change can be achieved. I'm using it as an inclusive term for all the different women's movements, groups, consciousness-raising, campaigns, arguments, research and practical experiments across three generations since the 1960s that are dissolving patriarchy and misogyny.

If you believe that real politics can only take a traditional form — a manifesto, a unified push to get office, adroit positioning, electoral discipline, winning and passing laws — then to propose feminism as a method produces a brain-jam. But over time feminism's dispersed nature, shapeshifting capacity, the vitality of its disagreements, and the force of its claims, led to change more lasting than much progressive legislation. It needed equal opportunity laws and legislation to protect women too. The pressure for them came from outside and not from within party leaderships. Conference motions and negotiated platforms were the result not the source of feminist influence.

In 1966, when most women were still confined to the family or at best had subordinate employment, and the second wave of feminism was about to take off, Juliet Mitchell wrote "Women: The Longest Revolution", a title in part inspired by Raymond Williams.[12] I'm not sure if she expected feminism to be as revolutionary or take so long. Hers was only one voice, and a theoretical one, in what would soon become a vigorous growth of claims and demands. One argument in her article became influential. She emphasised that the suffragettes showed that success on a single front, voting equality, did not lead to change elsewhere. Women's subordination needed to be reversed across the interconnected spheres of production, reproduction, socialisation and sexuality. This suggested the breadth of the struggles to come. So when I say that feminism inspires a method I mean a process that while not geared only to "taking power" is not "reformist" in the sense of making disconnected improvements that don't reinforce an overall project. Dedicated to lasting change, it embraces inclusivity and diversity while fighting for a principle and opposes mono-party, mono-cultural, mono-national, patriarchy.

Feminism is not, therefore, an "ism" in the usual sense of being programmatic. Norbert Elias observed: "Almost all programmes of social action [...] are geared to the notion that what happens in human societies can all be explained in terms of acts of will, of the deliberate actions and decisions of human beings as individuals and groups. Many social beliefs, a multitude of 'isms', are cut according to this pattern [...] Often enough, their fantasy-content outweighs by far their reality-orientation."[13] I don't agree that we should retreat from commitment until we "understand ourselves", as Elias preferred, because commitment is needed to achieve understanding. But his argument that the forced "wilfulness" of ideological change can be driven by fantasy rather than engage with reality is spot on. It is striking that the right has sought (and failed) to define feminism in just these terms of fantasy and will (for example, in accusations of feminazi).

The realisation that how we live and relate to each other has deep political implications has led to a lot of research, action and experience on the nature of personal transformation and social change. Even if it has not yet been integrated into an effective politics, its pioneers, such as Michael Edwards, emphasise the need for two things: a focus on the places where transformative action is located (families, schools, universities, workplaces, municipalities, local governments, community groups); and a need to create structures that can engage with differences positively, even when they are very deep-rooted (think Trump supporters). These are not contained within a conventional left-right frame.[14]

Shared Empowerment

Elias's case that campaigns for change can be damagingly wilful fantasies is important for all politics, right wing as well as left. In England at present, for example, the Johnson government's obsession with the popular "will" leads it to ride rough-shod over people's rights as well as the truth. It is arbitrary and careless. Yet its appeal derives from a desire by voters to "take back control" that locked the notion of "will" into the UK's popular politics, as if it was something one could "have". Trumpism appeals to the same spirit.

The fantasy aspect has yet to grasp that "sovereignty" has changed. Regulation, which plays an ongoing part in our lives, for example, has become a fourth branch of sovereignty, alongside the legislature, the judiciary and the executive.[15] It can also be empowering in that it gives us quality control over important aspects of our lives.

Capitalism too can empower us to express ourselves economically outside of the state. The desire to "take control" expresses a positive revulsion at being reduced to a marketing entity, or welfare recipient, or someone who can't speak their mind. The overall objective of a progressive government should be to assist and support shared empowerment as a way of achieving "government by the people" that isn't monolithic.

One way to communicate what I'm trying to get at is through describing what it isn't. Spin doctors like to appropriate the buzz of attractive words while depleting them of bite. In the 1980s, Neil Kinnock, the then leader of Britain's Labour Party, supported the idea of an "empowering state". The concept can be seen as bridging the pre-Sixties notion of a well-administered welfare state and the notion of the state as a delivery platform for market-style choice, as embraced by Tony Blair after 1997 — it draws on a Fabian model while it bows to individual "freedom".[16] I'm not proposing this or a policy for government; I'm seeking a way to describe achieving democracy that is empowered and shared and generated from below.[17]

Maybe we are at the consciousness-raising early stage of identifying the blockages amongst us that prevent such a movement. Just as the call for equality for women had implications in unexpected ways, revealed unintended discrimination in how we are brought up, a commitment to "shared empowerment" may enable people to make the best of our capacities in ways that we have still to discover — it may help to link equality and democracy, liberty and justice, in ways that are open without being directionless. Networked solidarity can join empathy, respect and equality. When two feminist analysts, Susie Orbach and Luise Eichenbaum, researched relationships between women, they found that "separated attachments and connected autonomy" described an ideal.[18] This is more than respect; it creates a solidarity — a form of love — that is also just and empowers the other.

A smaller-scale way to understand shared empowerment is through "the commons". Unmapped, many people are creating local projects, such as gardens or wild land, or allotments, without a framework of larger intent. Guy Standing has tried to reframe the economy in its terms with a Charter of the Commons.[19] It is a way of thinking that is helpful because it is practical. The commons is not limited to being small. Tim Berners-Lee chose not to copyright the

World Wide Web and consciously created a commons that the whole of humanity can use. Jeremy Gilbert makes an important observation:

> What is particularly useful about the idea of the commons as distinct from the idea of community is that it does not depend upon any presumption that the participants in a commons will be bound together by a shared identity or a homogeneous culture. Rather, they will be related primarily by their shared interest in defending or producing a set of common resources, and this shared interest is likely to be the basis for any egalitarian and potentially democratic set of social relationships.[20]

Such projects are hard, as anyone who has attempted to start one can testify. Shared empowerment can easily fail! The first thing you learn is how much you don't know. In a small way, you hit upon the issue of reflexivity and risk — that we can never know what humans will do next. Ulrich Beck conceptualised modernity itself as a "risk society"; something we all now understand, as parents everywhere assess probabilities when deciding whether to send their children to school during COVID. Shared empowerment is a suggestion for thinking about political power differently and in a practical way, as centred around self-renewing societies in a living world, to draw on Williams' notion of livelihood.

Institutional Inventiveness

Citizens' assemblies are an example of shared empowerment. These are deliberative bodies, selected by a process of sortition — which combines random selection with ensuring a representative cross section of a population — that debates the evidence and then decides on specific issues in the manner of a jury. There is a growing body of research on citizens' juries, citizens' assemblies, deliberative processes and the use of sortition, which have grown in this century and been mapped by Stuart White and others.[21] They show that political decision-making can indeed be democratised. Two outstanding examples are Ireland's decision to legalise equal marriage and the right to abortion, both passed by referendums (in 2015 and 2018) on the recommendation of well-publicised deliberative assemblies, after the political parties were unable to confront the issues.

While forms of direct democracy are beginning to show its effectiveness, representative institutions are fossilised, their stony procedures help make party politics repugnant. Since the 1990s, the Brazilian theorist and politician Roberto Unger has insisted on the need for "high energy politics" and an "acceleration of *democratic experimentalism* in all fields of social life".[22] If you look at the last half-century, the epoch of the great acceleration, so much has changed: our culture, communications, technology, the nature of companies, universities, our cities, our relationship to the land, and the nature of family life. But our political institutions remain much as they were. Apparently untouchable, it is not surprising they are out of touch. Their sclerosis assisted the neoliberal depoliticisation of society. If we want agency to return to politics, we need political institutions and decision-making to be opened up to the direct deliberation of voters.

Populist leaders attack "elite institutions" to delegitimise opponents, whereas democracy demands dialogue, participation, deliberation, engagement with facts and respect for one's opponents, as Jan-Werner Müller sets out.[23] In her outstanding overview, *Open Democracy, Reinventing Popular Rule for the Twenty-First Century*, Hélène Landemore takes the argument to a new level: our constitutions may claim to be democratic but are designed to limit democracy. As a result, "core to the constitutions of all modern democracies" is a "crisis of the electoral model of governance" itself.[24]

Landemore tries to rethink "democratic representation in a manner that opens it up to ordinary citizens". She works through questions of participation, deliberation, and transparency — "openness is to both voice and gaze [...] inclusive and receptive of people and ideas [...] a system that lets in ordinary citizens". She develops a theory of sovereignty that includes agenda setting and deliberation as well as "the final say", and draws on a close study of Iceland's elected citizens' convention and similar assemblies in France.[25] Participative frameworks can create arenas for invention and building new kinds of politics that go beyond the binary of "direct" versus "representative" democracy, in which the former poses a "threat" to the latter. Representative institutions were born out of a process where chambers, parliaments or congresses replaced royal rule. In so doing, they reproduced the division of sovereign and subject. Direct democracy — especially arbitrary referendums — reproduces it too, in reverse. In the age of the internet, this has become a pathological regression, not an advance. Deliberative processes — what Landemore calls "open democracy" — should replace the polarity of rulers and ruled.

This is the route we need to take to get to the economic solutions of Piketty, Raworth and others. The reason for the gap, the absence of agency, is that politics itself has been stripped of the traction that allows it to transform the way the economy is governed. The way to reverse this is not by — or at least not only by — altering the platforms of parties, that then win elections, whereupon a select few enter government, only to be captured by their departments. Instead, we need a focus on altering the means and methods of democracy itself. Piketty emphasises that one of the reasons for Germany's economic success is the high degree of participation of workers on its company boards. *Participation works.* It is also popular.

Breakthroughs may occur away from the gnarled states of the major powers. The European Union is struggling for democratic legitimacy as a multinational entity that has renewed not displaced its member states. Kalypso Nicolaïdis is working on the creation of citizen juries in the EU, "Our new democratic era calls for permanent citizens' participation" and she confronts an issue that exists within nations too: "when asked *what* is to be done, European publics want 'more Europe,' but when asked *how* that is to be done, they want it closer to home [...] The only path for resolving this tension is [...] [to] connect national democratic conversations horizontally rather than only vertically".[26] A parallel report proposes other forms of institutional horizontalism, such as a permanent European Citizens' Assembly and the connection of European cities and regions bypassing national governments.[27] Experiments in deliberative democracy in South Indian village assemblies are underway that draw on lost methods of tribal consensus.[28] At the beginning of the century, apart from the participatory budgets pioneered in Brazil's Porto Alegre, there was little to support Unger's case for high-energy experimentation. Today it is no longer a lonely call.[29]

You might think that this takes us a long way from voter registration in, say, Pennsylvania. It doesn't. Voting involves voting for a candidate you may never see, who issues adverts of dubious truthfulness, is not like yourself, and belongs to a system that is grossly unfair even if it promises to improve. Canvassing people to overcome their scepticism is hard. If the horizon of such engagement is confined to what seems a broken system, why bother? The effort to register and get out the vote needs to be sustained. This in turn demands a vision that opens up politics to real participation. Part of the reason for voting now is to achieve more and better agency. Examples of experiments from around the world may help to overcome the depoliticisation of the last forty years.

Naturally, the voice of those "who know" will denigrate the idea that there are better ways to create public policy than theirs. One good reason they may be wrong is that corruption flourishes where office holders remain in post for decades, debate is off the record and deals are done after being lobbied. Members of the public sitting in open, livestreamed forums, with no career in politics before them, are less likely to be corrupted. And corruption must be stopped if we are to enjoy democracy. The best, perhaps only way to achieve this is with new methods of decision-taking, which are open to the public, not the transfer of money.

The Nation

Families can't start to be "empowered" without the security of income, sustainable habitation and a safe environment. What use is "shared empowerment" if the air is unbreathable, the seas are toxic, food carcinogenic and the temperature unbearable — *for other families anywhere*? The right to breathe is more tangible than "the right to life" as a claim for living equality, and leads us to the right to speak.

In a recent essay on our current "age of contagion", Elif

Shafak writes about how from Brussels and Washington to New Delhi,

> a growing number of citizens feel left out, not so much forgotten as never noticed in the first place. As their disillusionment deepens, so does distrust even in the most basic institutions. More than half of the people living in democracies today say that their voice is 'never' or 'rarely' heard [...] And the biggest irony is that all this is happening at the time when we as humans – regardless of race, gender, religion, class or ethnicity – are supposed to be more connected and empathetic and free than ever before [...] To be deprived of a voice means to be deprived of agency over our own lives [...] In losing our voice something in us dies.[30]

She is right that to lose our voice is to lose our capacity for purpose. But this is different from "not being heard". The question is who is listening? How are they listening? Are those of us in democracies who feel their voice is never or rarely heard also concerned to listen and therefore, potentially, to be changed? Because listening is as important as speaking. When I read Shafak's words, I thought of Thomas Rainsborough, the Leveller, who first set out the call for modern democracy in 1647:

> I think that the poorest he that is in England hath a life to live, as the greatest he; and therefore truly, Sir, I think it's clear, that every man that is to live under a government ought first by his own consent to put himself under that government; and I do think that the poorest man in England is not bound in a strict sense to that government that he hath not had a voice to put himself under.

Rainsborough was debating with Cromwell's New Model Army after the Levellers had issued their *Agreement of the People*. His argument was rejected. His claim recognises the principle of consent, which became the mark of Anglo-Saxon government, but emphasises that it must come from everyone who "has a life to live" and not just property holders.

By voice he meant a vote in the sense of a say, one that is genuinely listened to in the creation of the national council. This was the common parliament (from the French *parler,* to speak, hence a gathering of speakers) that forms and authorises government. In this context the line between speaking and obeying is the slender line of liberty, that distinguishes a free human from a slave: a line written on a ballot paper that says we have the right to a voice over who shall make the laws that rule us.

To be heard is to have a say in how we are governed. Not that the government must do what you say, but that what you say is taken into account. Also, that if together those who think like you become the majority, the government is changed. This is a right — a *human* right. But humanity itself, currently 7.9 billion and counting, is far too great a number, with too many wonderful languages, to be the vehicle for our own government. The parliament one puts oneself under is that of one's nation.

Democracy and nationality are joined at the hip. Agency, voice, shared empowerment, livelihood, all express a claim of meaning within a national context. There are two interrelated arguments that need to be distinguished. One concerns the nature of the industrial and technological order created by capitalism, the other the relatively bounded nature of human identity.

In 1841, the German-American Friedrich List published

287

The National System of Political Economy. He explained "I perceived that the popular theory took no account of nations, but simply of the entire human race on the one hand, or of the single individual on the other."[31] He set out why Germany needed to build internal railways and throw up external tariffs so that it could develop its own industry and protect itself from English economic domination. He also argued that such economic competition between national economies would be mutually beneficial. In the 1980s, China adopted a List strategy of national development. Today, the United States under Biden has brushed up the List playbook almost word for word, as it seeks to protect and develop its internal resources, so as to catch up with China.

List infuriated Karl Marx, who wanted to end the cruel exploitation of workers under capitalism, not debate how it should expand. In 1845, Marx drafted a splenetic, unpublished response to List's book, writing, "The nationality of the worker is neither French, nor English nor German, it is *labour* […] His government is neither French, nor English, nor German, it is *capital.* His native air is neither French, nor German, nor English, it is *factory air*".[32] Seventy years later, many workers volunteered to take to the trenches, strongly aware of their separate national interests.

Marx's failure was twofold. On a world scale the expansion of capitalism is driven by its uneven and combined development organised by nation states. Capitalism as an economic system is inherently national, overseen by governments motivated by the imperative of catching up. The nation, its education system, its language and culture and its state, is the means whereby people, including both its capitalists and workers, raise their level to the standards of the leading societies.

If this is true, it has a devastating consequence. It means that our economic system is inherently irrational. Marxists believe that capitalism is inherently destructive because capital seeks its own accumulation but it sees capitalism as pursuing its own "rationality" and general interest. Neoliberalism, which is oddly like Marxism because it gives primacy to the economy, also sees capital as pursuing its own rational interests, only it holds that the outcome will be benign. But if nations and capital are symbiotically unified complex entities, it means there is no singularity called "capitalism", only competing national-capitalisms, and capitalism is a form of war, and not primarily class war, by economic means.

Second, nationality is not limited to economics for either capitalists or workers and their families. Writing in 2003, Tom Nairn argues:

> outside of economic textbooks, people have never wanted to live merely to reproduce themselves in less awful circumstances. Once change is imaginable, they want it to mean something, or to 'stand for something' (other than being bottom of the resultant heap). Post-1989 globalisation, unlike all its precursors, entered a world where change was universally imaginable, a daily summons to meaning and altered identity [...] Even before September 11th 2001, how could it have been imagined that homo economicus would not dissolve in the resulting tidal force?[33]

The desire to stand for something brings us back to voice, agency and participating in self-determination. It means becoming part of a larger social life while becoming identified with something particular — that tangible-intangible of "We the People".

It is extraordinary how persistently those who seek fairness and equality disregard this question and instead regard class and economic issues as "real" problems, while the question of their national form is somehow "unreal". A telling example, because he was such a fair-minded scholar, is Eric Olin Wright's *How to be an Anti-Capitalist in the 21st Century*. He presents his book as a search for a method for democratic socialism. He looks at equality and fairness, at democracy and freedom, and at community and solidarity, in relation to the capitalist state. He discusses agency and identity. But the issue of nations and nationalism is simply absent — as if one could have a theory of the state that does not ask why there are so many states and democracies, different and often competing ruthlessly with each other.[34] There can be no meaningful democracy or shared empowerment or superseding of capitalism, without nations. They are integral to participation and emancipation.

Nairn emphasised the dual nature of nationalism, which he dubbed a modern Janus after the Roman god with two faces, one looking forward the other to the past. He desired an anti-nationalist nationalism in which people "make and remake their own collective meaning in the here and now, [… so as to] open up collective identity to the creative involvement of as many participants and experiences as possible".[35] It's an ideal of a nationalism at ease with itself in the world. Its other face, that of a closed, belligerent militancy is more familiar. We all have versions of this conflict inside our own nations and know its hopes and dangers. The list is more than 200 long. It is an unavoidable part of being human. To become a voting citizen is to enter ongoing conversations and disputes about what kind of country you are a member of and how it will give you meaning in relationship to others. The particularities of geography, language, history, with all that this entails, are the basis of what we are. They are not epiphenomena, or random scars upon our essence and they will always be contested.

The issue may be dynamite. There is a short fuse between registering a Latino in Texas to prevent voter suppression and demands to close the border that might swing his or her vote. Human boundaries are always porous and often agonising. For those who have to leave, migration is a painful freedom. It can enhance life in the societies that are able to receive migrants but can be unsettling for them too and an easy excuse for authoritarians. Wealthy countries must help to raise the living standards of those that are poor. Shared empowerment meets reality on this defining ground.

This is why I have placed the general questions of the strategies for progress within the framework of today's national histories and the peculiar, fraught conjuncture of the present moment in the United States. I share Timothy Snyder's view that it is essential to "win back historical time for politics". If we accept ideas of timeless superiority, inevitability, claims that there is "no alternative", or globalisation as fate, or advocate a classless, nationless internationalism, then loss of agency and eventually of democracy follow.[36] What it meant to call for democracy in Russia in 1987, or England in 1997, is not the same as calling for it in the United States after 2020, nor will it be the same in the future. Humankind will go on being different, with distinct histories even while we live on one planet and need democratic internationalism.

To Conclude

The war-like insanity of our economic arrangements at a world level has been vividly confirmed by the failure of wealthy countries to immediately pay for vaccination programmes in poor and developing ones — a failure that increases the likelihood of a catastrophic variant mutation of SARS-COV-2. Similar madness has been evident across this century in the refusal to stop coal burning, methane release and flaring that cause intense emission of greenhouse gases when the cost of preventing this is a fraction of national budgets.

What is the impediment to achieving such obviously essential, easily affordable, international collaboration? It is not the people of the world. As I've tried to show, a humanisation of humanity has accompanied the growing capacity to respond globally which we have seen with the pandemic — in terms of rights, expectations, health, science and social understanding, including of risk and probabilities, as well as at a specialist level in finance. Yet politically the failure has been massive: the hyper-inequality and national competitiveness that have led us toward global disasters are if anything being exacerbated.

The prime cause of the problem is a state system where each national government claims to represent its people but is symbiotically both master and slave of its country's capitalism and their influential military sectors with supporting sub-cultures.[37] International organisations from the UN down, instead of becoming a framework for global fairness and mutual benefit, are arenas for nation-state competition and have given internationalism a bad name.[38] (Hence the genial but almost certainly futile idea of a "polylaterism" that cuts out nation states to generate a progressive globalisation via cities and non-government agencies.)

As the world still turns on America, if Trump or his supporters win in 2024 there will be little chance of an escape from toxic national competition. In striving for primacy over China, Biden regurgitates the familiar reflexes of polarisation

— as does China under Xi, with draconian, neo-Maoist domestic consequences. Yet pulling against this, Biden seeks collaboration with China over climate change which hopefully will be reciprocated, and desires an alliance of democracies, something only possible if America can legitimise itself by securing democracy within the USA from its bigoted minority.

It is a domestic contest of world-importance. Biden's bitterly opposed presidency has pitched his seven million plurality against a gerrymandered, racially-biased, corporate-funded American polity — which is also enough of a democracy to have produced his success. In the balance is the possibility of America becoming a genuine democracy, where people can live without fear or want — and the impact this can inspire across the rest of the world.

Throughout this book I have stressed the positive in order to resist the surrounding gloom, and because, while I admit the odds may be against it, the fact that the outcome is in the balance means that sustainable democracy is achievable both in the US and outside. What are the strengths of the forces that generate this possibility? The underlying one is that people are now wiser than those who govern us. The historic nature of this shift is not yet recognised. Not all "the people" in a singular way are wiser and not all "the elite", whatever exactly that may be, are more selfish and short term. But the principle on which the historic institutions of representative democracy were built in the eighteenth and nineteenth centuries has been upturned. The premise was: that those who govern must control the governed to secure a country's general interest, while retaining consent. Once there was wisdom in this claim as well as the self-interest of property holders. Only a fraction of the population was literate. Early industrialisation and urbanisation created ferocious conditions that could generate mob mentalities. But across the world in the twenty-first century those of us who were considered the "unwashed" practise good hygiene and have a long-term view of our interests, while elites, integrated into the military-industrial complex and the staggering wealth of fund-holders, are greedy and short-term in their decision-taking.

A turning point was the invasion and occupation of Iraq. It was a war of choice that the people would never have chosen. Between the decision to invade in early in 2002 (President Bush told three US Senators meeting with his National Security Adviser Condoleezza Rice, "Fuck Saddam, I'm taking him out"[39]) and the actual invasion in March 2003, a massive, concerted and duplicitous effort was mounted to secure public support for the use of force, while its purpose was the misconceived ambition of global hegemony. Even then, for the first time ever in history, there were vast demonstrations in the United States, as well as around the world, *before* a war, against the decision to launch it. It was not a protest against injustice or what had happened. It was a demand for a different and better judgment than the one we knew Bush and Blair, with the political classes in the US and UK in tow, were set upon and we wanted to prevent. The streets took the long view and were vindicated. We have earned the right to real democracy now.

To put it another way that points towards a solution: had there been a dispassionate, deliberative representative assembly of un-lobbied Americans who listened to the arguments on all sides, it would never had endorsed a war of conquest and occupation. Similarly, would a deliberative people's assembly, even if made up of a majority of Trump voters, have supported substantial tax cuts for the very wealthy to be funded by borrowing, as in Trump's Tax Cuts and Jobs Act of 2017, if the arguments on all sides had been presented in a disinterested fashion? Of course not.

The significance of this development is profound. Earlier, I noted how over two-thirds of voters, both Democrat and Republican think that "American democracy serves the interests of only the wealthy and powerful". Perhaps the other third thought that "only" was a step too far and "mainly" would have been more exact. The US political system has lost the positive consent of the public for good reason. Not because the public is greedy, stupid or short-sighted but because it can see what is happening – the starting point for wisdom.

Pull back and ask, what would be necessary to create positive consent? The answer, surely, is that the processes of government must be democratised, not just the outcomes. The time has come for even the poorest of us to have a voice in the government we put ourselves under.

And only by addressing the nature of the system can an appeal be made to many who vote for Trump because they feel he gives them voice and meaning. Liberals will need to discard their distrust of working people, and progressives their belief that they already know what working people need. The process can bring politics back to life and end the sterilisation of the political that has accompanied neoliberalism.[40] A democratic culture, institutional inventiveness, a spirit of experimentation, scientific awareness, an appreciation of the toughness of life, a capacity to make a claim on our societies with those we love, to empower ourselves and prevent an environmental catastrophe — COVID-19 has allowed us to see that such collective answers are possible.

Such a humanisation of humanity is possible yet it is also in question. Its premise is the moral equality of all humans. As

COVID has taught us, the health of one, however poor and lowly, can be the health of all. We are one species on the basis of which we can enjoy the conviviality of planetary differences, to use Paul Gilroy's attractive description. However, it was an authoritarian inhumanity that imposed the way we have come to dominate the planet and its resources. It trades on racism. Because of its history and composition, the epicentre of the conflict over ending racism depends upon Americans. To realise the danger, consider the fact that in 2021, 48% of white Americans believe that voting "can be limited" because it is "a privilege", and do not agree that it is "a fundamental right of every US citizen", according to a careful Pew Survey.[41] The bedrock principle of democracy is up against racial prejudice reinforced by the rigged US election system. On this issue too, a progressive alliance is essential.

To take up the words of Haile Selassie speaking to the UN in 1963, and refreshed by Bob Marley: Until there are no longer first-class and second-class citizens of any nation. Until the colour of a man's skin is of no more significance than the colour of his eyes. Until the basic human rights are equally guaranteed to all without regard to race… there will be war. Who wants this war? We have learnt repeatedly that the exhilaration of a call to arms is the route to self-destruction mastered by the far-right. Against this we do not want 'peace' which sounds dull and uniform, we want life. Nor is it just a matter of inclusion and fairness. Equality emancipates all of us. Notions of intrinsic pre-eminence over women have afflicted men and enslave both sexes. To believe that as Chinese you are superior to Blacks, or as Japanese that you are better than Koreans, or as Muslims that you are better believers than Christians, or that as Israelis you are more human than Palestinians, or that as a white American you can restrict the rights of other Americans, makes you a slave of your own supposed elevation.

If America can renew itself thanks to the cooperation of its progressive alliance – that's *if* – then its drive for global primacy can be dissolved in the openness of global pluralism. The rest of us may be alarmed by the possible outcome in the US but at the same time we can admire the resolve and creativity that is now engaged there. In my own country, England, the contrast is excruciating. Trapped in the breakdown of a political system which our rulers lack the courage to replace, they speak to us as if from their coffins, mouthing clichés and bad jokes, lacking even the energy and glamour of the undead.

Perhaps the country that best symbolises the fraught state of the world is Turkey, a large predominantly Muslim country strategically situated between Asia and the West. Its authoritarian president, Recep Erdoğan, has overseen an immense transformation into modernity of its poorest people that has created a loyalty to him. Currently he appears to have the upper hand. But it was only by cheating that he "won" a referendum in 2017 by — supposedly — 51%. It made him president with some control over the judiciary. The country remains balanced between authoritarianism and democracy. Erdoğan boasts of his legitimacy but knows that he has only minority support and, in Trump-like fashion, stirs up hatred of the Kurdish minority while seeking to cover up corruption to secure his position. His control of the state makes him strong enough to confine but not to crush democracy, a state of affairs symbolised by Erdoğan's imprisonment of Osman Kavala. Kavala is a philanthropist who represents humanisation at its finest and Turkey at its best.[42] In terms of his dedication to saving the environment, ending racial and national prejudice, supporting peace, democracy and the rule of law, and working for an honest knowledge of history, few can equal him. When Kavala was jailed in 2017 on absurd charges, I was confident he would be shortly freed. Instead, he remains behind bars because the forces he represents are such a threat to despotic rule. Today, I and all who know him work for his liberation — and will then seek the success of what he stands for because, as Rosemary Bechler says[43], it is the follow-up that really makes a difference, since this is when persuasion begins.

Epilogue: Socialism and the Syndemic

In Memory of Julian Perry Robinson

Around the world, most of us have a family member or friend who has died from COVID-19, or know those who have. We are told it is a "pandemic", which is a contagious disease that spreads exponentially through a population. At the beginning I accepted this description. But while writing this book the Delta variant took off in England and even some who have been vaccinated caught it. At the same time it was credibly reported that its spread was due to the Prime Minister deciding to keep the UK open to travellers from India, where Delta was known to be spreading, because he wanted to go there to sign a trade deal. As a consequence, in April 2021, over 40,000 went back and forth and between 500 and 1,000 carried the Delta variant to England from India, according to the BBC.[1]

Then there is the role of India's Prime Minister, Narendra Modi. He encouraged attendance at vast Hindu religious ceremonies which generated an intense reproduction of SARS-COV-2 (the name of the actual virus — COVID-19 is the name of the disease in humans). Experts had warned that crowded conditions that concentrate viral spread are ideal for generating new variants. This was apparently the origin of Delta.

Another cause of the rapid spread of Delta in England

was that many of those coming from India were returning citizens of the UK who live in overcrowded conditions and are unable to completely "self-isolate", so that young people from their households become carriers. In my country, bad housing suffered by immigrant communities has regenerated the disease. Are those who then catch it suffering from the modern slums of Bradford as well as COVID-19's Delta variant?

In the 1990s, Merrill Singer, an American medical anthropologist, and others, developed an approach designed to identify the social interactions behind the spread and mortality rates of disease, as well as the biological causes. They concluded that public conditions and personal circumstances interacted "synergistically" with a disease and its clusters. They termed the pattern of its mortality rates as a "syndemic".

Writing in the British medical journal *The Lancet*, its editor Richard Horton applied the term to what is happening with COVID-19. He observed, "we must confront the fact that we are taking a far too narrow approach to managing this outbreak of a new coronavirus". It was scything down people with pre-existing conditions who became a source of its transmission because of their need for treatment. "The vulnerability of older citizens; Black, Asian, and minority ethnic communities; and key workers who are commonly poorly-paid and with fewer welfare protections" meant that the mortality of the disease has "social origins" not just biological ones. "This is not a pandemic", Horton concluded, "it is a syndemic".[2]

What we are now experiencing around the planet is not the impact of a disease spreading evenly across human populations as a plague. We are living through the interaction of a range of causes. If we really want to manage and limit its impact, Horton concludes, we need to approach COVID-19 as a syndemic, so that we can gain "a larger vision, one encompassing education, employment, housing, food, and environment".

The Lancet article produced a conversation between medical experts. One wrote in agreement to add that ecological factors should be included. Another objected, saying it was wrong to call COVID-19 a global syndemic, because in countries like New Zealand, which had moved fast to isolate themselves from it, it was a regular pandemic and not a disease that interacted with other conditions. But she added, "I do not write this to dampen Horton's use of the term, as I believe COVID-19 is syndemic in my country (the USA). This is precisely because pre-existing conditions such as hypertension, diabetes, respiratory disorders, systemic racism, mistrust in science and leadership, and a fragmented health-care system have driven the spread and interacted with the virus. These synergistic failures have caused more death and devastation than many other contexts".[3]

By calling it a syndemic, we identify the combined determination of the spread and consequence of the disease. On their own, none of the social or political issues are "the" cause of COVID-19's devastation. Their *joint* impact is responsible: medical, political, social and economic.

Combined determination is one of the themes of this book's exploration of whether a more human, democratic world can emerge from the present inter-connected crises of inequality, ecology, biology and authority. Short-term policy decisions interact with long-standing problems which are always expressed in historically specific ways. For example, as mentioned in Chapter 5, in early February 2020 China's Xi Jinping and America's Donald Trump had an opportunity to collaborate in an effort to contain the virus. Had they done so both authoritarians might now be holding office. Instead,

Trump also became a cause of the deaths and suffering around the world as well as in America. The point is not to "blame" him — or to use him as a scapegoat for the wider issues that helped create him — but from now on to demand that voters and political leaders think and act "synergistically".

This could be another description of "socialism" — because it combines the interests of all with an approach that is not determined by the market. I've mentioned Raymond Williams' suggestion of using "livelihood" as a description of a future alternative to capitalism, when he felt the attraction of the word socialism slip away. Perhaps he did so because he had long argued that the left should talk about "socialisms" in the plural so as to recognise the complexity of any future that will release our "real energies", but there had been no take-up for such a perspective.

I've backed off using the term "socialism" to describe the arguments I'm making because their ambition is to reach out to anyone willing to embrace the moral equality of all humans whatever else they think. Also, for my generation it is hard to disassociate socialism from state power and vanguardist organisations that are the opposite of democratic — and I do not want to be dragged back into that history with its many scar tissues.

Ironically, however, a report on how the idea of socialism has returned to life in England has just been provided by the country's most venerable neoliberal think tank, the Institute for Economic Affairs. Concerned about rumours of the unpopularity of capitalism, it commissioned Kristian Niemietz to produce *Left Turn Ahead?*, an in-depth survey that asked young people between the ages of sixteen and thirty-four, a generation for whom the Soviet Union is something akin to the First World War, what they think about socialism. 67%

favour the idea. Even more, 75% believe that socialism has never been tried. The same number regard climate change as a problem of capitalism; 71% say capitalism fuels racism; and 73% that it fuels "selfishness, greed and materialism", whereas a socialist system would promote "solidarity, compassion and cooperation".[4]

Furthermore, the shifts of opinion across the nearly twenty-year span between sixteen-year-olds and those who reach thirty-four, showed them moving leftwards with age. Whereas students who enthused about Lenin and Mao after 1968 dropped their anti-capitalist ideas, the report's author claims, this generation, while less certain and strident, and with often confused views about what capitalism actually is, is becoming more consciously socialist.

In the US there is also a generational embrace of an open-minded notion of socialism as an alternative to capitalism, encouraged by the influence of Bernie Sanders. Felix Salmon of Axios reported on a 2019 survey that showed eighteen to twenty-four-year-olds had a more positive view of socialism (61%) than of capitalism (58%), whereas only 27% of those over sixty-five had a positive view. While this might seem surprisingly high for those who have lived through forty years of relentless anti-socialist propaganda, the old overwhelmingly endorse capitalism (69%).[5] A Gallup poll in 2019 showed a similar, relatively positive view of socialism by young Americans. It also showed that while they have a "subdued" view of big business they like "small businesses" and their reaction to the term "free enterprise" is overwhelmingly positive at over 90%.[6]

If this research is valid, Millennials and Generation Z sense the need for a "unified alternative" to capitalism, which they call "socialism" and see it as a way of living that embraces "solidarity, compassion and cooperation", that is opposed to racism, supports feminism and focuses on identity. At the same time they support free economic activity as a form of self-expression that serves the general good. They see no contradiction between "solidarity" and "enterprise": a combination that is culturally welcoming and attentive to the feelings of others but also bracing and energetic.

There is a long history of efforts to combine the benefits of competition and planning. They range from speculative and theoretical analysis of "market socialism" to cooperatives, mutuals and efforts to combine an open economy with a socialist state that began in the former Yugoslavia. There is also a tradition that Stuart White calls "Alternative Liberalism", which goes back to John Stuart Mill and is liberal but not neoliberal, in that it refuses to give the values of capital a defining role over society.[7]

All this suggests an ideal that is intrinsically participatory and democratic. If so, it needs to be the project of new socialists, not of new socialism. The difference is crucial. It is essential to grasp that there isn't a singular, future nirvana that awaits us on the other side of capitalism. Others have made the same warning. Its significance is that historically the structure of feeling associated with the idea of socialism has promised an escape into the future that must not be "betrayed", which then often permits, or has certainly been associated with, very oppressive behaviour in the present.

The dream goes back a long way and is intended to be emancipating. In his denunciation of the division of labour in *The German Ideology*, Karl Marx evoked a "communism" where we can "hunt in the morning, fish in the afternoon, rear cattle in the evening, criticise after dinner".[8] OK, he was just in his late twenties, he dashed it off, it was never published.

But cattle can't just be looked after "in the evening", any more than bringing up a child. Real life demands a positive division of attention and commitment. Instead, Marx expresses a passion for a realm of plenty that often haunts the notion of socialism: a desire for a future in which politics has been abolished, the state has withered away, all are equal and the rule of law can be discarded into its bourgeois dustbin. No socialist would openly advocate such a caricature perhaps, but the dream encourages contempt for any "concessions" to the present, as it idealises a future uncontaminated by our mortal history. In this way the dreamwork of revolutionary thought has contributed to a depoliticisation which is intrinsically disempowering.

We have to do better than actually-existing, hyper-unequal capitalism with its nation states, their corporations, violence, corruptions and militarism, that is currently destroying the world. In our different societies, the economy must be governed by priorities set by energetically democratic governments, hopefully motivated by solidarity, compassion and cooperation. We need to deliberate and act holistically, putting the values of humanity first. This is the lesson being taught us by the COVID-19 syndemic. Whether or not it will lead to socialisms across the world matters less than the need for politics in the here and now to become synergistic.

Notes

Introduction

1   Gabriel Sherman, "This is so unfair to me", *Vanity Fair*, 26 May 2020.

2   Adam Tooze, Chartbook #34, a preview of his argument in *Shutdown*, New York, 2021. https://adamtooze.substack.com/p/chartbook-34-how-we-paid-for-the

3   Achille Mbembe, *Out of the Dark Night*, Chapter 1, "Planetary Entanglement", New York, 2021, pp. 7–41.

4   In his eponymous Audible podcast, Misha Glenny, "The Rise of the Iron Men". https://www.audible.co.uk/pd/The-Rise-of-the-Iron-Men-With-Misha-Glenny-Podcast/B08GBVPC38

5   Donald Trump, "Speech 2020 UN General Assembly Transcript", 22 Sep 2020, https://www.rev.com/blog/transcripts/donald-trump-speech-2020-un-general-assembly-transcript

6   Alex Hochuli, "The Brazilianization of the World", *American Affairs*, Summer 2021.

7   On the threat of the Chinese model, Laurie Macfarlane, "A spectre is haunting the West – the spectre of authoritarian capitalism", *openDemocracy*, 16 April 2020.

8   Thomas Piketty, *Capital and Ideology*, Harvard, 2020, p. 17.

9   For example, David Sloan Wilson, *This View of Life*, New York, 2019.

10   Azar Nafisi, *Reading Lolita in Tehran*, New York, 2003, p. 132.

11   Philip Pullman, "Writing is despotism, but reading is democracy", *New Humanist*, 19 January 2015.

12   Anthony Barnett, "'The twots': Letter from a would-be New Statesman Editor", *New Statesman*, 16 April 2013.

13 Neal Ascherson, "Ancient Britons and the Republican dream",
    openDemocracy, 13 September 2018 (republishing his 1986 lecture).

14 See David Marquand's marvellous *Britain since 1918, The Strange Career
    of British Democracy*, London, 2008, for a history that includes this
    period and identifies the "democratic republican" as one of the four
    traditions of the country's politics.

15 Anthony Barnett, "Corporate Control", *Prospect*, 20 February 1999,
    and also "Corporate Populism and Partyless Democracy", *New Left
    Review 3*, May/June 2000.

16 "Trump's Red Guards", *Byline Times*, 11 January 2021.

17 Richard Parker, "Of Copernican revolutions", *Real-World Economics
    Review*, 96.

1. My Three Questions

1 Aaron White, "This election can't contain the rage of young
   Americans", *openDemocracy*, 29 October 2020.

2 Roberto Unger, *Democracy Realized*, London, 1998, p. 178.

2. The Shock of the 6th: Trumpism Frustrated but Defiant

1 Bellingcat Investigation Team, "The Journey of Ashli Babbitt", 8
   January 2021.

2 BBC News, "Chilcot report: What Blair said to Bush in memos", 6
   July 2016.

3 Evan Osnos, "How Greenwich Republicans Learned to Love
   Trump", *New Yorker*, 3 May 2020.

4 National Public Radio, 21 January 2021, https://www.npr.
   org/2021/01/21/958915267/nearly-one-in-five-defendants-in-
   capitol-riot-cases-served-in-the-military.

5 Todd C. Frankel, "A majority of the people arrested for Capitol riot
   had a history of financial trouble", *Washington Post*, 10 February 2021.

6   *Slate*, 13 February 2016, https://slate.com/news-and-politics/2016/02/jeb-bush-donald-trump-clash-over-george-w-bush-s-record.html.

7   Laura Basu, "The assault on the Capitol was shameful. But defending the status quo isn't the answer", *openDemocracy*, 8 January 2021.

8   Zack Stanton, "The Rise of the Biden Republicans", *Politico*, 3 April 2021.

9   https://www.theguardian.com/media/2021/jul/19/landslide-michael-wolff-rupert-murdoch-donald-trump-fox-news

10   Alexander Burns, "How Democrats Planned for Doomsday", *New York Times*, 24 January 2021.

11   Mary Fitzgerald and Aaron White, "How Democrats won Georgia and what happens now", *openDemocracy*, 9 January 2021.

12   David Runciman, "Biden wants unity and democracy", *Guardian*, 25 January 2021.

13   https://freebeacon.com/politics/46-times-president-obama-told-americans-thats-not-who-we-are/

14   Rep. Jamie Raskin's impeachment indictment, 10 February 2021.

15   https://nypost.com/2020/06/18/michelle-caruso-cabrera-getting-major-funding-from-wall-street-giants/

16   https://www.opensecrets.org/elections-overview/most-expensive-races

3.   Trumpism — Nativist and Minoritarian

1   Hal Foster, *What Comes After Farce?*, London, 2020, p. 34.

2   https://www.pbs.org/wgbh/frontline/article/the-state-of-americas-middle-class-in-eight-charts/

3   https://www.rand.org/pubs/working_papers/WRA516-1.html

4   "aggregate income for the population below the 90th percentile over this time period would have been $2.5 trillion (67%) higher in 2018,

had income growth since 1975 remained as equitable as it was in the first two post-War decades". As above.

5   https://www.bbc.co.uk/news/av/election-us-2016-35680694

6   Adam Ramsay, Anthony Barnett, "Behind Trump's lies is a hard truth about the US", *openDemocracy*, 14 October 2020.

7   Zack Stanton, "The Rise of the Biden Republicans", *Politico*, 3 April 2021.

8   Morgan Gstalter, "Kinzinger says relatives told him he has embarrassed the family name", *The Hill*, 16 October 2021, https://thehill.com/homenews/house/538943-kinzinger-says-family-members-told-him-he-has-embarrassed-the-family-name

9   Sarah Posner, *Unholy*, New York, 2020, p. 10–11.

10 Anne Nelson, "Jesus is just all Right", *Times Literary Supplement*, 22 January 2021.

11 *Mail Online*, 20 January 2021, https://www.dailymail.co.uk/news/article-9138429/Las-Vegas-casino-mogul-major-Trump-donor-Sheldon-Adelson-dies-aged-87.html.

12 Robert D. McFadden, "Sheldon Adelson, Billionaire Donor to G.O.P. and Israel, Is Dead at 87", *New York Times*, 12 January 2021.

13 Sheldon Alderson, "I endorse Donald Trump for president", *Washington Post*, 13 May 2016.

14 CNN Business, https://money.cnn.com/2013/08/27/news/companies/las-vegas-sands/, 27 August 2013.

15 Andrew Edgecliffe-Johnson and Mark Vandevelde, "Stephen Schwarzman defended Donald Trump at CEO meeting on election results", *Financial Times*, 14 November 2020.

16 Chibuike Oguh, "Blackstone CEO Schwarzman took home $610.5 million in 2020", *Reuters Business News*, 1 March 2021.

17 Kathleen Belew, *Bring the War Home, The White Power Movement and Paramilitary America*, Harvard, 2018, p. 106.

18 Peter Mair, *Ruling the Void*, London, 2013.

19 Paul Hilder, "They were planning on stealing the election", *openDemocracy*, 28 January 2019.

20 Glen Greenwald Substack, 12 July 2021, https://outsidevoices. substack.com/p/author-of-the-mega-viral-thread-on.

21 Reuters, 19 January 2021, https://www.reuters.com/article/us-usa-election-texas-republicans-insigh/trump-fraud-claims-open-republican-rift-in-texas-and-other-red-states-idUSKBN29O1XV.

22 Reid Wilson, "Republicans plan voting overhauls after Biden's win", *The Hill*, 25 January 2021.

23 Mary Fitzgerald, "I never thought Democrats could win Georgia. Could it happen twice?", *openDemocracy*, 3 January 2021.

24 https://www.forbes.com/sites/nicholasreimann/2021/03/08/georgia-gops-attempt-to-restrict-absentee-voting-prompts-boycott-from-its-own-party/?sh=90f553c575ad.

25 https://www.brennancenter.org/our-work/research-reports/voting-laws-roundup-may-2021.

26 Charles M. Blow, "Voter Suppression Is Grand Larceny", *New York Times*, 28 February 2021.

27 Ari Burman, "The Insurrection Was Put Down. The GOP Plan for Minority Rule Marches On." *Mother Jone*, March-April 2021. Aziz Rana, "It Would Be Great if the United States Were Actually a Democracy", *Jacobin*, 16 February 2021.

28 Timothy Bella, "A GOP Lawmaker Says..", *Washington Post*, 13 March 2021.

4. From Reagan to Trump: The Rise and Fall of Neoliberalism

1   "Read the full transcript of Trump's first solo press conference", *CNBC*, 16 February 2016, https://www.cnbc.com/2017/02/16/click-for-a-full-transcript-of-trumps-first-solo-press-conference.html

2   "Remarks by President Biden on the American Rescue Plan", 12 March 2021, https://www.whitehouse.gov/briefing-room/speeches-

remarks/2021/03/12/remarks-by-president-biden-on-the-american-
rescue-plan-2/

3   Mark Carney, "A chance to re-boot civilisation" *Financial Times*, 19
    March 2021.

4   "The Era of Big Government is Over", transcript of President
    Clinton's Radio Address, 27 January 1996, http://edition.cnn.com/
    US/9601/budget/01-27/clinton_radio/

5   Private email

6   James Meadway, "Neoliberalism is dying – now we must replace it",
    openDemocracy, 3 September 2021.

7   Quoted by Adam Tooze, *Crashed*, London, 2018, p. 574.

8   New York Times, 23 October 2008, https://economix.blogs.nytimes.
    com/2008/10/23/greenspans-mea-culpa/

9   Congressional Research Services, *Real Wage Trends, 1979 to 2019*, Table
    1, https://fas.org/sgp/crs/misc/R45090.pdf

10 Zachary D. Carter, "The End of Friedmanomics", *National Review*,
    17 June 2021 — a very useful survey of Milton Friedman's life,
    extremism and influence.

11 Stuart Hall, Doreen Massey, Mike Rustin, *After Neoliberalism? The
    Kilburn Manifesto*, London, 2015.

12 Wendy Brown, *Undoing the Demos*, New York, 2015.

13 Gordon Brown, Mansion House Speech, 6 July 2007, https://www.
    ukpol.co.uk/gordon-brown-2007-mansion-house-speech/

14 Adam Ramsay, "US defeat in Afghanistan marks the end of
    neoliberalism", *openDemocracy*, 17 August 2021.

15 See the SIPRI Military Expenditure Database and the Uppsala
    Conflict Data Program.

16 https://ourworldindata.org/global-education#all-charts-preview

17 James Vernon, "Heathrow and the Making of Neoliberal England",
    Past & Present, August 2021.

18 Anthony Barnett, "Corporate Control", *Prospect*, 20 February 1999, and also "Corporate Populism and Partyless Democracy", *New Left Review 3*, May/June 2000.

19 Diana Hambree, "CEO Pay Skyrockets To 361 Times That Of The Average Worker", *Forbes*, 22 May 2018.

20 Wendy Brown, *Undoing the Demos*, New York 2015, pp. 173 and 155.

21 Margaret Thatcher Foundation, Archive, https://c59574e9047e61130fl3-3f71d0fe2b653c4f00f32175760e96e7.ssl.cf1.rackcdn.com/FA5DB3D8544A461DACEDF181801765AE.pdf

22 Alan Travis, "Murdoch did meet Thatcher before Times takeover, memo reveals", *Guardian*, 17 March 2012.

23 The quote is from James Curran, in James Curran and Jean Seaton, *Power without Responsibility*, London 2010, p. 73. I discuss the episode in *The Lure of Greatness*, p. 203.

24 "Roy Greenslade, "Their Masters Voice", *Guardian*, 17 February 2003.

25 Peter Oborne, *Alastair Campbell: New Labour and the Rise of the Media Class*, London 2004.

26 Maggie Haberman and Steve Eder, "Clintons Earned $30 Million in 16 Months, Report Shows", *New York Times*, 15 May 2015.

27 Ian Schwartz, "Hillary Clinton: I Did Goldman Sachs Speeches Because They Paid Me; Notes Conference Sponsored By Goldman", *Real Clear Politics*, 31 May 2017, https://www.realclearpolitics.com/video/2017/05/31/hillary_clinton_i_did_goldman_sachs_speeches_because_they_paid_me_notes_conference_sponsored_by_goldman.html#!

28 I discuss this in even more detail in *Lure of Greatness*, London, 2017, Chapter 26.

29 Adam Tooze, as above, p. 281.

30 Robert Brenner, "Escalating Plunder", *New Left Review*, May/June 2020.

31 Lawrence Summers on "House of Debt", *Financial Times,* 6 June 2014.

32 David Stockman on *Reason.tv,* 3 Jan 2011, https://www.youtube. com/watch?v=Lq9NwyQSzhk

33 David Leonhardt, "18 Revelations From a Trove of Trump Tax Records", *New York Times,* 27 September 2020. It is not clear how much of the £427.4 million comes from his TV revenues.

34 *The Lure of Greatness*, p. 43.

35 Naomi Klein, *No Is Not Enough: Resisting Trump's Shock Politics and Winning the World We Need.* London, 2017, p. 257.

36 'What we Owe to Donald Trump', *globalinequality,* 7 November 2020, https://glineq.blogspot.com/2020/11/what-we-owe-to-donald-j-trump.html

37 Robert Reich, "Why isn't Joe Biden doing all he can to protect American democracy?", *Guardian,* 25 July 2021. See, https://www.forbes.com/sites/michelatindera/2020/04/17/here-are-the-billionaires-backing-donald-trumps-campaign-as-of-february-2020/?sh=6d3940de4f52

38 Jon Hilsenrath, "The Verdict on Trump's Economic Stewardship", *Wall Street Journal,* 14 October 2020.

5. Out of the Belly of Hell

1 Tom Burgis, *Kleptopia,* London, 2021.

2 See, for example, George Monbiot, "Pegasus spyware is just the latest tool autocrats are using to stay in power", *Guardian,* 27 July 2001 and continuous coverage in *Byline Times.*

3 "Investigate the Origins of COVID-19", Jesse D. Bloom and others, Letters in *Science,* 14 May 2021; Zeynep Tufekci, "Where Did the Coronavirus Come From? What We Already Know Is Troubling", *New York Times,* 25 June 2021.

4   A helpful analysis by David Frum of "The Pro-Trump Culture War on American Scientists", skewers the efforts by the Trumpites to bait US scientists and Fauci in particular as the "enemy within", *Atlantic*, 18 May 2021.

5   https://www.ncbi.nlm.nih.gov/pmc/articles/PMC2714797/

6   Andy Beckett, "A cavalier Tory leader and a botched pandemic response? It must be 1957", *Guardian*, 1 May 2020.

7   https://www.cdc.gov/flu/pandemic-resources/1968-pandemic. html?web=1&wdLOR=cEDA8E9E5-0006-184D-AAE0-0C9BD0F3256A

8   The Centres for Disease Control, "The 1968 Pandemic", https://www.cdc.gov/flu/pandemic-resources/1968-pandemic. html?web=1&wdLOR=c05C487C8-EBAD-FA45-A42F-B0EB78635694

9   A redacted account has now been published: GOV.UK, Department of Health and Social Care, *Annex B: Exercise Cygnus Report (Accessible)*.

10 Cheng Wang and others, *Lancet*, 24 January 2020.

11 Richard Horton, *The COVID-19 Catastrophe*, Cambridge, 2021, p. 46 — A striking account by the editor of the *Lancet*.

12 "Trump's Coronavirus Timeline", Lloyd Doggett's website, https://doggett.house.gov/media-center/blog-posts/timeline-trump-s-coronavirus-responses

13 Bob Woodward, *Rage*, New York, 2020, from the prologue.

14 Doggett's Timeline, as above.

15 NBC news, 9 September 2020, https://www.nbcnews.com/politics/donald-trump/trump-told-bob-woodward-he-knew-february-covid-19-was-n1239658

16 GOV.UK, "PM speech in Greenwich: 3 February 2020", https://www.gov.uk/government/speeches/pm-speech-in-greenwich-3-february-2020

17 Simon Walters, *Daily Mail*, 25 April 2021, also *Mail Online* https://www.dailymail.co.uk/news/article-9510133/Boris-Johnson-said-

bodies-pile-high-order-lockdown-sources-claim.html. Downing Street denied it, but the paper's reporter Simon Walters writes, "those who say they heard it stand by their claim", meaning he had more than one source.

18 Quoted by Nick Paumgarten, "The Price of a Pandemic", *New Yorker*, 20 April 2020.

19 "Lifting Lockdowns", *Economist*, 23 May 2020.

20 Peter Baldwin, *Fighting the First Wave*, London, 2020, p. 82.

21 https://www.worldbank.org/en/country/china/overview

22 Sweden was only partially the exception, the account by Peter Baldwin (as above) shows. Its government relied on the public cloistering themselves without legal enforcement. Many did, its economy shrunk just as badly as its neighbours, but enough didn't and the long-term impact of the disease was worse.

23 Victor Mallet and Roula Khalaf, "Emmanuel Macron says it is time to think the unthinkable", *Financial Times*, 16 April 2020.

24 Adam Tooze, "The debt hawks are flapping their wings", *Social Europe*, 17 May 2021, https://socialeurope.eu/the-debt-hawks-are-flapping-their-wingshttps://socialeurope.eu/the-debt-hawks-are-flapping-their-wings

25 Gabriel Sherman, "This is so unfair to me", *Vanity Fair*, 26 May 2020.

26 I discuss "combined determination" as opposed to monocausal explanations in Chapter 32 of *The Lure of Greatness*, London, 2017.

27 Jake Sullivan, "The New Old Democrats", *Democracy*, 20 June 2018, and "What Donald Trump and Dick Cheney Got Wrong About America", *Atlantic*, Jan/Feb 2021.

28 Paul Gilroy, "Declaration of Rights", Chapter 2 of *Darker than Blue*, Harvard, 2010.

29 Guy Aitchison, "Rights, citizenship and political struggle", European Journal of Political Theory, 25 March 2015.

30 Archie Brown, *The Human Factor*, Oxford, 2020, p. 227.

31 Samuel Moyn, *Not Enough, Human Rights in an Unequal World*, Harvard, 2018, pp. 182, 192.

32 Pankaj Mishra's essay on this "The Mask it Wears" in *Band Fanatics*, London 2020, provides a concise summary.

33 Katrina Forrester, *In the Shadow of Justice*, Princeton 2019, p. 272; "The Future of Political Philosophy", *Boston Review*, 17 September 2019.

34 Perry Anderson, *New Left Review 1*, Jan–Feb 2000. Elsewhere in London the first business plans for an anti-neoliberal website were being hatched, that would become *openDemocracy*.

35 Andrew Marantz, "Are We Entering a New Political Era?", *New Yorker*, 24 May 2021.

36 Gillian Tett, the Chair of the *Financial Times* Editorial Board foresees the growth of "conscious capitalism": capitalism that is conscious of externalities such as climate change and inequality. Gillian Tett, "The rise of conscious capitalism", *Financial Times video*, 17 February 2020, https://www.ft.com/video/0999613a-42f7-4c93-b4fe-5e042b7e85f6,

37 Samuel Moyn, "Biden pulled troops out of Afghanistan. He didn't end the 'forever war'", *Washington Post*, 17 August 2021.

38 Molly Ball, "The Secret History of the Shadow Campaign That Saved the 2020 Election", *Time Magazine*, 4 February 2021.

39 Andrew Marantz, "Are We Entering a New Political Era?", *New Yorker*, 24 May 2021.

40 https://www.nbcnews.com/news/nbcblk/how-black-voters-key-cities-helped-deliver-election-joe-biden-n1246980

41 Quotes taken from parts 1 and 3 of "Inside the Whale", George Orwell, *Collected Essays, Journalism and Letters, Volume 1 An Age Like This 1920-1940*, London 1968, pp. 540–578.

6. The Biden Surprise

1   Rana Foroohar, Heather Boushey, "The guardrails have come off the US economy", *Financial Times*, 21 July 2021.

2   Adam Tooze, *Chartbook #19* American Family Values and Biden's Families Plan, 8 May 2021, https://adamtooze.substack.com/p/chartbook-newsletter-19

3   James Polti and Colby Smith, "Crunch time for Biden's economic plan: 'Failure is not an option'", *Financial Times*, 17 September 2021.

4   See for example, Biden's National Security advisor, Jake Sullivan, "I Was Hillary Clinton's Chief Foreign-Policy Advisor. And I Have a #MeToo *Mea Culpa*. Men in positions of power need to do better. That includes me". *Foreign Policy*, 8 September 2017, for an expression of the sympathetic culture of learning in today's White House.

5   Barack Obama Interview, Ezra Klein, *New York Times*, 1 June 2021.

6   David Serota, *Daily Poster*, 1 June 2021, https://www.dailyposter.com/no-obama-wasnt-mad-about-bailing-out-his-wall-street-donors/

7   Edward Isaac-Dovere, "What Biden Didn't Realize About His Presidency", *Atlantic*, 25 May 2021.

8   Katie Rogers, "On Voting Rights, Biden Prefers to Negotiate. This Time, It Might Not Be Possible.", *New York Times*, 27 May 2021.

9   Ezra Klein, "Four Ways of Looking at the Radicalism of Joe Biden. It's unexpected, but it's not inexplicable", *New York Times*, 8 April 2021.

10 Brown University, "Costs of War", https://watson.brown.edu/costsofwar/figures/2021/human-and-budgetary-costs-date-us-war-afghanistan-2001-2022, and The World Bank, "GDP per capita – Afghanistan", https://data.worldbank.org/indicator/NY.GDP.PCAP.CD?locations=AF

11 The White House, *Interim National Security Strategic Guidance"*, 3 March 2021.

12 The White House, "Memorandum on Establishing the Fight Against Corruption as a Core United States National Security Interest", 3 June 2021, Presidential Actions.

13 https://www.state.gov/wp-content/uploads/2020/02/Agreement-For-Bringing-Peace-to-Afghanistan-02.29.20.pdf

14 https://www.nytimes.com/2021/04/17/us/politics/biden-afghanistan-withdrawal.html

15 Edward Luttwak, "Joe Biden was right all along", *Unheard*, 17 September 2021.

16 Ezra Klein and Robert Wright, 'The Foreign Policy Conversation Washington Doesn't Want To Have', *New York Times,* 27 August 2021.

17 https://www.sarahchayes.org/post/the-ides-of-august

18 Sarah Mimms, 'Congress Has a Caucus for Everything', *The Atlantic,* 18 April 2014

19 Isabella Weber, "Origins of China's Contested Relation with Neoliberalism: Economics, the World Bank, and Milton Friedman at the Dawn of Reform", *Global Perspectives,* 9 April 2020.

20 Isabella Weber, *How China Escaped Shock Therapy*, London 2021, pp. 7, 269.

21 Isabella Weber, "Origins…", as above.

22 *Economist,* 13 May 2021 and Simon Rabinovitch tweet, 11 May 2021.

23 "Document 9: A ChinaFile Translation", *ChinaFile*, 8 November 2013, https://www.chinafile.com/document-9-chinafile-translation

24 Quinn Slobodian, *Globalists, the end of empire and the birth of neoliberalism,* Cambridge, Mass, 2020, p. 276.

25 Anatol Lieven, "How the West Lost", *Prospect,* 31 August 2020.

26 Ivan Krastev, "A European Goes to Trump's Washington", *New York Times,* 30 November 2018.

27 "The Longer Telegram: Toward A New American China Strategy", by Anonymous, the Atlantic Council, 2021. I refer to the author as

"he" because the paper makes a great deal of calling for democracy internationally but makes no mention of feminism and the role of women although this now has a significant role in opposing macho authoritarianism. It is hard — although not impossible — to imagine a woman being the author and sustaining such an obvious omission.

28   Denghua Zhang, "The Concept of 'Community of Common Destiny' in China's Diplomacy: Meaning, Motives and Implications", *Asia and the Pacific Policy Studies*, 16 April 2018.

29   Paul Rogers, "China: the next military rival", *openDemocracy*, 26 May 2011.

30   Jack Detsch, "Pacific Commanders Want More Money for Biden's Asia Pivot", *Foreign Policy*, 8 June 2021.

31   Ezra Klein, "The Best Explanation of Biden's Thinking I've Heard", *New York Times*, 9 April 2021.

32   Hal Brands and Jake Sullivan, "China Has Two Paths to Global Domination", *Foreign Policy*, 22 May 2020.

33   Thomas Hale, Harriet Agnew, Michael Mackenzie and Demetri Sevastopulo, "Wall Street's New Love Affair with China", *Financial Times*, 28 May 2021.

34   Jennifer Harris and Jake Sullivan, "America Needs a New Economic Philosophy. Foreign Policy Experts Can Help. The United States cannot get grand strategy right if it gets economic policy wrong", *Foreign Policy*, 7 February 2020.

35   "Secretary of the Treasury Janet L. Yellen on International Priorities", *U.S. Department of the Treasury*, 5 April 2021, where she says coldly, "Our economic relationship with China, like our broader relationship with China, will be competitive where it should be, collaborative where it can be, and adversarial where it must be", repeating exactly the words of Antony Blinken's first speech as Secretary of State, 3 March 2021.

36   Tom Nairn, "The Modern Janus", *The Break-up of Britain*, Third edition, London 2021 p. 322.

37 Eric Levitz, "Adam Tooze on Climate Politics After COVID", New York, Intelligencer, 21 May 2021, https://nymag.com/intelligencer/2021/05/adam-tooze-on-climate-politics-after-covid.html

38 CNN.com: "Transcript of Blair speech to Congress", 17 July 2003.

39 John le Carré, "The United States has Gone Mad", *The Times*, 15 January 2003, and "A Predatory and Dishonest War", *openDemocracy*, 12 January 2003

40 George Monbiot has a magnificent column that makes this argument after the evacuation of Afghanistan, "Who's to blame for the Afghanistan chaos? Remember the war's cheerleaders", *Guardian*, 25 August 2021.

41 https://thehill.com/policy/defense/navy/566883-senate-confirms-bidens-pick-for-navy-secretary

42 Oiwan Lam, "The construction of Chinese patriotic masculinity: 'sissies will ruin the nation'", *Global Voices*, 15 September 2021.

43 Alec Ash, "China's New Nationalism", *The Wire China*, 8 August 2021.

44 Didi Tang, "Son of Deng Xiaoping cautions President Xi not to overreach", *Times*, 31 October, 2018.

45 See Edward Snowden, "The Insecurity Industry", 26 July 2021, on *Substack*, https://edwardsnowden.substack.com/p/ns-oh-god-how-is-this-legal

46 Peter Geoghegan, *Democracy for Sales*, London 2021, pp. 291–306.

47 Steve Coll, "The Spyware Threat", *New Yorker*, 2 August 2021.

48 On "caste" see Isabel Wilkerson, *Caste, the Lives that Divide Us*, London, 2020.

49 John Kruzel, "Threats of violence spark fear of election worker exodus", *Hill*, 2 August 2021.

50 https://www.americansurveycenter.org/research/after-the-ballots-are-counted-conspiracies-political-violence-and-american-exceptionalism/

51   I found Annie Olaloku-Teriba "Afro-Pessimism and the (Un)Logic of Anti-Blackness", *Historical Materialism*, Issue 26.

52   Barack Obama's full eulogy of John Lewis, CNN, 31 July 2020, https://edition.cnn.com/2020/07/30/politics/barack-obama-john-lewis-eulogy-full-transcript/index.html

53   Stacey Abrams: "Our democracy faced a near-death experience. Here's how to revive it", *Washington Post*, 7 February 2021.

54   Daniel Strauss and Sam Levine, "Top House Democrat Jim Clyburn: No way we'd let filibuster deny voting rights", *Guardian*, 7 March 2021.

55   Aris Folley, "Mike Lee says 'For the People' voting bill is 'as if written in hell by the devil himself'", *Hill*, 10 March 2021.

56   David Greenberg, "Was Nixon Robbed?", *Slate*, 16 October 2000.

57   https://fivethirtyeight.com/features/can-democrats-move-forward-a-voting-rights-bill-by-making-a-moral-case-for-it/

58   SUPREME COURT OF THE UNITED STATES: BRNOVICH, ATTORNEY GENERAL OF ARIZONA, ET AL. V. DEMOCRATIC NATIONAL COMMITTEE ET AL. For both the Majority and Minority opinions, https://www.supremecourt.gov/opinions/20pdf/19-1257_g204.pdf. Where I have quoted from them I have edited out the legal references.

59   Donald Ayer, "The Supreme Cort has Gone off the Rails", *New York Times*, 4 October 2021.

60   David Daley and Gaby Goldstein, "America is full of 'democracy deserts'. Wisconsin rivals Congo on some metrics", *Guardian*, 13 August 2021; and for the Harvard Electoral Integrity Project reports, https://www.electoralintegrityproject.com/

61   https://thehill.com/homenews/state-watch/566327-american-voters-largely-united-against-partisan-gerrymandering-polling

62   https://www.whitehouse.gov/wp-content/uploads/2021/06/Bowie-SCOTUS-Testimony.pdf

63   https://verfassungsblog.de/openers-for-interpretation/

64   Jonathan Martin and Jonathan Weisman, "Biden Throws In With Left, Leaving His Agenda in Doubt", *New York Times*, 2 October 2021.

65   David Frum, "Trump May Not Have to Steal 2024", *The Atlantic*, 28 September 2021.

66   Alex Shephard, "Why Isn't the Democratic Reconciliation Bill More Popular?", *New Republic*, 12 October 2021.

7.   The Argument Resumed

1   Timothy Snyder, *On Tyranny*, London 2017 and *The Road to Unfreedom*, London, 2018.

2   Joe Biden, "We Are Living Through a Battle for the Soul of This Nation", *Atlantic*, 27 August 2017.

3   Martin Wolf, "The struggle for the survival of US democracy" *Financial Times*, 11 May 2021.

4   Statista, "Prisoners in the United States, Statistics and Facts', https://www.statista.com/topics/1717/prisoners-in-the-united-states/

5   Ross Douthat, "Are we destined for a Trump coup in 2024", *New York Times*, 8 June 2021.

8.   Can Actually-Existing Democracies Become Democracies?

1   Anthony Barnett, *This Time*, London, 1997, p. 259

2   The Preamble states: "We the People of the United States, in Order to form a more perfect Union, establish Justice, insure domestic Tranquility, provide for the common defence, promote the general Welfare, and secure the Blessings of Liberty to ourselves and our Posterity, do ordain and establish this Constitution for the United States of America".

3   Elizur Wright Jr, *The Sin of Slavery and its Remedy*, New York 1833, quoted in Paul Gilroy, *Darker than Blue*, Harvard 2010, footnote 1, p. 185.

4   Nikolas Bowie, "The challenges of teaching the Constitution in the age of Trump", *Washington Post*, 18 January 2021.

5   As Aziz Rana shows in his important study *The Rise of Constitution*, Chicago 2022, and "How the US Constitution came to be venerated" in *Eurozine* with accompanying essays by others, in *Public Seminar* forthcoming.

6   Brank Milanović, *Capitalism Alone*, Harvard, 2019, p. 57.

7   Jane Meyer, "Inside the Koch-Backed Effort to Block the Largest Election-Reform Bill in Half a Century", *New Yorker*, 29 March 2021.

8   Speech in Cleveland, *Washington Post*, 27 May 2021.

9   Jonathan Guyer, "How Biden's Foreign-Policy Team Got Rich", *American Prospect*, 6 July, 2020; Eric Lipton and Kenneth P. Vogel, "Biden Aides' Ties to Consulting and Investment Firms Pose Ethics Test", *New York Times*, 15 December 2020.

10 Andrew Perez, David Sirota, "Biden Boosted A Pipeline, Now His Aide Could Reap A Windfall", *Daily Poster*, 12 July 2021, for both figures.

11 See, for example, David Potter the wealthy creator of Psion, "Let's welcome the enmity of Bankers", *openDemocracy*, 5 October 2012, https://www.opendemocracy.net/en/opendemocracyuk/lets-welcome-enmity-of-bankers/

12 David Gelles, interview with Carol Tomé, CEO of UPS, *New York Times*, 17 June 2021; although she is a steely engineer of profit making: Paul Ziobro, UPS Boss Preaches the Power of No, *Wall Street Journal*, 26 February, 2021.

13 https://twitter.com/PeteButtigieg/status/1176262794586533894

14 Veronica Stracqualursi, "Pete Buttigieg: 'Capitalism has let a lot of people down'", *CNN Politics*, April 16, 2019.

15 Igor Derysh, "Joe Biden to rich donors: 'Nothing would fundamentally change' if he's elected", *Salon*, 19 June 2019.

16 Branko Milanović, *Capitalism Alone, the future of the system that rules the world*, Harvard, 2019, pp. 185, 196–7.

17 Albena Azmanova, *Capitalism On Edge*, New York, 2020, p. 195–6.

18 Dylan Riley, "Capitalists Have Never Been Friends of Democracy", *Jacobin*, 12 April 2021.

19 Will Davies, *This is Not Normal, the collapse of liberal Britain*, London, 2020, pp. 238–242.

9. The Left from 1968 to Occupy

1 Marcus Gilroy-Ware, *After the Fact?*, London, 2020, p. 24.

2 I discuss the transformations of 1968 in "Out of the Belly of Hell: COVID-19 and the Humanisation of Globalisation", *openDemocracy*, 21 May 2020 https://www.opendemocracy.net/en/opendemocracyuk/out-belly-hell-shutdown-and-humanisation-globalisation/

3 Anthony Barnett, "It was more than 12 months", *Moving the Social*, Issue 64, 2020, special issue on "1968 in Britain".

4 Kristin Ross, *May '68 and its afterlives*, Chicago, 2002, p. 4.

5 In the UK, culture and commerce, fashion and music were transformed by the Sixties and had a world influence, but the country's political 1968 was confined to small numbers of us in a society still captured by the conceit that it has "won the war" and that all its institutions needed was a paint job. The result was an exceptional divergence between vigorously modernising business sectors and a society attached to a sclerotic political system which still persists.

6 David Graeber, *The Democracy Project*, London, 2013, pp. 276–7.

7   Andy Beckett, *When the Lights went Out*, London, 2009,
    p. 209.

8   *Wikipedia*, Trilateral Commission, accessed 6 July 2021.

9   Michel Crozier, Samuel P. Huntington, Joji Watanuki, "The Crisis of
    Democracy", *The Trilateral Commission*, pp. 18, 26, 61, 113.

10 As above, pp. 62, 114, 115.

11 Zachary D. Carter, "The End of Friedmanomics", *National Review*,
    June 17, 2021; a very useful survey of Milton Friedman's life,
    extremism and influence.

12 Mark Fisher, "Acid Communism (Unfinished Introduction)", in
    K-PUNK, London, 2018, p. 754.

13 Jeremy Gilbert, *Common Ground*, London, 2014, p. 212.

14 *National Security Archive*, Allende and Chile: "Bring Him Down",
    3 November 2020, https://nsarchive.gwu.edu/briefing-book/
    chile/2020-11-06/allende-inauguration-50th-anniversary

15 Anthony Barnett, Isabel Hilton, "Democracy and openDemocracy",
    openDemocracy, 11 October 2005.

16 In unmatched and wrongly ignored columns in the *Observer* and his
    novel *The Bellringers*. I worked with him on the 2009 Convention on
    Modern Liberty, https://www.modernliberty.net/

17 Naomi Klein, "The Screen New Deal", *Intercept*, 8 May 2020.

18 The United Kingdom is the latest example; now the victim of the
    process of elite corruption it perpetrated on so many others, as the
    shame of selling off its public assets like its water and power as well
    as its industry to global speculators is covered up by the bragging self-
    importance of its government, while ancient checks and balances are
    discarded.

19 www.rtve.es/noticias/20110806/mas-seis-millones-espanoles-han-
    participado-movimiento-15m/452598.shtml.

20 https://www.economist.com/europe/2011/07/14/europes-most-
    earnest-protesters.

21 *15 May Revolution* website, "Translation of the conclusions of Manuel Castells on May 27 at *the AcampadaBCN — Plaza of Catalonia,* https://15mayrevolution.wordpress.com/2011/06/06/translation-of-the-conclusions-of-manuel-castellson-may-27-at-the-acampadabcn-spanishrevolution-15m/

22 Interview with Beatriz Pérez, "We have broken the silence: Fresh from Madrid, a member of the Communications team of the 15 May Movement", *openDemocracy,* 30 May 2011.

23 https://hyd.org.tr/en

24 Cited in James Curran, *Media and Power*, London, 2002, p. 182.

25 Originally published by Penguins and now online at the TNI, https://www.tni.org/en/publication/how-the-other-half-dies

26 https://www.amnesty.org/en/documents/eur30/013/2011/en/

27 Susan Richards, "The World's Fair", *openDemocracy,* 5 February 2003, https://www.opendemocracy.net/en/article_950jsp/

28 Znet, 20 February 2005, for the "Manifesto", https://archive.is/20051112235616/http://www.zmag.org/sustainers/content/2005-02/20group_of_nineteen.cfm#selection-399.4-399.114, and for a discussion of it Solana Larsen, "The WSF in Search of Itself", *openDemocracy*, 25 January 2006, https://www.opendemocracy.net/en/wsf_3211jsp/.

29 For the signatories see https://en.wikipedia.org/wiki/Porto_Alegre_Manifesto

30 Naomi Klein, "Cut the Strings", *Observer,* 1 February 2003.

31 Patrick E. Tyler, "A New Power In the Streets", *New York Times,* 17 February 2003.

32 Michael Levitin, *Generation Occupy, Reawakening American Democracy.* The quote is from a draft review by Todd Gitlin — himself a veteran of the Sixties and the author of an early, far-sighted account, *Occupy Nation: The Roots, the Spirit, and the Promise of Occupy Wall Street*, New York, 2012.

33   *New York Review of Books* Newsletter, https://email.nybooks.com/t/
      ViewEmail/y/62D2058FCDE51FEE2540EF23F30FEDED/0EF30
      309AE226424F1E87EB810D8F10A

34   Emily Tamkin, "How Slovakia halted its democratic descent", *New
      Statesman,* 24 June 2021.

35   See Dan Hancox and Guy Aitchison, Siraj Datoo, Cailean
      Gallagher, Laurie Penny, Paul Sagar (editors), *Fight Back! A Reader on
      the Winter of Protest,* openDemocracy, 1 February 2011. The first book
      to be produced by an "editorial kettle" — all seven of its editors were
      under 30 and kettled by the police — I contributed a forward.

36   Gerbaudo, Paolo, The "Movements of the Squares" and the
      Contested Resurgence of the "Sovereign People" in Contemporary
      Protest Culture, 20 May 2014, available at SSRN: https://ssrn.com/
      abstract=2439359 or http://dx.doi.org/10.2139/ssrn.2439359

37   Judith Butler, "Occupy as Form", *ARC Muses,* 2 February 2012,
      http://arcdirector.blogspot.com/2012/02/occupy-as-form-judith-
      butler.html

38   David Graeber. *The Democracy Project A History A Crisis A Movement,*
      London, 2013, p. 149.

39   Naomi Klein, "Why now? What's next?" in discussion with Occupy
      Wall Street activist Yotam Marom, *Nation,* 9 January 2012; *Red Pepper,*
      19 January 2012,

40   Naomi Klein: "We Have to Rebuild From the Wreckage of
      Neoliberalism", interview with Grace Blakeley, *Tribune,* 29 September
      2020.

41   Interview with Blakeley, as above. The Leap Manifesto is at, https://
      leapmanifesto.org/en/the-leap-manifesto/#manifesto-content.

42   Naomi Klein, *No Is Not Enough,* London, 2017, p. 296.

43   Ece Temelkuran, *Together, 10 Choices for a Better Now,* London, 2021,
      pp. 69–71.

44 Heather McGhee, *The Sum of Us*, London 2021, p. 237. She also notes the pushback to make people fear the demonstrations were violent when they were not, led by Trump's White House.

45 Steve McQueen, interviewed by Gary Younge, *Tate Etc.*, spring 2021.

10. America's Multilayered Crisis

1 Anthony Barnett, *This Time*, as above. I dedicated the book to Tom Nairn who in response dedicated his *After Britain*, "For Anthony and the Next Time".

11. Shared Empowerment and Humanisation

1 Raymond Williams, *Towards 2000*, Section V, "Resources for a Journey of Hope", London, 1983, pp. 243–269. *The Long Revolution*, is the title of his book published in 1961, and republished by Parthian in Cardigan, in 2011.

2 Oliver Balch, "Buen vivir: the social philosophy inspiring movements in South America", *Guardian*, 4 February 2013.

3 Thomas Piketty, *Capital in the 21st century*, Harvard, 2013, p. 34.

4 Thomas Picketty, *Capital and Ideology*, Harvard 2019, p. 1036. For a critique of his earlier book and a reflection on capital as power: James K. Galbraith, "*Kapital* for the Twenty-First Century", *Dissent*, Spring 2014.

5 Kate Raworth, *Doughnut Economics Seven ways to think like a 21st century economist*, London, 2017, p. 287.

6 Guy Standing, *The Precariat, Covid-19 Edition*, London, 2021.

7 George Monbiot, *Out of the Wreckage*, London, 2017, pp. 14–15.

8 https://www.rfi.fr/en/france/20210228-citizen-s-climate-convention-slams-french-government-response-to-reducing-carbon-emissions-ccc-emmanuel-macron and https://www.rfi.fr/en/france/20210706-french-senate-blocks-referendum-on-climate-change

9   Quoted in Adam Tooze, Chartbook, 1 September 2021, https://adamtooze.substack.com/p/chartbook-on-shutdown-keynes-and.

10 Jeremy Gilbert, perhaps Labour's outstanding cultural intellectual, tried to warn them, was not listened to and is now not thanked for pointing it out.

11 Lola Seaton, "The Experience of Defeat", in Grace Blakeley (ed.), *Futures of Socialism*, London 2020, pp. 18–19.

12 Juliet Mitchell, "Women: the Longest Revolution", *New Left Review I-40*, Nov–Dec 1966 and "Raymond Williams: Tomorrow is also yesterday's day", *European Journal of Cultural Studies*, 15 July 2021.

13 Quoted in, Stephen Mennell "Some political implications of sociology from an Eliasian point of view", Chapter 20 in Florence Delmotte and Barbara Górnicka (eds), *Norbert Elias in Troubled Times: Figurational Approaches to the Problems of the Twenty-First Century*, New York, 2021.

14 Mapped and critiqued by Michael Edwards in the Transformation section of *openDemocracy* he edited for eight years.

15 Anthony Barnett "Why Brexit won't work: the EU is about regulation not sovereignty", *openDemocracy*, 25 June 2018.

16 When Gordon Brown became Labour Prime Minister in 2008 he resurrected the formula. To borrow a phrase, one could say that power empowered is power retained.

17 For just three of many examples: Same Skies Think-Tank https://sameskiesthinktank.com); Neighbourhood Democracy Movement (https://dememove.org); the new municipalist movement https://minim-municipalism.org

18 Susie Orbach and Luise Eichenbaum *Bittersweet: Love, Competition & Envy in Women's Friendships*, London 1987, released as *Between Women*, New York 1988.

19 Guy Standing, *Plunder of the Commons, A Manifesto for Sharing Public Wealth*, London, 2019.

20 Jeremy Gilbert, *Common Ground*, London, 2014, p. 165.

21 Stuart White, "Citizen's Assemblies and Republican Democracy", in Bruno Leipold, Karma Nabulsi, Stuart White, *Radical Republicanism*, Oxford, 2020, an overview of the current state of play in developing active, popular sovereignty, see also the work of Graham Smith, https://www.westminster.ac.uk/about-us/our-people/directory/smith-graham#publications, and James Fishkin https://politicalscience.stanford.edu/people/james-fishkin.

22 Roberto Mangabeira Unger, *Democracy Realized: The Progressive Alternative*, London, 1998, pp. 190, 275, and *What Should the Left Propose?*, London, 2006.

23 Jan-Werner Müller, *Democracy Rules*, London 2021.

24 Hélène Landemore, "Remaking the UK Constitution", Bonavero Institute of Human Rights, Oxford University, 23 February 2019, https://livestream.com/oxuni/remaking-uk-constitution/videos/187826199 (1:04 in).

25 Hélène Landemore, *Open Democracy, Reinventing Popular Rule for the Twenty-First Century*, Princeton 2020, pp. 11, 13.

26 Kalypso Nicolaïdis, "The Democratic Panopticon", *Noēma*, 6 July 2021.

27 Luke Cooper, Roch Dunin-Wąsowicz, Mary Kaldor, Niccolò Milanese, Iavor Rangelov, *The Rise of Insurgent Europeanism*, London School of Economics, https://www.lse.ac.uk/ideas/Assets/Documents/reports/LSE-IDEAS-The-Rise-of-Insurgent-Europeanism.pdf

28 Ramya Parthasarathy, Vijayendra Rao, Nethra Palaniswamy, "Deliberative Democracy in an Unequal World: A Text-As-Data Study of South India's Village Assemblies", *American Political Science Review.* 2019.

29 I'd like to salute the work of Paul Hirst whose arguments for Associational Democracy were highly inventive and practical, Paul Hirst, *From Statism to Pluralism*, London, 1997, pp. 87; I proposed a different kind of experimentalism, calling for sortition in the House

of Lords: Anthony Barnett, Peter Carty, *The Athenian Option*, Demos, 1998, published in an expanded book form, London, 2008; as part of the publishing project of Keith Sutherland, author of *A People's Parliament*.

30   Elif Shafak, *How to Stay Sane in an Age of Division*, London, 2020, pp. 7–8.

31   *The National System of Political Economy*, by Friedrich List, 1841, translated by Sampson S. Lloyd M.P., 1885 edition, Author's Preface, p. xxvi (reference lifted from *Wikipedia*).

32   *Marx, Engels Collected Works,* Vol. 4, p. 280.

33   Tom Nairn, "Postscript 2003", *The Break-Up of Britain, Third Edition,* London, 2021, pp. 406–7.

34   Eric Olin Wright, *How to be an Anti-Capitalist in the 21st Century,* London, 2019.

35   Rory Scothorne, "Tom Nairn: The prophet of post-Britain", *New Statesman,* 28 July 2021.

36   Timothy Snyder, *The Road to Unfreedom*, London, 2018, p. 9.

37   Paul Rogers calls them the "military-industrial-academic-bureaucratic-complex" which includes, "arms companies, senior military personnel and civil servants, trade unions, think tanks and university researchers, arms sales, profitable enterprises and a hunt for new enemies", *Losing Control, 4th Edition,* London 2021, p.145 and p.266.

38   See Mark Mazower's gloomy conclusion to *Governing the World*, London 2012.

39   http://edition.cnn.com/2003/ALLPOLITICS/03/24/timep.saddam.tm/

40   Eliane Glaser calls for a "pro-political left" on these lines, *Anti-Politics,* London 2018.

41   Pew Research Center, 'Wide partisan divide on whether voting is a fundamental right or a privilege with responsibilities', 22 July 2021, https://www.pewresearch.org/fact-tank/2021/07/22/wide-

partisan-divide-on-whether-voting-is-a-fundamental-right-or-a-privilege-with-responsibilities/

42   Anthony Barnett, 'Osman Kavala, Turkish Democracy on the Anvil', *openDemocracy*, 3 November 2017.

43   Rosemary Bechler, "When Saying No Isn't Enough", *openDemocracy*, 29 September 2021.

Epilogue: Socialism and the Syndemic

1   Rachel Schraer, "Covid: Why has the Delta variant spread so quickly in UK?", BBC News Health, 20 June 2021, https://www.bbc.co.uk/news/health-57489740

2   Richard Horton, "COVID-19 is not a pandemic", *The Lancet*, 26 September 2020.

3   Emily Mendenhall, "The COVID-19 syndemic is not global: context matters", *The Lancet*, 22 October 2020.

4   Kristian Niemietz, "Left Turn Ahead? Surveying attitudes of young people towards capitalism and socialism", IEA, July 2021.

5   Felix Salmon, "Gen Z Prefers 'Socialism' to 'Capitalism'" *Axios*, 27 January, 2019.

6   Lydia Saad, "Socialism as Popular as Capitalism Among Young Adults in U.S.", *Gallup*, 29 November 2019.

7   Stuart White, "Alternative liberal solutions to economic inequality", *openDemocracy*, 5 November 2014.

8   Karl Marx, *The German Ideology, 1845*, https://www.marxists.org/archive/marx/works/1845/german-ideology/ch01a.html

Index

Acknowledgements

I hope the reader will enjoy and continue the arguments I've set out, they are part of an ongoing discussion with the living (and the dead). Among those who have helped or inspired me, often by downright disagreement, I thank:

Tariq Goddard, Josh Turner and James Hunt of Repeater for their publishing, production and editing, Rebecca Wright for her apt cover and Marcus Gilroy-Ware for linking us up.

For sometimes crucial moral and/or practical support: Henrietta Batchelor, Portia Barnett-Herrin, Tamara Barnett-Herrin, Bob Borosage, Mary Fitzgerald, Paul Gilroy, Peter Geoghegan, Paul Hilder, Michael Mitchel, Seb Smith, Daniel Trilling.

For this and some big bold points as well: Jay Basu, Rosemary Bechler, Mike Davis, Mike Edwards, David Edgerton, Henry Porter, Peter Jukes, Roman Krznaric, Richard Parker, Adam Ramsay, Jonathan Rée.

And for both plus invaluable specific comments and corrections: Guy Aitchison, Hugh Brody, Tony Curzon Price, Todd Gitlin, Jamie Mackay, Andrea Pisauro, Rory Scothorne, Hilary Wainwright, Stuart White.

And always and in all ways, Judith.

Repeater Books

is dedicated to the creation of a new reality. The landscape of twenty-first-century arts and letters is faded and inert, riven by fashionable cynicism, egotistical self-reference and a nostalgia for the recent past. Repeater intends to add its voice to those movements that wish to enter history and assert control over its currents, gathering together scattered and isolated voices with those who have already called for an escape from Capitalist Realism. Our desire is to publish in every sphere and genre, combining vigorous dissent and a pragmatic willingness to succeed where messianic abstraction and quiescent co-option have stalled: abstention is not an option: we are alive and we don't agree.